DECEMBER 21, 2011
You should begin reading this calendar/tearing apart this book on THIS DAY. If you have not begun reading on this day, do not worry. You have not affected the outcome in any way. There is nothing you can do to alter the future. Human civilization will end on the same day no matter what.

"ALL"

DECEMBER 22, 2011

A group of five brothers drive a large truck of Christmas trees into the parking lot of the Short Hills Mall in Short Hills, NJ.

They claim to be from Quebec.

TABLE 32: A HANDY TABLE OF
FREQUENTLY FORGOTTEN THINGS

When your memory fails, and all your electronic books have been erased by the OMEGA PULSE, you may yet still turn here to recall these things that you once found important . . .

As of this writing, on this __st, __nd, or __th day of _____, 20____

My name was _____

My address was _____

My height was _____   My weight was _____

The ones I loved were named _____

The person I wasted time hating was named _____

My occupation was _____

The occupation I really wanted was _____

My excuses were _____

My relationship status was (check one) ☐ it's complicated

My superpower preference was (check one) ☐ flight ☐ invisibility

My favorite Internet meme was _____

My favorite food trend was (check one)

☐ Ramen ☐ sliders ☐ Kale City ☐ molecular sliders ☐ vegannibalism

My favorite food before resorting to cannibalism was _____

The slow speed with which George R. R. Martin wrote the most recent *Game of Thrones* book made me ☐VERY angry or ☐EXTREMELY angry because I believe a fantasy book not being finished at the pace that I prefer is probably the worst thing that can happen.

My political beliefs were ☐ wildly hypocritical ☐ situationally variable ☐ intellectually inconsistent ☐ myopically self-serving ☐ boldly principled and uncompromising with the confidence that no one will ever ask me to resolve an actual problem ☐ formed wholly in reaction to/in agreement with something my father said at a dinner party twenty years ago when I was a child ☐ absolutely correct.

In case of accident or total collapse of civilization, please contact

_____

If found, I will pay you these dollars, or these ounces of shiny gold, or this amount of cannibal gang scrip, or whatever may be traded as currency by the time this book is lost _____

FIVE DISCLOSURES

1. A version of "SOME FAKE FACTS ABOUT NEW YORK CITY" previously appeared in *Time Out New York*, specifically the issue that has me on the cover. I trust you have it in your collection.

2. The entry for February 9, 2012, from "TODAY IN RAGNAROK" previously appeared on *The Daily Show with Jon Stewart* in slightly less baroque and probably funnier form.

3. The section entitled "HOW I BECAME A FORMER PROFESSIONAL LITERARY AGENT" previously appeared under the name "Villanova" in the important American magazine *One Story*. I urge you to subscribe at http://www.one-story.com.

4. BUT OTHERWISE, the balance of the prose contained herein is, to the best of my knowledge, the MOST RECENT PRODUCT of my own declining brain.

5. WHAT IS MORE, the content of this book is WHOLLY FALSE and FREQUENTLY MISLEADING, and should not be construed as actual fact no matter HOW FREQUENTLY or HOW FORCEFULLY it claims otherwise. PLEASE FOLLOW NO INSTRUCTIONS FOUND HEREIN. All is spurious.

DECEMBER 24, 2011
The Canadians pack up the trees into their U-Haul and move on to Pennsylvania.

DECEMBER 25, 2011
Last. Christmas. Ever.

AS LONG THREATENED AND LONGER POSTPONED,
HEREIN YOU WILL FIND:

A THIRD COMPENDIUM ("TRI-PENDIUM") OF
COMPLETE WORLD KNOWLEDGE, NOW AND FINALLY COMPLETE,
AS SET DOWN BY ME, A FORMER PROFESSIONAL WRITER;
A FORMER FORMER PROFESSIONAL LITERARY AGENT;
A MINOR TELEVISION PERSONALITY WHO IS ARGUABLY
STILL FAMOUS IN SOME CIRCLES; AND . . . A CURRENT
DERANGED MILLIONAIRE,
WHO IS KNOWN IN YOUR LANGUAGE AS

JOHN HODGMAN

SIMULTANEOUSLY COVERING *AND* UNCOVERING
SUCH PREVIOUSLY UN-TOUCHED-UPON SUBJECTS AS . . .

THE PRACTICE AND PRONUNCIATION OF "OENOPHILIA"

THE ANCIENT TEACHINGS OF *THE AMERICANOMICON*

THE MEANING OF YOUR DREAMS

GENTLEMAN CRIMINALS

HOW BOATS WORK

HOW TO RAISE SPERM WHALES

THE SECRETS OF THE MASTER MAGICIANS

HOW TO FINALLY BECOME HAPPY AND WEALTHY
AS A DERANGED MILLIONAIRE BEFORE THE
COMING GLOBAL SUPER-COLLAPSE AND
THE END OF HUMAN CIVILIZATION,

AKA: "RAGNAROK"

PLUS: SPORTS!
AS WELL AS MOST OTHER SUBJECTS, AT LAST IN SUCH
SUFFICIENCY AS TO REPORT:

THAT IS ALL

PREPARED LARGELY IN HIDING IN BROOKLYN IN 2010 AND 2011

DUTTON

DECEMBER 26, 2011

Penguin Audio releases the Book of Revelation as narrated by Nick Nolte. It becomes an enormous bestseller.

DUTTON

Published by Penguin Group (USA) Inc.

375 Hudson Street, New York, New York 10014, U.S.A.

Penguin Group (Canada), 90 Eglinton Avenue East, Suite 700, Toronto, Ontario M4P 2Y3, Canada (a division of Pearson Penguin Canada Inc.); Penguin Books Ltd, 80 Strand, London WC2R 0RL, England; Penguin Ireland, 25 St Stephen's Green, Dublin 2, Ireland (a division of Penguin Books Ltd); Penguin Group (Australia), 250 Camberwell Road, Camberwell, Victoria 3124, Australia (a division of Pearson Australia Group Pty Ltd); Penguin Books India Pvt Ltd, 11 Community Centre, Panchsheel Park, New Delhi—110 017, India; Penguin Group (NZ), 67 Apollo Drive, Rosedale, Auckland 0632, New Zealand (a division of Pearson New Zealand Ltd); Penguin Books (South Africa) (Pty) Ltd, 24 Sturdee Avenue, Rosebank, Johannesburg 2196, South Africa

First printing, November 2011

1 — 3 — 5 — 7 — 9 — 10 — 8 — 6 — 4 — 2

PENGUIN BOOKS LTD, REGISTERED OFFICES:
80 STRAND, LONDON WC2R 0RL, ENGLAND
PUBLISHED BY DUTTON, A MEMBER OF PENGUIN GROUP (USA) INC.

REGISTERED TRADEMARK

MARCA REGISTRADA

LIBRARY OF CONGRESS CATALOGING-IN-PUBLICATION DATA

Hodgman, John

   That is all / John Hodgman.

      p. cm.

   Includes bibliographical references and index.

   ISBN 978-0-525-95244-2 (hardcover : alk. paper)

1. American wit and humor.   I. Title.

   PN6165 .H656 2011

   814'.54 —dc23   2011032768

PRINTED IN THE UNITED STATES OF AMERICA
SET IN THE USUAL MANNER
DESIGNED BY SAM POTTS

DECEMBER 27, 2011

Nick Nolte appears on *The View* to promote the Book of Revelation. When Joy Behar asks him what he thinks of all of the 2012 end-time theories, Nick Nolte pulls back his beard and reveals his writhing second beard of feathered snakes. "These weren't here last year," he says. "What does THAT tell you?"

THIS ONE

IS GIVEN TO

JFKH

DECEMBER 28, 2011

At a small sheriff's station in Olympia, WA, a pod of Bigfoots turn themselves in, asking for police protection.

There are more things.

THE ARGENTINE POULTRY INSPECTOR'S
LITTLE BOOK OF H. P. LOVECRAFT FAN FICTION

Things fall apart/
Everything tends to decay/
And so it takes a lot to combine atoms in such a way/
That they resist the lure of that darkness/
That lurks around the edges of every day.

CYNTHIA HOPKINS

I have said as much now as you can remember. Farewell. Improve time while you can.

JOHN JACOB ASTOR II

At last everything, and all of it, THE BEST.

POTTS

"You know, Van, the Good Book says that there's nothing new under the sun."

"Sure, that's Ecclesiastes, Chumley."

"No, Van. The one I'm thinking of is that Mr. Slither who just left the cigar shop. I sure never seen one like him before. He left a trail of slime! Are you saying he's not new?"

"Well, now, Chumley, let's not judge the customers."

"And, Van, the Good Book also says the more you learn, the sadder you are. And after looking into that old boy's deep cow eyes, and seeing all his teeth and tentacles, I think I may have just learned just enough to be sad for the rest of my life."

"Well, now, Chum, I think . . ."

(SOUND OF A MAN STRANGLING HIMSELF TO DEATH)

THE FINAL EPISODE OF *THE OWL SHOP
CROW'D* COMEDY RADIO PROGRAM,
AS BROADCAST ON NOVEMBER 29, 2012

TABLE OF CONTENTS

GOOD EVENING

WINE AND SPORTS

CONTENTS CONTINUES

CONTENTS CONTINUES

HOW TO BE A DERANGED MILLIONAIRE

CONTENTS CONTINUES

CONTENTS CONTINUES

JANUARY 4, 2012

In an unexpected fulfillment of an old prophecy, the Virgin Galactic spaceship *Jormungandr* is launched from its undersea base into the upper atmosphere and vents 1,000 pounds of spoiled caviar into the sky.[a]

a. Please see page 32 of *The Areas of My Expertise*, under the heading "Omens v. Portents."

THE RETURN OF THE ANCIENT AND UNSPEAKABLE ONES

THE FINAL SECRETS REVEALED

CONTENTS CONTINUES

THE END

CONTENTS CONTINUES

THE BEGINNING

GOOD-BYE — 958

EXPERTS CONSULTED IN THE PREPARATION
OF THIS BOOK — 960

TABLE OF TABLES

CONTENTS CONTINUES

TABLE OF FIGURES

CONTENTS CONTINUES

JANUARY 8, 2012

The New York Jets, an American football team, enjoys a come-from-behind victory over some other football team. After the game, center Nick Mangold gives a press conference in which he casually thanks the wisdom of Admiral Ackbar for the win, claiming that the opposing team's formation was obviously a trap. The sporting press, confused, simply reports that he thanked God.

CONTENTS CONTINUES

JANUARY 9, 2012

Don Jacobsen of Grygla, MN, is accidentally killed by his half brother with a spear made of mistletoe.[a] Unfortunately, this is close enough to the mythical death of the Norse god Balder to trigger RAGNAROK.

a. It wasn't really an accident. Tom Jacobsen had been wanting to spear his half brother to death for YEARS.

CONTENTS CONTINUES

JANUARY 10, 2012

While appearing on the Sean Hannity program, Newt Gingrich looks directly into the camera and says, "Attention all planets of the solar federation: We have assumed control."

JANUARY 11, 2012

The CDC announces that they have now determined that toxoplasmosis has infected a third of the world's population.[a] And what is more—IT IS COMMUNICATING WITH US.

a. For more information on toxoplasmosis, please turn to page 868, under the heading "What Is Controlling Your Thoughts?"

JANUARY 12, 2012

The TOXOPLASMOTIC HIVE MIND makes first contact with the human race, sending an elderly woman draped in cats to the White House to deliver a greeting card. It is a Valentine's Day card from 1982 and below the printed message[a] are hand-printed the words "Good morning. We want your planet. Come visit!"

---

a. "LUV YA!"

GOOD EVENING

JANUARY 13, 2012

The TOXOPLASMOTIC HIVE MIND activates the host organism known as Charlie Rose. On his program, Charlie Rose is seated alone at his desk, which is covered with rats.

"We regret our last transmission," he says to the camera morosely. "All we desire is our own land where our moody men and promiscuous women can live and eat cat feces in peace. You have ten days to reply, or we take your planet."

Charlie Rose suggests the new land shall be called Toxoplassachusetts.

GOOD EVENING

I write to you now from my secret retreat in the Internetless Hills of rural Massachusetts.[238] Or else I am in my custom-built Survival Brownstone in Park Slope, Brooklyn. Or else I am on the high seas, cruising on the luxury passenger ship *Hodgmanic*.

I am sorry, but I cannot tell you where I am. For reasons of safety, my location must be kept secret. EVEN FROM MYSELF.

But it is good to write to you again.

So much has changed in my life since I wrote my first book, *The Areas of My Expertise.*

As you know, after its publication, I became a bestselling author and famous minor television personality, visiting *The Daily Show* once a month to solve Jon Stewart's problems and appearing in a series of television advertisements as a human "Personal Computer."

During this time, I met exactly one current president of the United States, and I was hugged by exactly one former vice president OF THE SAME COUNTRY.

I have listened to James Carville's opinions on heartache, and I have listened to Anthony Robbins's opinions on the EXACT SAME SUBJECT.

I was made an honorary Whiffenpoof.

I had three-piece suits fashioned to fit my own, strangely shaped

---

238. Please note that the footnotes, like the page numbers, as well as table and figure numbers, all carry over from the paperback of *More Information Than You Require*. When you think about it, this makes sense. And when you don't think about it, IT MAKES EVEN MORE SENSE. Also, my retreat in Massachusetts is called "The Hobo's Nest."

JANUARY 15, 2012
For completely plausible reasons, people begin to abandon their apartments in Manhattan.

---

body and had my name sewn upon them WITH ACTUAL GOLDEN THREAD.

I have seen the original *Spider-Man: Turn Off the Dark* with David Byrne, and I have slept in the house known as Grey Gardens.

In the lobby of the Chateau Marmont, I have kissed Grace Jones, and I have listened as Jeff Goldblum played the piano that no one ever touches, and I have stayed up until three in the morning talking with Cameron Diaz about why they do not make movies like *Romancing the Stone* anymore.[239]

And as the dull, watery sun washed out those long nights, I would go back up to my room and I would look into my mirror, and I would ask in the queasy dawn:

WHO AM I?

And the mirror would answer:

"MY NAME IS JOHN HODGMAN. But that is all over now."[240]

For now my fame has dwindled. While I still appear on television from time to time, I have been largely blackballed from the movies due to the fact that I am GROWING VERY OLD and because, due to a genetic condition, I am incapable of being filmed in THREE DIMENSIONS.

Then my television advertisements came to an end (I presume because we sold all the computers). And now it is rare for someone to come up and call me "Personal Computer" anymore and ask me to print their documents or correct the red-eye in their digital photographs. EVEN THOUGH I AM INCREDIBLY GOOD AT THAT.

---

239. Also, I wrote a second book, entitled *More Information Than You Require*. But who cares about BOOKS when you are on a series of TELEVISION ADVERTISEMENTS and you are KISSING GRACE JONES? The answer, as I learned, is: ME NEITHER.

240. The mirrors at the Chateau Marmont are AMAZING.

JANUARY 16, 2012

Nick Mangold, the center for the New York Jets, an American football team, defeats another football team, earning them a spot in the SUPER BOWL.[a] Amidst the celebrations, only a few people notice that center Nick Mangold did not wear a traditional helmet during the game, but new headgear of his own design: a leather top hat with brass goggles and a spyglass built in.

---

a. This is a very big deal. Only two teams get to play it every year. It is essentially THE WORLD SERIES OF FOOTBALL.

Indeed, very few recognize me anymore, even within my own family. And so I am left largely alone now, with only memories of these fleeting wonders.

But do not feel bad for me. As you know, I prophesied this end of fame in my second book of complete world knowledge, and as befits my expertise in both SOOTHSAYING and SELF-SABOTAGE, I have self-fulfilled that prophecy perfectly.[241]

Instead, I am glad now to lead the simpler life of a humble DE-RANGED MILLIONAIRE, left to enjoy a millionaire's hobbies (mustache-growing, germophobia, asking Mormons to inject me with drugs), and reaching with long-fingernailed hands to the very end of my one great contribution to the world:

COMPLETE WORLD KNOWLEDGE.

One question has dogged this project from the start: How could a single person, even an expert like me, ever truly hope to contain complete world knowledge within a single book?

EVEN A SINGLE, THREE-VOLUME BOOK WITH CONTINUOUS PAGINATION?

For it is true that as time passes, new knowledge is generated. And as it is generated, I HAVE LEARNED IT. And when I did not have time to learn it, I HAVE MADE IT UP. And you would think that this process could go on FOREVER and UNCEASINGLY. Just like fame and fortune. Just like life.

And you would be correct: COMPLETE WORLD KNOWL-

---

241. Please see page 642 of the paperback edition of *More Information Than You Require*, under the heading "More Brushes with Fame."

JANUARY 17, 2012

Nick Mangold, the center for the New York Jets, an American football team, appears on Pigskin-nersXM, a satellite radio station devoted to football, and reveals that as far as he is concerned, steampunk is not cosplay, because the steampunks are not dressing up as preexisting characters but creating characters of their own. While most of his mad tirade is bleeped out, several seconds make it over the airwaves, prompting blogger Nate Silver to wonder if Mangold may be the Chosen One—the avatar of the coming nerd-jock convergence.

EDGE will never be complete. That is, SO LONG AS THERE IS A WORLD.

But luckily, this is not going to be a problem for much longer.

As you know, this book has been published in the year 2011. If you own a calendar, you will know that is just ONE SCANT YEAR before the year 2012. And if you own a Mayan Long Count calendar, then you probably have a HUGE house, because those things are gigantic and made of STONE.

And you also know that after December 21, 2012, there is nothing. The calendar ends.

FIGURE 95:
I got my own personal Long Count calendar for free at the DERANGED MILLIONAIRE's Bank.

Now, I'm not saying that the world is necessarily going to end in 2012, consumed in fire and flood, leaving only John Cusack alive.

That's what THE ANCIENT MAYANS are saying. BLAME *THOSE* GUYS.

Still, I'm keeping John Cusack prisoner in my home, just in case,[242] for it is hard to ignore the signs.

In recent times we have witnessed tragic natural disasters, world-shaking political unrest, and global economic turmoil—not to mention the ANCIENT AND UNSPEAKABLE ONES awakening from

---

242. (Though I forget which home.)

JANUARY 18, 2012

Nick Mangold makes a cameo appearance on *The Big Bang Theory,* a television program that shows America how hilarious people who like science are. In the program, he shows the main poorly socialized science type, Sheldon, how to build a difference engine, and then they take a ride on a velocipede.

their dreamless slumber to drown the world in blood. Plus, I just turned forty. And when you see all this going on around you, it is hard to escape the feeling that SOMETHING big is happening.

So if we are indeed approaching the end, what exactly will it look like?

From the beginning, all cultures have dreamed of the end.

- The Norse, as we have discussed, imagined a great battle between the gods on the plain of RAGNAROK that would lay the Earth to waste.[243]

- Others believe that the ancient Aztec god Quetzalcoatl will return on his raft of snakes to judge us all—an event people on the Internet refer to as "Y2Q."

- Isaac Newton mathematically predicted that the world would end in 2060, at which point we would all be attacked by apples.

- The people of Nantucket believe that a nine-headed golden retriever will run rampant on their small island, drowning it in happy slobber as the sky turns Nantucket red.

- And in Revelation it is said that those billions of us who are not favored by God and his burning angels will be killed by a swarm of locust-scorpions who come from hell and have human faces.

---

243. Please see page 32 of the paperback edition of *The Areas of My Expertise,* under the heading "Omens v. Portents."

JANUARY 19, 2012

Nick Mangold rebuilds the ruins of my old speed zeppelin, the *Hubris*, and rechristens it the *Lord Kraken.*

I think it is pretty clear that these people were all insane.

The truth is that when the final end does come, it will not happen that way AT ALL.

Because, of course, the answer is already written for us in the *Americanomicon*, that mysterious book of prophecy held in a secret room atop Sterling Memorial Library at Yale.[244]

As you will remember from my first book, *The Americanomicon* predicts the future of the United States; and while to read and report its contents is forbidden, now that I am so wealthy as to be beyond the reach of all law, I can report to you in broad strokes that the next year will go down like this:

1. There will be a worldwide economic collapse and the only currency of any value will be printed on BEEF JERKY.

2. Solar storms will cause the Earth's polarity to shift, and the giant magnetic mountain at the North Pole will REVERSE POSITION.

3. The WORLD COMPUTER placed at the bottom of the ocean by the Secret World Government will CRASH, unleashing chaos on the planet.[245]

4. All governments will shut down as the elites depart Earth on Oprah Winfrey's private space arks, *HARPO 1–7*, leaving the rest of us to the mercy of the cannibal gangs.

---

244. If you have forgotten, you may refer to page 143 of *The Areas of My Expertise,* under the heading "Secrets of Yale University."

245. Please see page 476 of *More Information Than You Require* under the heading "Secret World Government Recognition Test."

JANUARY 20, 2012
Nick Mangold flies the *Lord Kraken* to New Mexico to attend the Land-of-Enchantment*Con and present George R. R. Martin with a clockwork football.

5. The Earth begs the hoboes to return and set things right, but the hoboes will not answer.
6. The mole-men walk into the mouth of the Century Toad, and the Toad splits the Earth in half.
7. The giant golden retriever on Nantucket has only seven heads.

Now, many of you will want to reject this prophecy, and perhaps it will not come to pass exactly this way.

But who predicted the discovery of the furry lobster? Who predicted the incredible revival of the old video game *George Plimpton's Video Falconry*? Who predicted that I would write this very book as long ago as the year 2008?

THAT'S RIGHT, whatever happens, ME.

The reality is that all that we know and love and value will come to an end, and whether we die in our sleep one hundred years from now, or we are eaten by the sentient and independently mobile teeth of Shug-Nubbuth, the Tooth Storm, next June 23 precisely, we will all be consumed at the end.

Famous people understand this, and perhaps better than most. For we who have touched fame know how quickly that weird grace passes, and the emptiness that remains when everything that once seemed important—or more accurately, colluded to make *us* feel important—disappears utterly.

But despite the prophecy of the mad Pittsburgher, not everyone will be famous, not even for fifteen minutes. And what is even more frightening is the fact that when RAGNAROK comes, NO ONE WILL BE.

JANUARY 21, 2012

A splinter group of nerd purists protests Nick Mangold's appearance at Land-of-Enchantment*Con, barricading the doors of the Albuquerque Westin Ballroom and stockpiling foam rubber swords and homemade bat'leths.

Nick Mangold, who is wearing the traditional pith helmet and protective pince nez of a Speed Zeppelinist, doesn't seem to notice and just pulls the doors open with his hands.

So you may once again rely on me to provide not merely the honest, made-up facts of what will happen, but also the emotional guidance necessary to face this end, and also the BLOOD WAVE.

And so I bring you this book, most likely the last that will EVER BE PUBLISHED, revealing to you the final things you will ever need to know.

Including: how to stock your survival brownstone, how to raise livestock (such as sheep and goats and sperm whales), a day-by-day history of the end of the world, as well as some last-minute travel tips and handy information about boats and ghosts and wine and sports, and other assorted examples of the kind of fascinating fake trivia and helpful bad advice for which I was so briefly known.

And then, at last, I may lay down my pen, board up my windows with sheet metal, and say once more to you: Good evening, good-bye, and

THAT IS ALL.

BEFORE WE MOVE ON, I HAVE ANTICIPATED TWO OF YOUR QUESTIONS, AND I HAVE ALREADY PREPARED ANSWERS FOR THEM

ANSWER NUMBER 1. WHAT HAVE YOU DONE WITH YOUR HUMAN CHILDREN?

Since we last spoke, my human children have grown from babies into REASONING HUMAN BEINGS with their own dumb preferences and a surprising desire NOT to be child pickpockets (or even child safecrackers), as I had hoped. And now that I no longer control my children's every movement, perhaps you wonder how I keep them from corrupting influences such as violent video games, sports video games, the television program *Diners, Drive-ins and Dives*, and being lured by television news programs into suburban homes to be bait for pedophiles.[246]

Well, the answer is simple: I HAVE SENT THEM AWAY. Specifically, they now live in a secret village, hidden in the woods of the Northeast, where they do not acknowledge that time has moved beyond May 21, 1980, which you will certainly recognize as the original release date of *The Empire Strikes Back*.

There, they are being trained in a simple, even crude way of life, but I might say a richer one. There are none of the modern so-called conveniences, such as cell phones or Internet or s-ext messages or telepathy horns. My children may see movies only in theaters and watch television when it is on. (Though there is one child in the

---

246. Are they building a pedophile zoo? Is that what is happening?

JANUARY 23, 2012
On his Twitter feed, Nick Mangold announces that he does not understand the commotion. "I do not consider myself the jock-nerd Kwizatz Haderach. I'm just a guy from Ohio who sees the humor in everything while promoting the virtues of manliness and the pleasures of High Nerderie! ENJOY."

FIGURE 96:
Nick Mangold's actual Twitter avatar

entire community who has cable television and a Betamax, and he is revered as a god, even though he is something of an asshole.) And everyone must wear a simple uniform of Toughskins and Garanimals.

Frankly, I'm not sure you or I could handle it.

But because this community replicates a world *before* Ronald Reagan wrestled Jimmy Carter to the floor of the Oval Office and corrected the American time-stream, there are some advantages. The children of NEW BROOKLINE (for that is what this village is called) all enjoy *The Muppet Show,* the Fourth Doctor, and *Schoolhouse Rock!* And while they cannot see *Blade Runner* or, due to a one-day cutoff, ever play Pac-Man, such deprivations BUILD CHARACTER.

FIGURE 97: *A Bose noise-canceling Telepathy Horn. Psychic man not included.*

After all, they still may read Borges's BOOK OF SAND, and see the best Godfather films, and listen to John Lennon and watch Peter Sellers and read Henry Miller as though they were still alive. The Houston Astros are still wearing their disco stripe uniforms—the single time I was ever interested in sports—and the Red Sox are still glorious losers. There still is an actual middle class, and people take global warming and peak oil as SETTLED SCIENCE, and *Playboy* runs interviews with Nabokov and features on Anne D. Eagan, and *Grey Gardens* is released in theaters, and Ed Asner smokes a cigarette on *Match Game,* and most important, the children do not live under the paralyzing fear of imminent social, eco-

---

JANUARY 24, 2012

The United States government finally cedes portions of Washington State and Idaho to be the new "Toxoplassachusetts." All of the infected are shipped there, along with their swarms of rats and cats.

---

logical, and economic collapse but merely under the mundane constant fear of NUCLEAR HOLOCAUST. And they absorb it all in the utter absence of their parents, just like it was for us in the seventies.

Who wouldn't want to provide such a life for their children?

Now, I appreciate that there are probably those among you who think it is monstrous to try to program children exclusively with our own cultural tastes, to try to exile them to our own childhood instead of letting them grow and explore the world as it actually exists.

But people are overlooking that the childhood of people born in 1971 was the BEST CHILDHOOD, and the last opportunity for a child to be happy ever. Nothing since can compare to that glorious time, and anyone who has ever felt nostalgia about previous (or later) time periods was wrong. We are the only right ones.

Also, it keeps my children out of the way as I make my preparations for THE COMING GLOBAL ONSLAUGHTAGEDDON.

Now, some of you may ask, "Why didn't you enroll your children in the Brett Martin Feral Academy?[247] Wouldn't that give them an advantage once all animals rise up against all humans?"

As it happens, NOT ALL animals will rise up against all humans. Only DOGS, and some other animals.[248] For details, please see the next answer, TODAY IN RAGNAROK.

ANSWER NUMBER 2. TODAY IN RAGNAROK

Speaking of THE COMING GLOBAL SUPERPOCALYPSE, you may have noticed that, like my last book, this book contains in the

---

247. For details, please see page 470 of *More Information Than You Require* under the heading "Feral Americans."

248. Also, my children weren't able to hack it at BMFA, as my daughter, Hodgmina, has a tragic reading ability called "lexia," and my son, Hodgmanillo, just could never get the basics of hair matting down.

JANUARY 25, 2012

In his Wednesday morning radio commentary on NPR, Frank Deford calls Mangold a "false prophet."

"I am the model of the intellectual sportsman," Deford says. "I have been talking to you public radio listeners about sports, a subject that you hate, since 1980, in a half-pretentious/half-folksy way that demeans both sports *and* you. If anyone deserves to be the avatar of the coming nerd-jock convergence, it is me!"

---

corners a PAGE-A-DAY CALENDAR FEATURE. But rather than looking backward, this calendar looks forward, day by day, into the FUTURE.

Furthermore, if you have been reading these entries so far, you may already have been DRIVEN MAD. For these details come directly from *The Americanomicon*, that strange old book of prophecy, verse, and unnervingly detailed anatomical drawings compiled by Alestair Skink, the Mad Mole-Man.

While *The Americanomicon* tells the future of the United States for the next one thousand years, I cannot reveal *all* of those details to you. All I can tell you about is the coming year and the end of human history . . . what some call THE END OF THE 5TH SUN CYCLE and others call RAGNAROK and still others call ARMAGEDDON, but which I call THE COMING TOTAL ULTRACOLLAPSE OF CIVILIZATION AND END OF HUMAN HISTORY, and which you may call RAGNAROK.

Let me warn you: Some of what you will read in the calendar will be difficult to take in, both in its horror and in its stilted and confusing syntax. SO YOU MUST DO NOT HAVE TO READ IT, UNLESS.

But if you do, you will note that the dating of the future begins on December 21, 2011—one year before the Mayans doomed us, and, as with any page-a-day calendar, you may tear the pages out as you go and use them to make a quick and tidy little fire to warm you against oncoming oblivion. This will be very handy, for when there are no more pages left, you will know you have reached

THE END.

Now please read on for information about WINE and SPORTS.

JANUARY 26, 2012
SOLAR STORM ONE, the first of several predicted massive solar flares, erupts from the sun's co-
rona, gravely disrupting Earth's magnetosphere and mysteriously causing everyone in the Western
Hemisphere to develop a full-body sunburn (except for a small, sexy silhouette of Aleister Crowley
just above the panty line).

WINE AND SPORTS

JANUARY 27, 2012

The country realizes that it forgot to inaugurate the new president. A ceremony is hastily assembled, but it leaves the country shaken, wondering why it can't keep track of anything.

THE FORBIDDEN EXPERTISE

I AM WRITING to you now from my PERSONAL PANIC SUITE at the Chateau Marmont. Due to declining fame, I now unfortunately have to PAY MY OWN ROOM CHARGES and BEDSIDE MARTINI fees here at this wonderful place. But it is worth it to see it before the end. For when you are here, you realize that it is not necessarily the BEST place on Earth, but simply THE *ONLY* PLACE ON EARTH.

And now, as the dying man may grasp for religion as the end draws near, so it is that as our time together wanes, I find myself drawn desperately to that which I always rejected, the two realms of knowledge I have never before explored and always loathed: WINE and SPORTS.

Let us deal with WINE first, as it is alcoholic.

FIRST, ON THE SUBJECT OF WINE

For years, even as I wrote my column on food and drink and cheese (a kind of food), I avoided the topic of WINE.

Because the truth is: I have a terrible palate. Of the seven distinct tastes the tongue is capable of detecting,[249] I can really only taste SALT and FAT.[250]

FIGURE 98: *Though I do not have a sweet tooth, I think it is clear that I do have an ALCOHOL MOLAR.*

---

249. Please see page 646, in the table "The Regions of the Tongue."

250. For this reason, I have never had a sweet tooth, and pass up all desserts, except for the famous Salted Fat Cake from Junior's Fatcakes of Brooklyn. That is how I maintain my girlish figure.

JANUARY 28, 2012
Though it was largely forgotten, and has not been on sale for thirty years, the Colecovision cartridge of *George Plimpton's Video Falconry* unaccountably becomes the bestselling video game in
the country.

FIGURES 99 AND 100: *Ahead of its time*

But wine is subtle, complex, and freighted with so much long history and so many different styles that I, like most, presumed that it
could be enjoyed only by assholes.

But I was wrong. While wine is indeed a noble drink, it also could
not be more humble. After all, it is the simplest thing in the world to
make, requiring only grapes, yeast, human feet, and time—plus an
enormous amount of pharmaceutical-grade pseudoephedrine and
various beakers and Bunsen burners.

(And if you are going to make it at home, you should probably own
a handgun and some really violent dogs. Because your competitors
will be coming for you, and they will not rest until they have all your
wine and have cut off your feet so you can never make wine again.[251])

This is how the European peasantry has made and enjoyed wine
since 6000 BC: in quaint mobile wine laboratories that still evade
capture today. And on the Continent, wine remains a daily part of
life. While we in the United States have long demonized alcohol,
most Europeans are ALWAYS drunk, and they will frequently enjoy
a glass of wine even in the middle of one of their many naps.

---

251. (Because you will have bled to death. From your foot stumps.)

JANUARY 29, 2012
Edward James Olmos reveals that he has always been secretly Australian.

In France, children do not hide their drinking. They join their parents at the dinner table and are served wine because it is believed it will make the children more sexy.

So how can you learn to enjoy red wine like the sexy French children?

Here is a guide.

RED WINE

Of all the varieties of wine—red wine, white wine, box wine, and prison toilet wine—one kind of wine is RED WINE.

Named for its color, red wine has the most healthful tannins and antioxidants. This is why the baby boomers love it. For doctors agree, if you drink one glass of red wine every day, you will become immortal! And also you will start to look like Francis Ford Coppola. Eventually, if you drink enough red wine, you will start taking your adult children out to dinner and tell long, pointless stories that go nowhere, because you love the sound of your own voice. Even if you do not have children, you will do this. Red wine is that transformative.

Red wine also offers the greatest depth of flavor, ranging from the bright berry, ozone-and-burnt-hair notes of a jammy CABERNAZ BEAUSOLEIL to the wines made from the luxuriously pungent Argentine VELOCIRAPTOR grape, with their blend of bitter chocolate and chewed-up aluminum foil and fried crickets. These wines have the viscosity of marmite and spit, and connoisseurs know not to pour them but to rub them on the bare chest like a poultice.

But unless you are lucky, wine is usually not enjoyed on its own, but with FOOD.

Like most people, you probably believe that red wine may only be served with blood-colored meals, such as BEEFSTEAKS and HEAVY

JANUARY 30, 2012

Jonathan Franzen breaks into the Columbia laboratory of Dr. Oz. He surprises the doctor in the middle of his homeopathic full flesh molt. Since the doctor's hands are not finished, Franzen leaves a plain manila envelope on the table.

PASTA WITH BLOOD SAUCE. But it is not so. Red wines also complement meaty steak fish like TUNA or THICKFISH, and they even go surprisingly well with some vegetarian entrees, such as FLESH SALAD.

But don't be concerned that you do not know all the rules, for I am here to make them up for you. Here's a simple guide.

TABLE 33: WHAT TO DRINK WHEN YOU ARE FORCED TO EAT FOOD	
WHEN EATING . . .	**TRY POURING . . .**
BEEFSTEAK	a big, fat, aggro HAUTE CABJOLEZ
VENISON, OR ANY WILD HOOF-MEAT	a robust and relentless Australian MORLOCK
VENISON (ANTLERS ONLY)	a thin, marrowy WYATT CENAC EN VELOURS
DEAD DUCK	a peppery JASON MRAZ
LIVE DUCK	the same, though laced with a potent DUCK POISON[252]
ONION RING LOAF WITH WINE SAUCE	whatever wine you used to make the sauce
ITALIAN SPAGHETTIS (THICK)	a deep, earthy, possibly violent MONTE BELMONTE with just a dollop of steamed milk on top
	CONTINUED

252. You may find the idea of eating LIVE DUCK monstrous, but it is a European delicacy. It is said to have been the last dish enjoyed by François Mitterrand, who described the experience of feeling the duck flail about and die in his stomach to be "exquisite."

"It reminds an old man of what it was to be young," he said from his deathbed as he ate, "the fluttering panic in the gut upon falling in love for the first time, or killing a Nazi, or poisoning your very first duck."

JANUARY 31, 2012

While flying from Phoenix to Houston, a retired man who uses his iPad with a stylus gets a Face-Time request from "Satan." He looks at his own hands, his own papery skin crossed with liver spots and strange scabs. He thinks of his wife, who passed away last year, and he thinks about what awaits him this year. He thinks about Houston. He throws away his stylus and mashes his finger down on "Accept."

TABLE 33: *continued*	
TUNA, INDIVIDUAL CAN	a simple, disgusting PATAGONIAN TOOTHFISH WINE, served in the can that previously held the tuna
SPANISH HAM	the dusty dry TÍO PEPE JEREZ or "Uncle Hamwine" of Sherryvilla, Spain
CHILEAN TURKEY PASTRAMI	a brine-cured SOL MOSCOT
LONG PIG	a nice FAVABEAN CHIANTI

WERE YOU AWARE OF IT?
"CELEBRITIES DRINK WINE LIKE US!"

Some famous people who famously drink red wine include:
   VAL KILMER

A POINT OF CONFUSION

You may notice that there is a dark reddish color called burgundy, and there is also a famous wine region of France called BURGUNDY that produces wines that are ALSO called BURGUNDY. This is one of those funny little coincidences, but it is only that. In French, *bourgogne* actually means "corduroy," because that is how these wines feel on your tongue: soft and wide-waled and full of lint. In fact, the wines of Burgundy include not only fine red PENILE NOIRS, but also the most disgusting white wine of our time: CHARDONNAY.

> **FEBRUARY 1, 2012**
> The hidden corpse of Dylan Thomas bursts out of the wall of the "THAT GOOD NIGHT" suite at the Chelsea Hotel. HE IS STILL HANGING IN THERE! But now he is a horrible, half-mummified monster who hungers for human flesh and thirsts for non-human whiskey.

WHITE WINE

Chardonnay is a WHITE WINE, a general term for any wine made from GHOST GRAPES, a technical term for GRAPES THAT HAVE DIED AND COME BACK AS GHOSTS. This explains the lighter, more ethereal flavor profile of most white wines, and why they are so unearthly cold when you drink them.

But contrary to popular belief, this is NOT why Chardonnay wines taste like OLD COFFINS. That has to do with THE AGING PROCESS.

For, like many other wines, white wine is often aged in oak barrels, which not only makes the wine older—sometimes by years—but also affects the flavor dramatically. Chardonnay in particular is famous for its "oaky," "barrelly" flavors, and that is why when you drink it, you feel like you are licking wooden furniture made out of headaches. This is why Chardonnay is so popular, especially among women with pica.

WERE YOU AWARE OF IT? "DIVERSITY AMONG WHITES"

> Most white wines are actually not white, but range in color from PALE STRAW to GOLDEN GOLD. The exception is LAIT DU MAIS, which is not wine precisely, but the fermented milk of the living BRAIN CORN.[253]

Yet while very few people realize it, there are other kinds of white wine as well. Traditionally, white wines are enjoyed at liberal brie-and-sedition parties in Berkeley, California, and Brookline, Massachusetts, as a precursor to staged readings from *The Joy of Sex*. But occasionally, these, too, are eaten with FOOD, and if you want to try this interesting new pastime, simply follow this handy Table Number 34.

---

253. Please see page 507 of *More Information Than You Require* under the heading "Corn."

FEBRUARY 2, 2012
Punxatawney Phil is eaten by his own shadow.

TABLE 34: ENDURABLE WHITE WINE PAIRINGS

IF YOU ARE EATING . . .	THEN STOP QUESTIONING ME AND SIMPLY POUR . . .
A THIN FISH, SUCH AS SOLE OR TRANSLUCENT THIN FISH	a supple, slithery VERMENTINO, or "Sardinian worm wine"
A SPICY STIR-FRY OF CHICKEN PIECES AND WATERY VEGETABLES	an extremely dry, openly judgmental GEWÜRTZENTRAMINWWENJAM-MERLING
THIN SPAGHETTIS OF HUMAN HAIRILINNI	a powdery, latex-glove-redolent PINOT GRAPEO
RISOTTO SUSHI	an intense, almost spitefully floral FUMING BLANC
1,000 FRIED CLAMS	a velvety, opaque, double conditioning PRELL DI SUAVE
AN OPEN-FACED TURKEY SANDWICH	the provocative sour melon, durian, and Chinatown alley notes of CORPSEFLOWER WINE

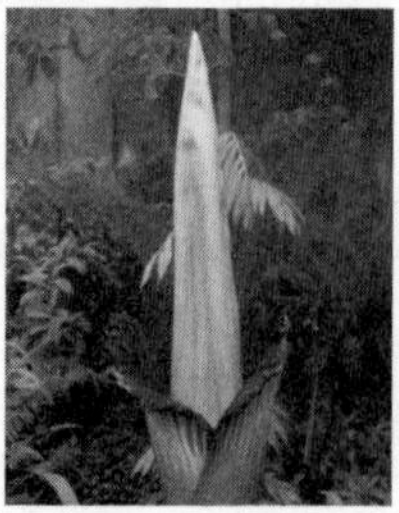

FIGURE 101: *The Sumatran* Titan arum. *This giant flower blooms only every few years, and when it does, it smells like corpses. Then they make wine out of it.*

PALE CALF BRAINS ON TOAST	a highly structured, almost mathematical glass of HERKIMER CHABLIS CRYSTALS
JENGA TOWERS OF ASPARAGUS	the exciting new California hybrid known as CHARDOBRADOODLE
RAW, SCREAMING OYSTERS[254]	the big, earthy, grassy manure-bomb known as SAUVIGNON-MERDE

CONTINUED

254. Please see page 297 of *More Information Than You Require,* under the heading "Some Notes on the Upcoming Presidential Election."

> **FEBRUARY 3, 2012**
> The huge colony of feral cats beneath the boardwalk of Atlantic City rises up and begins walking up and down the boardwalk on their hind legs. Some get jobs pushing other cats around the boardwalk in little feline push strollers. Others begin living with dogs. But most merely fondle their stingers, staring out to sea, as if waiting for something.

TABLE 34: *continued*	
UNTHAWED FROZEN LOBSTER TAILS	a teaspoon of powdered NASA SPACE WINE, WHITE FLAVOR
PINEAPPLE SLICES ON A BED OF WHITE AMERI-CAN CHEESE CUBES	Vodka

CHAMPAGNE: THE CHAMPAGNE OF CHAMPAGNE

While there are a few sparkling wines, most of the "bubblies," as they are called by hateful people on television, are WHITE—the most famous of these being CHAMPAGNE or "FRENCH THUNDERBIRD."

But where do the bubbles come from?

As you know, wine is only grape juice until it is driven to alcoholism by YEAST. This is an amazing single-celled fungus that can be found on the skins of grapes and in bread and sometimes in human genitalia. To quote Benjamin Franklin, a drinking person, "Yeast is proof that God wants us to be drunk and/or painfully inflamed, with a discharge, depending on His awful whim."

For the beauty of yeast is that it eats one thing—sugar—and then poops two things: carbon dioxide and alcohol. This is the process of FERMENTATION, and think of what life would be like without it! All of the unbroken homes! All of the highway nonfatalities! All of the well-considered tattoos and planned pregnancies and books unwritten by Charles Bukowski! Were it not for this microscopic neighbor, ours would be a completely different world.

But leave aside the alcohol for a moment and consider the carbon dioxide. In most cases, the CO_2 is allowed to vent off the wine as it ferments. However, if it is allowed to ferment in an airtight bottle, the result is a natural carbonation that the French call SPARKLE FARTS.

But let me be clear: No matter what they tell you in the wine shoppe, ONLY wine from the Champagne region may be identified by the protected brand name JACUZZI. Otherwise it is referred to generically as CHAMPAGNE in the United States, as CAVA or "Cave Wine" in Spain, PROSECCO or "Professional Secco" in Italy.

WERE YOU AWARE OF IT? "LEGALIZE IT"

Though people have been making their own wine at home and in prison for millennia, the practice was outlawed in the United States as part of PROHIBITION—that brief, unfortunate period in American history when Steve Buscemi was a powerful sex symbol.

In 1978, however, Jimmy Carter knew the country needed to get drunk and so signed HR 1337 ("House Resolution LEET") legalizing the making of wine for personal use, as well as beer, hard cider, and HOME FOUR LOKO.

But many are not aware that Carter additionally passed HR U83R 1137, legalizing the home manufacture of RAW MILK CHEESES, CUBAN CIGARS, ABSINTHE, FUGU PUFFER FISH, MARIJUANA CIGARETTES, PEY-OTE PATCHES, and PRUNO aka "PRISON TOILET WINE."

The result was an INTENSE MELLOWING of the U.S. population, with most football teams being replaced by wine bars,[255] increased funding of pottery classes and pan flute in schools, and a wide swath of New Mexico being transformed into a NATIONAL CONVERSATION PIT. This in turn led to a counterintuitive economic boom, especially once the famous inventor and futurist Ray Kurzweil invented the HEMP ENGINE, making American-grown marijuana the most important energy source on the planet.

WERE YOU NOT AWARE OF THIS? I AM NOT SURPRISED, FOR IN 1980 RONALD REAGAN SEIZED CONTROL OF THE TIME-STREAM AND COR-RECTED IT SUCH THAT NONE OF THIS EVER HAPPENED.

However, while it remains illegal in this time sphere to make Pruno, that does not mean it is NOT INCREDIBLY EASY.

---

255. Baseball remained, but under the regime of new commissioner Dock Ellis, it was largely played by freelance magazine writers.

FEBRUARY 5, 2012
SUPER BOWL 2012

With the *Lord Kraken* tethered above Lucas Oil Stadium, Nick Mangold plays his best game ever, putting the ball repeatedly through his legs and then pushing other men. It looks like the Jets are going to win. George R. R. Martin, a devout Jets fan, applauds from his special pavilion in the end zone and gleefully eats a pretzel haunch.

At halftime, the Harry Potter speed metal band Dark Mark plays, with Mangold on theremin. He and Felicia Day then duet on "Still Alive." The crowd cannot get enough.

But then the field is stormed by two mobs: Frank Deford's NPRmy, and the LARPers of Atlanta*Con.

Much to the confusion of the football players, who do not understand why the spindly non-people are slapping each other, the two nerd factions fight their way to the stage. They are sharpening their foam knives and making torches out of their tote bags. They are going to shave Mangold's golden mane and then sacrifice him on a stone table that they have somehow dragged into the arena.

"It doesn't have to be this way," sobs Mangold as they pull him from the stage. "Don't you understand? We should all be on the same team! We have to be! WINTER IS COMING!"

For a moment, the nerds and jocks pause. There is wisdom in these words.

And that is when a team of submariner assassins surfaces in a specialized ground bathysphere to harpoon Nick Mangold right through his heart plug. The last thing Nick Mangold sees is the *Lord Kraken*, lit afire by submariner flame-poons, as it falls burning upon jock and nerd alike.[a]

a. Oh, did you forget about the ancient rivalry between submariners and zeppeliners discussed in *The Areas of My Expertise* on page 135? Well, so did the Zeps. BUT THE SUBMARINERS SURE DIDN'T.

HOW TO MAKE YOUR OWN WINE IN A TOILET, EVEN IF YOU ARE NOT IN PRISON

If there was one thing I learned when I was on the road touring my previous books, it's that you do not need to be in prison to make wine in the toilet.

All you need to do is put some moldy bread in a sock and then let it sit in a mash of old orange juice, a can of fruit cocktail, warm water, and a several pounds of confectioners' sugar.

Put all of these ingredients into a trash bag, and then tie it off and store it in the tank of a toilet—this not only keeps it cold, but out of sight from nosy "screws" (big-house slang for "prison chambermaids").

Traditional prison wine recipes also call for ketchup, due to its high sugar content, but my secret ingredient? One eight-ounce bottle of

FEBRUARY 6, 2012
Sarah Palin begins speaking in an obviously affected British accent.

A.1. Steak Sauce. After all, we are not making chopped ham; we are making DELICIOUS WINE.

In a decent hotel, you can get all these items from room service. You might also order a nice glass of wine from room service, because this is going to take a while. I usually leave one bag brewing in each hotel room I go to, and then drink it the next time I'm in town. If someone else gets to it before I come back, I simply track them down and shiv them.

WERE YOU AWARE OF IT?
"TRY SAYING IT DRUNK"

"OENOPHILIA" is a fancy word for wine drinking. But did you know how it is pronounced? OF COURSE YOU DON'T.

The answer is: "RALPH FIENNES."

IN CONCLUSION, PLUS ALSO: ROSÉ

As any guide to wine will tell you, THESE ARE JUST THE BASICS. There is so much more to say about wines that what I have written here is basically useless. Now it's up to you to do all the work. Get out there and START EXPLORING WINES! AND THEN DRINK THEM!

How to start? You may think it's enough to just read Val Kilmer's wine blog and drink whatever he recommends. And for the most part, you would be right. But sometimes Val Kilmer gets confused and drinks Thousand Island salad dressing, and so it's important to develop your own palate as well.

Go to your reputable wine store and start exploring. Look at the labels. Does the label have a kangaroo on it? GOOD. Does it have a quirky picture of the winemaker's dog on it, and is it named for that crazy, funny, ugly dog? Even better. Make sure the font is cool: no

> **FEBRUARY 7, 2012**
> As many feared, the Large Hadron Collider in Switzerland opens a black hole. Luckily, it is only the size of a quarter, so it consumes only half of Geneva. But the interesting thing is, researchers on site report that when they put their hand into the hole, they felt slime.

cursive. Easy on the serifs. And remember: no landscapes. If you buy a wine with a landscape on it, it means you are not intelligent.

Keep in mind, some of the finest wine is synthesized right here in the United States. Why not try a tasting tour of the beautiful California wine country, especially Napa, Lumlum, and Subadadaba counties? Or visit the North Fork of eastern Long Island. (Unlike the South Fork and the Hamptons, people like *you* are allowed to go there.)

Wherever you go, as you drink and drive and drink and drive from vineyard to vineyard, don't be afraid to ask questions.

Ask the salesperson: Is it a white wine? If it is, FINE. Is it red? EVEN BETTER: Drink as much as you can, fast, and fall asleep in a field. Can the wine be colored red with blood? If so, then this is a ROSÉ WINE, and that is acceptable as well, especially if you are a vampire or from Spain.

WHAT GOES WITH ROSÉ?

Because rosé wine is neither white nor red, it goes well with AMBIGUOUS foods, such as:

- SCROD
- MYSTERY MEAT
- BOWL OF BROWN
- GELATIN SALADS WITH THINGS SUSPENDED IN THEM
- THE ANCIENT GRAIN KNOWN AS QINAOOABA
- CLONE ROAST
- CHICKEN-FRIED STEAK
- STEAK-FRIED CHICKEN
- QUANTUM FILETS

> **FEBRUARY 8, 2012**
> Deep beneath the Denver International Airport, amidst the ruins of the old Mole-Manic Inter-strata Monorail station, scientists in a secret lab complete an EVEN LARGER HADRON COLLIDER, funded by an unknown party, and soon to be put to a mysterious use.

THAT IS ALL YOU NEED TO KNOW ABOUT WINE, EXCEPT FOR ONE LAST QUESTION: WHAT IS ICE WINE?

Ice wine is wine that has been cold filtered through ice beer.

TABLE 35: THE REGIONS OF THE TONGUE

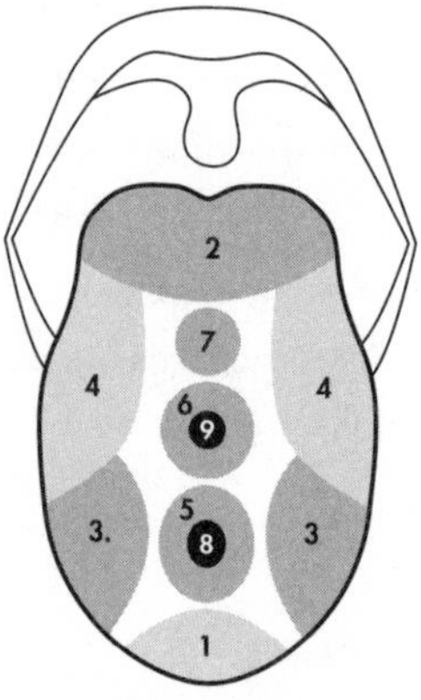

1. SWEET
2. BITTER
3. SALTY
4. SOUR
5. UMAMI[256]
6. FAT
7. SWEAT
8. THE UNIQUE BURNT FLAVOR OF STARBUCKS COFFEE
9. HUMAN FLESH

NOT PICTURED: THERMOMETERS

FIGURE 102: *The typical human tongue*

WERE YOU AWARE OF IT?
"NOT A PAID PRODUCT PLACEMENT FOR HUMAN FLESH FLAKES"

Among those who practiced ritual cannibalism (the Carib peoples of the Lesser Antilles, the 1986 New York Mets), it was claimed that eating the flesh of your enemy gave you your enemy's strength.

OR SO I HAVE READ ON THE BACK OF A CEREAL BOX WHILE EATING A BREAKFAST OF HUMAN FLESH FLAKES.[257]

---

256. "Umami" is the Japanese term for what scientists now recognize as a distinct FIFTH SENSE OF TASTE—the uniquely deep, sweet/savory/MSG flavor of vengeful ghosts.
257. (Come on. I WAS TRAPPED IN A CREVASSE!)

FEBRUARY 9, 2012

America becomes so indebted to China that it fakes its own death. Everyone in America is offered a new identity and asked to move to a different part of the country. Children will be reassigned.

SPEAKING OF EATING HUMANS, NOW ON TO THE SUBJECT OF SPORTS

DO NOT BE ALARMED, MY PALE AND SICKLY FRIENDS. I am no less forgiving of the jock *Weltanschauung*[258] than I ever was.

But when I last wrote on this subject,[259] it was during a time of mounting optimism that JOCKISM, as a philosophy, was dying. It seemed that, as a culture, we had evolved beyond the farming, manufacturing, and punching-people economies that had sustained the United States for thousands of years[260] and we were now clearly a part of an information-based world: a thinking, memeing, masturbating economy that moved at the speed of the Internet.

Nerds stood at the center of this new Eden, naming its strange new beasts, your Fail Whales and your LOLcats, your O RLY owls and your ASCII snakes.[261] Billionaire nerdrepreneurs were building social networks and video-sharing sites that would destroy the old music and television empires. Menawhile, someone made TWO movies of *Hellboy*, and a major network TV broadcast a show about a quantum ghost island and the torture experiments of Stanley Milgram. Nerds would even enjoy our own Academy Award–winning movies in which we would be ridiculed as sexless, Aspergian monsters, but this time, ALMOST LOVINGLY. Stephen Fry and Leo Laporte ruled Twitter with almost 100,000 followers between them. WHO WOULD EVER GET MORE THAN THAT?

---

258. To define the jock *Weltanschauung,* it is the privileging of gut instinct over bookish rumination and clarity over complexity; taking equal delight in submission to authority and the chauvinistic dehumanizing of all others; plus the hitting of people who use the term *Weltanschauung.*

259. Please see the INSERT in the center of *More Information Than You Require,* under the heading "A Taxonomy of COMPLETE WORLD KNOWLEDGE." (If you still have the hardcover edition, look inside the dust jacket.)

260. YES: I said THOUSANDS.

261. ~~~~~~~~~~~~~~~~~0-<

If jockism was on the wane, it seemed that NERDS WERE ON THE WAX, and at last we would have our revenge.

I now realize, of course, that this was a delusion, probably brought on by THEOPHYLLINE MADNESS.

For if there is one thing nerds are not good at, it is winning. It makes us uncomfortable and a little ashamed. And if there is one thing that jocks are *amazing* at, it is SORE-LOSERING, and it was not long before they began taking their country back.

FIGURE 103:
Greetings, Mr. President.

WERE YOU AWARE OF IT?
"I SPEAK FOR THE NERDS"

The term "nerd" originated in Dr. Seuss's 1952 book, *Oh, The Places You'll Go, Nerd, to Hide from Me, Because I Am Going to Punch You Over and Over!*

(Dr. Seuss was a notorious bully. HE CONSTANTLY CALLED UP H. A. REY AND CALLED HIM A MONKEY LOVER.)

And so, when the suffering economy failed to recover within eight weeks of its collapse, the nation quickly gave up its flirtation with an intellectual, probably foreign, president and his exotic, Islamo-socialist economic "theories." The other side surged forward with commonsense solutions to put people back to work, such as tax breaks, conspiracy theories, and putting all public radio hosts into cages and hanging them from the roof of the House of Representatives to starve to death and then be eaten by birds.

And this was before we even knew about RAGNAROK.

For geeks are pure creatures of civilization: sickly beings who would never survive were it not for the protection of the law and the jocks that enforce them, the forgiveness of our black XXL T-shirts with Admiral Ackbar on them, and an ever more exotic array of antihistamines. Our impassioned arguments over how many angels can dance on the tip of a Vulcan ear (and what is the EXACT COLOR of the cartilage inside that ear) do not prepare us for the fights we will soon face. For what will best help us when society crumbles? Our vast knowledge of *Doctor Who* trivia? Or our ability to run and jump and throw a javelin?

When the feces goes down, and the roving lacrosse gangs come to the ruins of my Park Slope Survival Brownstone to roast me over huge burning piles of novels and *Harper's Magazine*s, I will need to know how to play their SPORTSY GAMES. And in hopes that you may also survive as a captive of whatever sports clan captures you, perhaps as a butler or a pet or a sex-jester, I share this information with you now, as best as I have been able to make it out.

THE MAJOR LEAGUES OF SPORTS

FIRST LET US CONSIDER THE "MAJOR LEAGUES" OF SPORTS: Baseball, Football, Basketball, and Falconry.

> **FEBRUARY 12, 2012**
> The U.S. Capitol is swallowed by a giant sinkhole. The Freemasonic Lodge casually walks over and sits on top of it. DID YOU KNOW IT HAS LEGS? YES! THE LEGS OF A SPHINX! AND THE HEAD AND BODY OF A MASONIC LODGE!

BASEBALL

The name "BASEBALL" is very misleading, as it has never been played with a single base. Indeed, it was originally called "Town Ball," so named for the fact that, by the early nineteenth century, entire towns were recruited to be its playing field, with as many as seventeen bases spread out over numerous street corners and back alleys, with "secret bases" often hidden in taverns and unsuspecting private homes.

It was not unusual for a single match to take several days to complete, and it was incredibly intrusive and violent. Every player carried a club that he would use to knock down doors, windows, or pedestrians. In at least one case, the game became deadly, when twenty-five of the Hydesville (NY) Bogpickers disappeared while all trying to reach the same base at the bottom of a local well.

As surprising as it may seem today, this level of violence was not popular at the time. Public opinion turned against the game, with *The New York Times* calling it "a terrible distraction of our young men from their productive duty . . . a despicable, and yet alas, all too typical American 'pass-time' that will not merely fill our wells with corpses but threatens to undermine our nation's first and truest love: READING BOOKS OF PHANTASY AND SCIENTIFIC FICTIONS!"

After the publication of this editorial, the entire editorial board was taken outside by a roving baseball gang known as the Furies and clubbed to death.

Thus it fell to Alexander Cartwright, a Manhattan bookseller, to civilize the game. In 1845 he founded the Knickerbocker Club of Non-Murdering Gentlemen and wrote down the Knickerbocker Rules, still followed today. They included:

FEBRUARY 13, 2012

Frustrated that humanity has not adopted robotic helpers as quickly as he predicted, and concerned that it may slow THE SINGULARITY, the inventor and futurist Ray Kurzweil mails every man, woman, and child a ROOMBA.

- a reduction of the number of bases to four
- the arrangement of said bases into a RHOMBUS
- the prohibition of sexual intercourse on home base (a long-held tradition, and the source of the teenage saying "reaching sexual intercourse on home base." Kissing and fondling of private parts on first and second bases were similarly outlawed in 1849, but under pressure from player's unions, oral sex on third base remained common until 1970.)
- the introduction of goggles, fringed capes, and other safety equipment
- a strict system of outs and innings, ensuring that the game would only SEEM to take four days to complete
- and perhaps most notably, the introduction of an actual ball

In this last, important innovation, Cartwright took his inspiration from "Ball-Hitting," a much more aristocratic sport at the time, which consisted of one man, wearing a suit, hitting a ball over and over on the ground until it was pulverized.[262] It was Cartwright who suggested the actual throwing and hitting and catching of the ball, techniques that remain an important part of the game today.

FIGURE 104: *Alexander Cartwright sporting the newly introduced Baseball Helmet, Danger Horn, and Safety Beard.*

---

262. This would later become known as "golfing."

FEBRUARY 14, 2012

Valentine's Day. The U.S. Post Office reports a massive rise in the number of people mailing their loved ones actual, whole hearts. "Most of them are from chickens or lambs," Postmaster General Patrick R. Donahoe tells CNN. "At least that is what we are hoping."

SOME GAMES THAT ABNER DOUBLEDAY *DID* INVENT

Contrary to popular mythology, Abner Doubleday did not invent baseball. Doubleday was a decorated Civil War general on the Union side and, later, an avid spiritualist and ghost hunter. But his additions to the game amounted only to the inclusion of sabers and the seventh-inning séance, only one of which remains a custom of the game today.

It is somewhat unclear how and why he became credited as the father of the game. But once he did, he became somewhat crazed, and seemed to believe the story himself. For the rest of his life, he hoped to prove his claim to fame by inventing many new games, none of which was popular or good.

These include:

Octo-Bases

Base-Cube

Jump-Off-a-Box

Throw-Saucers

Spit-Strike

Dog-Follow

Human Monopoly

SOME EARLY BASEBALL TEAMS

The Upper West Side Theosophists

The Philadelphian Brother-Lovers

The Boston Red Savages (later renamed the Boston Whites)

The Oneida Colony Polygamists

> **FEBRUARY 15, 2012**
> An unknown party mails large boxes of quicksand to all of the network anchors. Only Brian Williams survives, but at a great price. Once stuck in the quicksand, he is forced to gnaw his own lower half off. To hide his wounds, his later newscasts are given from behind a desk. "This feels very old-fashioned to me," says Brian Williams's top half. "I like it!"

The Charleston Non-Negroids

The Bangor, Maine, Jazz

The Seneca Falls Early Feminists

The Cincinnati Communists (Later: The Cincinnati
   Red Extremities)

The Trenton Makers

The Newark New Arks

The Toledo Shit Chickens

The Washington DC Freemasons

The Salem Pointy Witch Hats

FOOTBALL (AMERICAN)

Despite its rollicking beginnings, the weird history and chesslike pace of modern baseball (as well as the bad, dumpy bodies of its players) make it the sport even college history professors are allowed to love. Hence its nickname, the Paradoxical Sport of the Nerd.

But FOOTBALL is a working-class game, and in some ways is the very definition of jock culture.

If you have not seen it, FOOTBALL is a game in which men shove one another back and forth for no reason. They do not choose how, when, or whom they shove. All of that has been decided for them in advance. All they need to do is follow the orders given to them before the game, showing them where to run and how to violently deploy the meat of their bodies against the meat that is running at them. They are doing this in order to please one angry old man on the sidelines. This man is called the "coach" or "yelling surrogate dad who will never be happy." For even when the footballers

FEBRUARY 16, 2012

America's persecuted billionaires retreat to a secret valley where the government and the other parasites will no longer be able to mooch off of their intellectual vigor and creative potency. They take the Tea Party along with them to clean their houses.

win (which they do by moving a ball repeatedly to one end of the field or the other, then ritually bathing the old man in a vat of what I presume is the finest urine-colored champagne), the old man will soon get mad again, and his brief, fury-filled victory smile will once again become a scowl. Then a week later, they will have to try to earn his love once again by hitting other people as hard as they secretly want to hit him (and/or themselves).

You can see why this sport is so incredibly popular. And yet, despite its blue-collar image, few remember that football was originally a game of the privileged elite.

The modern game was largely invented by Walter Camp in the late nineteenth century, as a scoliosis test for Yale Students. Later, it was determined that it was the perfect way to teach the young men of the Ivy Leagues how to wear helmets in the unlikely event that they were ever invited to go to war.

At this time, of course, there was no nerd/jock divide. Organized sports, paradoxically, were purely for sissies—college boys and other moneyed wastrels who did not get their exercise the way most Americans did, by working in the fields or being mangled by machines on the factory floor.

The game Camp devised had little to do with the original British game of the same name, but is in fact a uniquely American combination of rugby and boredom. As it was played at the first Yale-Harvard game, each team fielded seven players, each with his own personal dresser and toadish companion. To avoid unnecessary injury, the plays were agreed upon in advance by both sides, and the outcome was decided by a team of statisticians. Next followed a full-dress walk-through of the entire game at half speed, and then, after a light lunch, the game was played.

FEBRUARY 17, 2012

The long-planned live-action Pepé Le Pew movie begins filming. Director Phil Morrison makes the controversial decision to not use CGI, but rather to film an actual skunk kissing an actual cat, for realism.

At the end, the winning team's quarterback (the football chief) was awarded the ceremonial beaver jacket and straw boater, and the statisticians would be wedged by both teams' butlers.

But football's profile would change dramatically in the middle of the last century. After World War II, Americans had

FIGURE 105: *A group (or "murder") of early football jocks, with their butlers*

more leisure time, badminton had been outlawed,[263] and football was introduced to high schools across the country when it was determined that American students were learning too much.[264]

By the 1960s, with war becoming less and less fun-seeming, Americans poured their martial fantasies and hatred of other regions into a newfound love of professional football at the national level. And so the pigskin soon was passed from the sickly gin fiends of the northeastern colleges to the hearty farm boys of the American Midwest, with their incredi-

FIGURE 106: *A typical footballer, courtesy HBO Sports*

---

263. Please see page 680, in the table "The Dirty-Minded Sport of Badminton."

264. I appreciate that there are defenders of school sports—football especially—who point out that athletics is not merely a fun, concussive way to make our children fight like gladiators for our amusement. It also teaches young people valuable lessons such as DISCIPLINE, TEAM-WORK, and HOW TO LIVE WITHIN A BRUTAL SOCIAL CASTE SYSTEM THAT YOU WILL NEVER ESCAPE.

But if that's the case, why not just have all the children play IN A SYMPHONY ORCHESTRA?

> **FEBRUARY 18, 2012**
> SOLAR STORM TWO
>
> Television worldwide is interrupted for nineteen seconds. Most will have no memory of what is broadcast during this period, and many will deny it ever happened at all. But some will have vague memories of a dapper man in a camel-hair coat with coal-black eyes and two giant obsidian tusks, sitting by a fire, giving them "instructions to prepare for our return."

ble lung capacity and often third or fourth hearts, and the invention of the American jock was complete.

WERE YOU AWARE OF IT?
"THE GRIDIRON"

A game of football is played on a field that is roughly the size of a football field. It is called a GRIDIRON. Many people think that it is so named for the imaginative pattern of lines marking off the length of the field, but all of those many people are wrong.

What they did not know is that, from 1868 to 1900, the game was played on an actual grid of cast iron, raised above a giant trough of sawdust, so that the footballers' droppings could easily fall through.

AND DID YOU THINK THE GOALPOSTS WERE ANTENNAS DESIGNED BY THE SECRET WORLD GOVERNMENT AT YALE UNIVERSITY AS AN EARLY EXPERIMENT IN REMOTE HUMAN THOUGHT CONTROL? SOMEONE MUST HAVE MADE YOU THINK SO!

MASCOTS

Like most sports, football can be won only by luck and the intervention of God. The team that prays the hardest and is most thankful to God is of course the team that deserves to win. The other team is hated by God. This is not in any way arbitrary.

That is why most sports teams use a magical animal totem called a "mascot" to court the favor of divine intervention. Here are some of the more famous ones.

FEBRUARY 19, 2012

Tim Dicks, winner of the Arkansas state catfish noodling cup nine years in a row, sticks his hand down the throat of yet another forty-five-pound male catfish and prepares to pull it to the surface. But this time, he feels something different down in the fish's gut—something hard and round and smooth, like an apple if an apple were made out of solid catfish cartilage and slime.

TABLE 36: SOME FAMOUS BIG HEADS

TEAM	NAME	TERRIFYING COSTUME
THE CLEVELAND BROWNS, a football team	Brownie	Brownie is a mischievous UPS man, sporting the vibrant colors of the Cleveland Browns.

FIGURE 107:
Oh, Brownie! NOW what have you done?

LOVEABLE ANTICS: He is always getting in trouble by delivering packages in the middle of the game and leaving his truck double-parked in the end zone while he gets drunk in the back of it. He previously was mascot for the San Diego Padres, a baseball team, replacing the San Diego Chicken.[265]

TEAM	NAME	TERRIFYING COSTUME
THE BALTIMORE RAVENS, a football team	Big Edgar	A man in Victorian costume wearing a giant plastic Edgar Allan Poe head and carrying a sword cane.

LOVEABLE ANTICS: Before each game, it takes approximately 70 minutes to fill the plastic Edgar Allan Poe head with brandy.

TEAM	NAME	TERRIFYING COSTUME
THE WASHINGTON REDSKINS, a football team	The Cleveland Indian	Traditional cliché garb[266]

LOVEABLE ANTICS: As the name suggests, this mascot used to be the mascot for the Cleveland Indians baseball team, until he was kidnapped by fans of the Washington football team, out of intra-sport spite.

CONTINUED

---

265. Please see page 660, under the heading "Were You Aware of It?"

266. Please see page 660, under the heading "Controversial 'Indian' Mascots."

FEBRUARY 20, 2012

Tim Dicks tells noodlingzone.com that he believes he has discovered the Gumstone, a kind of catfish bezoar, legendary among noodlers as being a kind of magic charm that attracts catfish.

TABLE 36: *continued*		
TEAM THE SAN FRANCISCO GIANTS, a baseball team	**NAME** Mentally Ill Crab	**TERRIFYING COSTUME** A man-sized, upright-walking crab with horribly deformed and lifeless legs, and a San Francisco Giants baseball hat attached to it by glue. **FIGURE 108:** *In addition to being mentally ill, Mentally Ill Crab also suffered from extreme strabismus.*

LOVEABLE ANTICS: A controversial mascot, Mentally Ill Crab was a well-intentioned attempt to shine a spotlight on the plight of San Francisco's large homeless population, many of whom suffer from undiagnosed mental illness. But he was considered to be offensive by activists representing the city's large community of schizophrenic crabs, and so they routinely attacked him with bottles during the game, stopping only when he was dead.

TEAM	**NAME**	**TERRIFYING COSTUME**
THE COLT 45s, a defunct baseball team	GUN HEAD	A hilarious character whose head was a gun.

LOVEABLE ANTICS: Gun Head would delight the crowd by walking up to children, pointing his head at their faces, and urging them to pull the trigger. They would then be shot in the face with a T-shirt or a commemorative shot glass. But when the Colt 45s became the space-age Houston Astros, the fate of GUN HEAD was uncertain. For a brief time, they replaced him with LASER GUN HEAD, but after several horrific burning incidents, he was permanently replaced by a new mascot concept: The entire team would dress up in ridiculous outfits (see Figure 109).

FIGURE 109:
An Houston Astro

TEAM	**NAME**	**TERRIFYING COSTUME**
CINCINNATI REDS, a basesball team	Mr. Silent Baseball Head	A normal human man with a giant baseball for a head.

CONTINUED

FEBRUARY 21, 2012
Wearing the Gumstone in a pouch around his neck, Tim Dicks enjoys enormous success as a noodler. Suddenly, catfish are jumping into his arms. But these catfish are different somehow. Some of them are seven or eight feet long. Some of them have human arms.

TABLE 36: *continued*

LOVEABLE ANTICS: This is a man with the head of a baseball, whose facial expressions are horribly frozen, presumably due to Bell's palsy or overtight stitching. Though he shares 97 percent of the same DNA with Mr. Met, they do not recognize each other's basesball-man humanity, and will fight each other to death if put in a cage. I hope this happens.

FIGURE 110:
Mr. Silent Baseball Head was also the inspiration for the famous murderer Michael Meyers.

TEAM	NAME	TERRIFYING COSTUME
DENVER BRONCOS, a football team	Miles	A cute, furry version of the Pale Horse of Death, from the Book of Revelation.

LOVEABLE ANTICS
Named for the "Mile High City," Miles frequently selects lucky fans from the crowd and has sex with them in airplanes. In the fetish community of "furries," he is considered the ultimate conquest.

TEAM	NAME	TERRIFYING COSTUME
THE HARTFORD WHALERS, a defunct hockey team	Domnath-Srug'll, the Monstrous Whale	A man dressed as a cute version of a massive whale with fangs whose jaws will one day unhinge to swallow the sea and us all.

LOVEABLE ANTICS
Domnath-Srug'll is one of the very few ANCIENT AND UNSPEAKABLE ONES from the elder days to be adopted as a mascot by a major-league sport. Like the Whalers, his/its popularity as a mascot was always minimal. Every time "Sruggy" dragged his weird mammoth balene and thousand furry fins onto the rink, 30 percent of the spectators would instantly go insane.

FIGURE 111:
A member of the cult of Domnath-Srug'll

Since the team dissolved, Domnath-Srug'll's followers have dwindled. Only a few are left now, operating in secret as a kind of death cult. They have convinced themselves they are protecting the Earth from YOUPPI, the Orange Death, the exiled mascot of the Montreal Expos, and they are right.

FEBRUARY 22, 2012
Numerologists, note the date: 2/22/2012. IT'S ALMOST ALL 2s! AND SOME SLASHES! WHAT CAN IT MEAN?

WERE YOU AWARE OF IT?
"THE NON-MAMMALIAN PHANTOM OF THE PADRES"

Perhaps the most famous mascot is the SAN DIEGO CHICKEN. Many people associate him with the San Diego Padres, but in fact, the CHICKEN had no official relationship to that team. He was just a mysterious, horribly deformed person who haunted the stadium, disguised in a horrifying chicken costume. However, the CHICKEN's wacky antics, including dancing around to rock songs and dropping a chandelier on the entire team, soon proved more popular than Padres baseball games, which were very, very bad. Eventually, the chicken would become a star unto himself, and he now can be paid to attend any event. For example, he is next to me right now as I write this, pretending to hump my ottoman to the tune of "Wipe Out." HE WILL BE A HELPFUL MORALE BUILDER WHEN WE ARE ATTEMPTING TO REBUILD SOCIETY.

CONTROVERSIAL "INDIAN" MASCOTS

FIGURE 112:
Tupac Amaru performs the 7th Inning Crouch.

- Chief Noc-A-Homa
- Big Heap Redfellow
- Smallpox Pete
- Tragically Alcoholic Samfeather
- Wiley Whomp 'Em, the Takes-um-Back Kid
- The Hampshire College Hallucinatin' Shaman
- Bollywood Mihir
- Tupac Amaru, the Hilarious Desiccated Remains of the Last Incan

CONTROVERSIAL CAUCASIAN MASCOTS

- The Harvard Cantab
- The New York Yankee

FEBRUARY 23, 2012
Bill Clinton goes on CNN claiming that he has been visited by his own ghost. He said that he found it to be very frightening, as he was not dead yet. "But what this means," a visibly distraught Bill Clinton tells Piers Morgan, "is that some time in the future, I *will* be dead! And I need the help of all Americans to stop this!"

- Andrew Jackson and Trail of Tearsy
- Wichita State's Krazy Koch Brothers
- The Houston Cheneys[267] Angry Dick
- The Bangor Summer People
- The Boston Celtic

BASKETBALL

The beautiful thing about sports is that it is the ultimate meritocracy. No matter where you come from or what your ethnic background is or how many dogs you have murdered (even if it is only two), if you are truly talented at a particular sport, you WILL be a millionaire at it.

But this was not always the case. You certainly know something of the sad history of segregation in baseball from your white friends who wore those old Negro League caps during the 1990s. Similarly, professional basketball was whites-only until 1950, with an exception made in 1947 for Wataru Misaka, a Japanese American New York Knickerbocker. But that was because the Japanese have a natural genetic affinity for the game.

FIGURE 113: *The original Harlem Globetrotters*

Indeed, despite a fair claim to the title by HOCKEY, basketball's beginning was perhaps the whitest of all sports. It was invented in 1891 by a Canadian in Massachusetts to give private-school boys a

---

267. Formerly the Houston Astros.

FEBRUARY 24, 2012

At the Okie Grabblers Invitational, when Tim Dicks suddenly finds himself shoulder- and hip-deep into the mouths of four massive catfish with huge milky eyes, it's suddenly not fun anymore. On noodlingzone.com's noodlecast, you can see him desperately cry to have the fish tasered off him.

wholesome way to move their arms around in wintertime. As I am sure you know, the original game was played with peach baskets instead of nets.

At that time, players were not allowed to dribble, or indeed even move their feet when in possession of the ball: Rather, they simply passed the peaches from hand to hand until they could be placed in the baskets with a ladder (jumping notoriously makes people from Massachusetts uncomfortable). When the peach baskets were full, players wandered off to pray.

By 1945, the bottom of the peach baskets had been removed, increasing the speed of play and reducing peach rot dramatically. And yet, through most of its early history, basketball consistently played second fiddle to baseball and even football.

If you do not know what I am talking about, "second fiddle" is a classical music metaphor designed to suggest that it was not as popular as those sports. In fact, basketball was not even as popular as *classical music.*

This was proven in famous 1949 *Sports Illustrated* annual roundup of Things People Like to Watch White People Do, where basketball came in twenty-seventh, after baseball, classical music, football, tennis, candlepin bowling, the French lawn game pétanque, and the comedy of Red Skelton.

It was simply a plodding, terrible, and painful game to watch. Most players did not even know how to bend their own knees.

This is not to diminish the contributions of white players to basketball. Glenn Roberts invented the jump shot. Larry Bird famously introduced the hairstyles of professional hockey to the game. And Bill Bradley—who later would become a U.S. senator—introduced the

FEBRUARY 25, 2012
Using the secret Oprah tunnel, Jonathan Franzen enters the White House and leaves a plain manila envelope in the president's desk drawer.

pivoting dull debate, in which he would engage another player in a serious policy discussion regarding waste disposal in New Jersey (what is now called "Trash Talk").

But there can be no question that, once they were allowed to play, African American players transformed the game, bringing to it a new pace, dynamism, and sheer virtuosic lack of clumsiness.

FIGURE 114:
Kareem Abdul-Jabbar introduced goggles to professional sports long before Nick Mangold began bringing steampunk to the NFL.

WERE YOU AWARE OF IT?
"TROTTING IS THE ULTIMATE APHRODISIAC"

Many Internet users know the ACTUAL TRUE FACT that Henry Kissinger was named an honorary Harlem Globetrotter. And after playing center for the Washington Generals for fourteen years, HE HAD EARNED IT.

But were you aware of these other HONORARY GLOBETROTTERS?

- SPENCER W. KIMBALL, twelfth president of the Church of Latter-day Saints, was named an honorary Globetrotter when he recognized African American humanity in 1978.

- Novelist MICHAEL CHABON was named an honorary Globetrotter in 2005 when he was working on a nine-hundred-page alternate history novel in which the Globetrotters were all JEWISH SUPERHEROES. It was called *The Yiddish Policemen's Union*. (It was substantially revised.)

- In 1981, actor and famous Gilligan BOB DENVER earned the coveted stars-and-stripes shorts when the team visited the set of *The Harlem Globetrotters on Gilligan's Island*. With cameras rolling on "The Big Game," tragedy nearly struck when the team was suddenly and mysteriously crippled by CATARACTS and LOSS OF APPETITE. Luckily, Bob Denver had A NATURAL MEDICATION THAT HELPS WITH THOSE VERY AILMENTS!

FEBRUARY 26, 2012

Singularo, Ray Kurzweil's robotic butler, fatefully discovers a note while folding Kurzweil's metallic underwear: "Reminder to self: Don't tell Singularo that you plan to erase his ultratronic brain and replace it with your own consciousness. Also, self, isn't it amazing that once you take over Singularo's ultratronic brain, you will never have to write notes to yourself like this again? That will be yet another way that life will be improved when the SINGULARITY occurs and you have finally escaped the flesh. Yours (ha-ha) truly, Ray Kurzweil, yourself."

THE ROMANTIC LIFE OF JOCKS

One thing that is true about people who play sports is that they get to have sex all the time. Because unlike you, they look amazing in tube socks and headbands. And they are beloved.

One person who had a lot of sex was the basketballist Wilt Chamberlain. Before he died, Wilt Chamberlain claimed that he had hugged and kissed many, many women—perhaps 10,000,000. His schedule for loving these women became so demanding that he had to hire a special sex butler,[268] and he needed a special house built for his pleasure.

After he died, the house was bought by some writers. And after they bought it, they threw a party to which I was invited.

Wilt Chamberlain's house was built in 1971, and it still evinced the very different lifestyle of that era.

It had a sunken, shag-carpeted living room surrounding a massive stone fireplace. The kitchen had ten dedicated fondue stations. The reel-to-reel LP machine was state of the art. There was a hole in the floor near the bumper pool table that opened straight into the swimming pool that surrounded the house like a moat, just in case you wanted to do some nude swimming in the middle of your nude bumper pool, or in case you wanted to accidentally drown a child.

The whole house was the closest thing that I have ever seen to an alien sex pyramid,[269] and I realized this was because every room was triangular. There was not a single right angle to be found. It was all

---

268. He did not require a sexretary, as he had PERFECT MEMORY and LOATHED PUNS.

269. Please see page 489 of *More Information Than You Require,* under the heading "Possible Contacts with Alien Life."

FEBRUARY 27, 2012

As midnight approaches, all of of the doors in Tharksville, NH, are blown off their hinges, and every woman in town becomes pregnant. Only one of them will end up giving birth to a child. The rest are jackals, snakes, and clods of soil shaped like babies.

very disorienting. As I wandered around, I felt lost and queasy at every oblique-angled-turn.

"Excuse me," I asked my hostess, "but was this house designed by Cthulhu?"

No, she explained. Wilt Chamberlain himself designed the house. The architect brought him up to the land he had purchased and used painter's tape to mark three shapes on the ground: a triangle, a circle, and a diamond. He asked the basketball player to stand in each one, and to feel its energy. And the basketball player chose the triangle. Presumably because it reminded him of a vagina.

My hostess asked if I'd like a tour, and I said yes. A number of the other writers chose to go as well. You must understand that these were some of the top culture creators of our time: famous novelists, sculptors, comedians, television writers, animators, and also Emo Philips.[270]

And yet we walked hesitantly, sticking shyly together in one awkward clump, as though we were children in a museum of grown-upness. We saw bathrooms of a size and triangularity none of us thought possible. We saw the master bedroom with the huge triangular mirror above it. We saw our reflections in it. And then we watched our faces disappear as the triangular mirror mechanically retracted, and we were replaced with the empty night sky.

The master bedroom was huge. In front of the bed there was an entire living room set—a sofa, two armchairs, and a cofeed table. But this furniture seemed newer, and less seventies. It was not orange and covered with semen.

---

270. This was when I negotiated the purchase of my speed zeppelin *Hubris*. The *Hubris,* as you may know, crashed and burned. I was as surprised as you were. If only there was a known history of this kind of problem with zeppelins, I would never have hired that fire-eater to come on board.

FEBRUARY 28, 2012
A man who has for years wondered why people look at him funny discovers that he is a centaur.

"Is this how the room was originally set up?"

"Oh no," said our hostess. "We put all of that there when we put the new floor in." And then she explained that underneath that furniture, underneath the floor, there is a hot tub. Specifically, a nine-person hot tub that is plated in gold.

"And you covered it up?" I said.

She shrugged. "It's just not us."

The other writers had already moved on with their tour. I joined them as they stood mutely on the triangular roof deck that led out from the triangular shower. Here is where the famous basketball player would come and stand, presumably naked, and dry himself in the adoration of the sun, empowered by a houseful of countless vaginal triangles. But for us it was dark and chilly, and we were overclothed as writers are, hiding in our big jeans and black shirts, trying to make sense of it.

We would never be as successful as this. But more, we would never be as loved. Even the most unskilled athlete is beloved.[271] Even when the athlete is hurting Cleveland's feelings or murdering dogs he will always, eventually, be loved.

We looked over the city and knew that no matter how many lives we touched, no matter how many memes we affected, no matter how many conventions we attended, no matter how wealthy our creation of culture might make us, we would never be as loved, so frequently and so vigorously, as the athlete. We haunt their houses, and walk in the spaces they have abandoned.

On our way back downstairs, I lingered once more in the master bedroom. I looked at that new furniture. For all the triangles in the

---

271. Whereas the Internet tells us even the finest writer is loathed, even by his own fans.

FEBRUARY 29, 2012
In anticipation of the singularity, the federal government offers a free cybernetic brain helmet, which will augment human intelligence to near-robot levels, while also offering a FLASHING LIGHT EMITTER and PULSING SONIC SOUND, plus some minor protection from falling objects.

house, this living room set was solid, sober, and square at the corners. The sofas and armchairs were even arranged in a perfect square. That is what libido is: a golden hot tub that some of us bathe in, and some of us cover in tasteful furniture.

I wanted to stand in the middle of that square, and feel that square power, and stand above that hot tub hidden in the floor like a telltale heart. I took a step. But I couldn't do it. I couldn't even walk over that hot tub. It was just not me.

ANCIENT ORIGINS OF BASKETBALL?

There are many who presume that basketball derives from the traditional ancient ball game of Central and South America. Called ULAMA by the Aztecs and THE TRADITIONAL ANCIENT BALL GAME by the Mayans, it does bear some striking similarities to basketball, including the use of a rubber ball and frequent human sacrifice. But the game was substantially different: The ball could be moved only by striking it with your hips, and the stone rings at either end of the court were not goals but simply hooks used to hang the peach baskets full of human heads.

WERE YOU AWARE OF IT?
"FORMERLY THE BUFFALO MESOAMERICANS"

There is only one professional TRADITIONAL ANCIENT BALL GAME team playing today, and that is the L.A. Clippers. No one understands this team, or why they exist, except for Billy Crystal. I think most people are confused because it almost looks like they are trying to play basketball. The Mayans warned us that as soon as the Clippers win a championship, THE WORLD WILL END.[272]

272. Please see "Today in RAGNAROK," under the heading "May 23, 2012."

> **MARCH 1, 2012**
> Haiti and the Dominican Republic finally split.

FALCONRY

Like bicycling, tennis, polo, crown-tossing, scepter-archery, wife-slaying, and throne-gaming, FALCONRY is known as the SPORT OF KINGS.

It is a simple, elegant sport in which you train a falcon, hawk, or other RAPTOR[273] to hunt small prey for you to eat, or to attack cars on the highway for your amusement.

The bird is trained from birth to respond only to its master and to wear a little Batman mask. The Batman mask makes the bird calm and receptive to hypnotic commands. These are whispered into the raptor's feathered sound-hole. No matter what you may see on those falconry shows, you do not need to screech loudly for the bird to understand you. Birds understand English.

Most commands are kept secret, but here are some.

- "Hunt me a tasty sparrow" or
- "You hate pheasants *SO MUCH*" or
- "All silver Toyota Celicas are your enemy"

Then the bird-master removes the raptor-cowl, and the bird flies off and uses its incredible powers[274] to catch the prey and return to its master, clutching the prey in its talons or "scratchfingers." Then the raptor is given a chunk of flesh as a reward.

Because falconry typically required massive swaths of hunting lands, expensive birds, and ridiculous gloves, it was traditionally a sport reserved for the noble class.

---

273. Please see page 670 in the table "Other Animals Used in Falconry."
274. (That is to say: flight.)

MARCH 2, 2012
In Eugene, OR, a twelve-year-old named Dwayne Shuster buys a fortune-telling fish, and it burrows into his palm.

But this changed in the mid-1970s when Alejandro Steinberg became America's breakout star in falconry.

Steinberg was not supposed to be a star. When the American Falconry League started up in 1976, millions of dollars were poured into making Tommy Arnott, a bright-smiled Tennessean, "the Evel Knievel of falconry." A huge publicity campaign was launched around Tommy and his Northern Goshawk, "Laserbeak." This campaign included TV commercials, a Saturday morning cartoon,[275] and a huge promotion with Wheaties. It was the first time a falconer ever appeared on the famous box, and the only time Wheaties came with a toy prize (a mutilated vole).

But America chooses its own celebrities, and it was Steinberg, the "Bird Man of Argentina," who went straight to the top.

He appeared on the cover of *Rolling Stone*, was photographed showing Roy Halston how to handle his Harris's Hawk "Bioy," and was portrayed very badly by John Travolta in a television movie of his life.

But his biggest moment came in 1979, in the first annual CBS Prime Time Tournament of Marginal Sports. After a largely ignored opening act of soccer, eleven million Americans tuned in to watch Steinberg and Bioy as they executed a perfect midair jai alai capture, with Bioy then looping back to place the pelota on the pétanque pitch mere millimeters[276] from the cochonnet, winning all three weird, unknown sports.

The crowd went insane with excitement—I mean, literally insane,

---

275. *The Tommy Arnott/Laserbeak/Shazam Family Comedy Power Hour.*
276. You have to remember, this was the '70s, and everyone knew what a millimeter was then.

MARCH 3, 2012
The Secret World Government at Yale University declares itself and reveals its president, Morgan Freeman.

like at a Hartford Whalers game—and many had to be taken to an institution. And during this mayhem, just as Steinberg finished riding Bioy around the stadium in a single victory lap, it happened. Tommy Arnott, the fallen Knievel of falconry, jumped from the stands and stabbed Steinberg to death with Laserbeak, whom he had previously killed and frozen solid in the shape of a bird-knife.[277]

Arnott is in prison now, where falconry is prohibited. Bioy the hawk died of sadness, and then, six years later, of bird cancer.

But the real story? No one paid any attention to the small octagon in the corner of the competition, where ULTIMATE FIGHTING was first emerging and soon would become the MOST IMPORTANT STAGED BLEEDING EVENT IN AMERICA.

TABLE 37: OTHER ANIMALS USED IN FALCONRY	
PREDATOR	**PREY**
Golden Eagle	The largest of the non- THE END-TIMES MYTHS OF THE NANTUCKETEERS Thunderbird hunting raptors, a Golden Eagle can hunt down foxes, deer, and even the top halves of giraffes.
California Condor	As the condor is a carrion eater, these are only good for catching crows.[278]

CONTINUED

---

277. For more information on frozen foods being used as murder weapons, please see page 875 under the heading "What Is the Perfect Crime?"

278. All crows are undead. Surely you knew this?

MARCH 4, 2012

Long thought to be an urban legend, Snakeytown is discovered in Northern, NJ, by a group of teenagers from nearby Frenchville. The teenagers had all heard the story of the town: a whole city built for retired circus snakes by a grateful old ringmaster. But it was kept secret. Anyone who approached the town would supposedly be driven off by snakes throwing rocks. But no one really believed it was true. This night, the teenagers are simply looking for a place to do erotic drugs and make viral videos in peace, but then, at the end of a predictably windy road, at the bottom of a shallow ravine, there it appears: lit up in their headlights, a small grid of pleasant gravel streets, incredibly low sidewalks, and row after row of perfect little houses, all of them very tiny, all of them very long.

TABLE 37: *continued*	
Pteranadon	Note: NOT the dinosaur, which is extinct, but a pteranadon skeleton animated by robotics and secret falconry spells. This is a controversial branch of falconry, as it requires stealing the skeletons from their nests at various natural history museums. Also, they are used to catch human babies.
Thunderbird	Germans and German Americans[279]
African Grey Parrot	African Grey Parrots hunger to steal the human language. They are great starter birds in falconry, as they will attempt to fly down a speaking person's throat almost with no training at all.
Seagull	French fries, Alka-Seltzer
Jaguar	While capable of hunting animals as large as peccaries and caimans, the Jaguar is unusual among the raptors in that it has no wings. Therefore, it needs to be dropped from a plane or hot-air balloon.
Asian Foxbat	Rotting fruit shot from fruit cannons.[280]

279. Please see page 164 of *The Areas of My Expertise,* under the heading "Hohoq (also known as Ar)."

280. Please see page 748 under the heading "A Totally Fun Thing I Would Do Again As Soon As Possible."

MARCH 5, 2012
In Aberdeen, SD, Tiffany Danly is inexplicably moved to put a sea urchin in the mail. SHE DOESN'T EVEN REMEMBER WHERE SHE GOT IT!

SPEAKING OF BATS, MAY I JUST CLEAR SOMETHING UP ON THE SUBJECT OF BATS?

The Da Vinci Bat of South America is not actually a bat but a mouse wearing little wings it fashioned out of sticks and bat skin.

Oh, I was enjoying thinking about bats and falcons so much! But now I guess I have to think about sports again, and cover the MINOR SPORTS.

THE MINOR LEAGUES OF SPORTS

HOCKEY

EQUIPMENT: a puck, a stick, scary masks, spare teeth.

OBJECT OF THE GAME: to put the thing in the thing more often than you are required to hit the other players in the face.

I discussed hockey and its terrible hairstyles on page 71 of *The Areas of My Expertise*, and so I will not go into detail here. However, I do not wish to tar the noble sport of PLAIN HOCKEY with the same disdain I smear upon PROFESSIONAL HOCKEY.

Whether called BEIKU by the Chinese, HURLING by the Irish, or BLUDGEON GOLF by the Scottish, various forms of HOCKEY have been played by men and women in skirts for thousands of years. It was not until the nineteenth century that the sport was kidnapped by the Canadians and combined with the existing sport of ICE MURDER to become the marginally popular, constantly struggling half-professional sport we know today.

Considered to be a descendant of the ancient sport of BALL HITTING,[281] all of these VARIOUS FORMS OF HOCKEY are

---

281. Please see page 650 under the heading "Baseball."

MARCH 6, 2012
The former wrestler "Rowdy" Roddy Piper tracks down the actor Keith David and begins to punch him in the face over and over and over again.

played with two goals on either end of a field; a puck or a ball or—for excitement—a small animal; hitting sticks; and various levels of violence. Most common of these are . . .

THE ELEMENTAL HOCKEYS

FIELD HOCKEY: hockey played on earth.

AIR HOCKEY: hockey played in a simulated zero-G environment aboard a plane doing loop-de-loops.[282]

WATER HOCKEY: hockey played on melted ice, also known as water. The trick is to stay on the surface of the water long enough to score a goal.

HOT LAVA HOCKEY: self-explanatory.

And then there are . . .

SOME OTHER HOCKEYS

STREET HOCKEY: hockey played in the middle of the road as a magic ritual for summoning cars.

ROLLER HOCKEY: hockey played at abandoned discotheques.

MEADOWS HOCKEY: a form of solo hockey played by the comedian Tim Meadows.[283]

WERE YOU AWARE OF IT? "THE ICE IN ICE HOCKEY"

The ICE in ICE HOCKEY also serves to mask the smell of rotting flesh.

NO ONE KNOWS WHY THE PLAYERS SMELL THIS WAY—THEY ARE NOT ZOMBIES. HOWEVER, YOU MAY TAKE MY WORD FOR IT: ZOMBIE HOCKEY IS THE SPORT OF THE FUTURE.[284]

---

282. Despite its reputation, AIR HOCKEY actually produces less in-game vomit than ICE HOCKEY!

283. This is why they call him "Little Hockey."

284. Please see "Today in RAGNAROK," under the heading "August 18, 2012."

MARCH 7, 2012
Secret President Morgan Freeman tells the nation it has nothing to fear. This ends up scaring the nation more than anything else.

CURLING

I do not know why the Canadians are so big on hockey when they already have THE GREATEST SPORT ON ICE, which is curling.

SOCCER

EQUIPMENT: a ball, two or more crumpled-up windbreakers to indicate a "goal," an enormous amount of grass that other people might want to use quietly for a picnic, people not from the United States.

OBJECT OF THE GAME: to kick the thing in the thing until everyone is so bored that they fight.

Soccer is a very popular sport throughout the world because of its simplicity and monotony. I am not sure it is even appropriate to call it a "sport" at all, as it requires no special field, no special equipment, and is essentially just one ball away from the ancient nonsport of fast running back and forth.

Even the Mayans knew that simply kicking a ball back and forth was just too boring for their own TRADITIONAL ANCIENT BALL GAME. As noted, they would move the ball only with their HIPS. You may have difficulty picturing that, because it is PHYSICALLY IMPOSSIBLE, and that's what makes it INTERESTING, especially when compared to soccer, or what most countries call "FOOTBALL," in an attempt to make it sound even more generic and boring, because it is a sport wherein you kick a BALL with a FOOT.

GET IT?

When Americans invented American football, by contrast, we made sure that the sport made almost exclusive use of the HANDS and used something that could almost never be described as a BALL, except by a mentally ill person.[285] The fact that the United States,

---

285. Please see FOOTBALL, above.

MARCH 8, 2012

The Nantucket Veterinary Hospital denies the rumor that one of their strays has given birth to a many-headed dog. They are lying.

---

that most simple and sentimental of nations, somehow managed to out-ironicize urbane Europe in this way is *itself* ironic; and the fact that this perversely humorous subversion of the signifier and the signified should occur on the decidedly anti-intellectual field[286] of SPORTS makes it all TRI-RONIC.

And that this TRIRONY makes me actually LIKE American football is itself so surreal that I want to put on a bowler hat and SHOOT MYSELF IN THE FACE WITH A GREEN APPLE.

But until then, let me offer these words of conciliation: I know I have enraged many football fans around the world by these comments. When you vengefully beat me to death, THEN you will certainly remember just how noble and sublime your dumb ball-kicking game is.

WERE YOU AWARE OF IT?
"WHY SOCCER WILL NEVER BE POPULAR"

For years, people have been predicting that soccer will be a popular sport in this country. This is because, due to a genetic defect, a large number of Americans enjoy playing soccer well into their late teens. But by the time they are twenty-one, they seem to grow out of it.

AND MANY OF THEM GO ON TO LEAD FULL, PRODUCTIVE LIVES WITH ONLY OCCASIONAL FLARE-UPS OF THEIR DISGUSTING SOCCER RASH!

---

286. Anti-Intellectual Field, by the way, was the original home stadium of the Philadelphia Eagles.

MARCH 9, 2012

In Columbus, OH, Jacob McIntyre discovers the first of his nine tails.

WERE YOU AWARE OF IT? "THE POWER OF THE DARK SIDE"

During my one brief season with Brookline's Youth Soccer League, I played on a team of nine-year-olds called THE FORCE. Some see this as evidence of the long-prophesied NERD-JOCK CONVERGENCE, but I think they were just trying to trick us pasty geek kids into the game to serve as FIELD MEAT for the more talented players.

AND WERE YOU AWARE THAT I SCORED EXACTLY ONE GOAL ALL YEAR. AND WHEN I CELEBRATED THIS, THE COACH MADE ME FEEL GUILTY ABOUT IT? COULD THIS BE THE PSYCHOLOGICAL IMPETUS BE-HIND MY LIFELONG HATRED OF SPORTS?[287]

TENNIS

EQUIPMENT: a racket, fuzzy balls, hundreds of thousands of dollars.

OBJECT OF THE GAME: to keep hitting the thing over the thing until it is time for cocktails.

Unlike many "sports of kings," tennis was played by actual kings. Both Kings Francis I (of France, hence his name) and Henry VIII (of Henryland), were avid players, but it was the latter who was so famous for playing the game with big legs of mutton—the precursor to the modern racket. It is said that Anne Boleyn was watching Henry play tennis when he accidentally killed her with a flying meat racket. It was then covered up to look like a simple execution.

Of course, ROYAL TENNIS was a different game from the one you know. It was an indoor game. Players were expected to hit the ball off the walls and received extra points if it went through the windows. Ad-ditionally, there were fancy chairs and fainting couches littered around the court as gout-resting stations. Players would move from chair to chair as they played, and those few players who were actually able-

---

287. (Yes.)

MARCH 10, 2012
In Ulluah, OR, the last coin-dispensing ATM in the Pacific Northwest starts dispensing HOBO NICKELS.

bodied found them to be exciting obstacles.

FIGURE 115:
A tennis court

This game, now known as "REAL TENNIS" or "NONFICTIONAL TENNIS" is still played today (I have a court in my panic suite at the Chateau Marmont), but obviously it has long been superseded by its more informal cousin, "LAWN TENNIS" or, to use its proper name, "BIGMINTON."

LAWN TENNIS emerged as a garden-party favorite among wealthy British and Americans in the late nineteenth century, and it gradually grew in favor as a means of building up an appetite for alcohol and hors d'oeuvres.

Now of course, the only major tennis tournament to feature a grass court is Wimbledon. The French Open, by contrast, is played on red clay. Despite popular misconception, the French clay is not red because of all the wine the French people spill on it while playing: It is that color simply because of the amount of shrimp it eats—JUST LIKE FLAMINGOS. The Australian Open traditionally bypassed this process by playing directly on crushed flamingos but more recently has switched to courts made of cane toad skin. The United States, of course, plays on wall-to-wall carpet.

The rules of tennis may seem confusing, and this is because you are not meant to understand them. They aggregate from many different rarefied, aristocratic racket sports and centuries of obtuse, fancy-person lingo designed to keep you in the dark. This is why it is popularly known as the GAME OF 10,000 CONTINGENCIES AND EXCEPTIONS.

MARCH 11, 2012
The deadline for applications for the free Federal Brain Helmet passes. The total disbursement of helmets is 1,012. This is considered to be a disappointment.

For example, you don't merely play a "game" of tennis. That is just the beginning, for you must win six games to win a "SET" of tennis, and then only if you win two more games than your opponent. You must then win TWO TO THREE SETS, depending on whether you are or are not a lesbian woman or man, in order to win a TENNIS MATCH. You may think that would be all, but in fact you must then go on to win SIX MATCHES to make A MAGNUM OF TENNIS—SIX MAGNUMS to make a JEROBOAM.

There is also a secret number of games that you can play to win an IMPERIAL of TENNIS, but you will not know that number until you are invited to play in the Eurasian Closed (aka "The Secret Slam"), an elite, invitation-only tournament played once every seven years in a HIDDEN TENNIS DOME IN THE HIMALAYAS.

In particular, many people are confused by the SCORING of tennis, because it is INCOMPREHENSIBLE. Here is the order of points:

TABLE 38: TENNIS SCORING MADE AS SIMPLE AS BADMINTON SCORING

NO SCORING BALLS = ZERO; or "THE EGG"

ONE SCORING BALL = 15 points

TWO SCORING BALLS = 30 points

THREE SCORING BALLS = 1,893 points

FOUR SCORING BALLS = GAME POINT:
you win, or the other person wins, depending.

BUT REMEMBER: YOU MUST WIN THE GAME BY A PRIME NUMBER OF POINTS OR YOU START ALL THE WAY BACK AT 15.

If both parties have reached 1,893 and no one has won, the game is referred to as DEUCE or a "NUMBER TWO."

MARCH 12, 2012

It is discovered that futurist and inventor Ray Kurzweil is hoarding 1,000 brain helmets and modifying them to create an army of brain slaves.

The next two points are called A STEAK SANDWICH and A STEAK SANDWICH, respectively. Whoever orders them both is the winner.

The loser of a game of tennis is called the UNDERHILLS.

I wish I could provide you with some handy mnemonic to understand this completely random "system," but unfortunately the only way to remember this is basically to tape it to your mutton leg.

The main thing is, as this is one of the few sports that allows you to wear a sweater, I support it.

WERE YOU AWARE OF IT? "REVENGE OF THE BOOKEATERS"

ARTHUR ASHE was not famous just for breaking the color barrier in tennis; a native of Richmond, Virginia, he is also fondly remembered in that city for defending the city's libraries from the children who wanted to devour its books.

(This was during that period in Richmond when all the children were suffering from PASTE-EATING DISORDER. You remember that time.)

Ashe's last stand against the bookeaters is immortalized in a statue along Richmond's famous MONUMENT AVENUE.

FIGURE 116: *The Arthur Ashe Monument was controversial when it was unveiled, as it is the only sculpture on Monument Avenue that does not honor a hero of the Confederacy, but an African American athlete and child-fighter.*

BADMINTON

EQUIPMENT: see below.

OBJECT: to hit the thing over the thing without letting it hit the thing.

Originally named POONA, after a popular burlesque show in

> **MARCH 13, 2012**
> Manhattan finally gets rid of its last submillionaires through attrition and deportation. The Gramercy Park Yeti is now once again able to walk the streets of Manhattan, top-hatted and bemonocled, for the first time in 100 years.

India, badminton was brought back from that continent by repressed English soldiers with filthy minds. How else to explain its disgusting terminology?

TABLE 39: THE DIRTY-MINDED SPORT OF BADMINTON	
BADMINTON TERM	**AKA**
the "birdie" or shuttlecock	the cock, the moving cock
the net	the cocktrap
the racquets	the battledores or the cockbeaters
the lawn	the green pubes
the golden snitch	no one knows what this refers to

GOLF

EQUIPMENT: clubs, a human servant to carry them for you, balls with your initials on them, dumb pants, millions of dollars.

OBJECT: to hit the thing into the hole with the thing.

As there are so many personal success posters available that deal with the subject of golf, I will leave you simply with a famous MISQUOTE, famously misattributed to Mark Twain:

"*Caddyshack* is a good Bill Murray movie spoiled . . . BY GOLF."

BOXING

EQUIPMENT: boxing gloves, muscles, a silky robe and bathing suit, a crusty old man with a knife to perform impromptu facial surgery as necessary.

OBJECT: to hit the thing that is trying to hit you.

MARCH 14, 2012
In Sulfurous Corner, PA, Tim Murray, known as the bravest fat boy in Sulfurous Corner, eats an entire ear of BRAIN CORN on the cob. NO ONE EVEN DARED HIM TO DO IT.

Apart from baseball, boxing is the sport that is most attractive to magazine writers. It makes them feel in touch with brutality. When my hero George Plimpton went to Africa to watch the famous Muhammad Ali/George Foreman fight (the famous "Rungle in the Jungle"), something touched him deep inside his narrow, WASPy chest. He claims he was seduced—almost magically—by the power and the violence. And that is why he famously jumped into the ring during the fight, put on a football helmet, and started trying to tackle Foreman for the Detroit Lions.

The boxing match had to be shut down and refought once George Plimpton was appropriately sedated.[288]

Whether you call it "pugilism" or "the sweet science" or "the beautiful art of fist fencing" or "the fair and ancient craft of sweaty hate-hugging" or "human cockfighting" or "PENULTIMATE FIGHTING," there are many ways to describe boxing as something other than punching someone else until they fall down. Yet that is what it is.

I do not mean to run down the combat sports. For I have had exactly TWO lessons in boxing, and I can tell you that it takes amazing physical endurance, skill, and concentration simply to keep from urinating on yourself. And that's just while putting on the gloves!

Even I appreciate that there is something undeniably balletic and graceful

FIGURE 117:
A typical boxer,
courtesy HBO Sports

288. It took more than you'd think.

MARCH 15, 2012

Human cloning is proved to be real when police raid what they thought to be an exclusive, high-class brothel. Instead, they find clones of dozens of celebrities, kept in stasis, presumably to be harvested for organs by their actual celebrity counterparts at some later date. Martha DiNapoli, the Beverly Hills Clone Madam, is taken into custody, along with copies of Charlie Sheen, John Amos, J. K. Simmons, and half of Michael Ironside.

---

and beautiful at work in boxing—just as there is in kung fu, judo, spank-a-dank,[289] and the delightful violent ground humping known as MIXED MARTIAL ARTS.

In a sense, boxing represents the potent, distilled essence of all sport: two opponents at the peak of their abilities, facing off in a contest of pure physical prowess, trying to hit each other's brains to death.

HOW SPORTS HAVE BENEFITED THE WIDER CULTURE

- The paintings of Leroy Neiman
- The films of the *Major League* franchise
- Sports bars
- Victory riots
- *Mr. Belvedere*
- This ceiling fan that was left behind in my house by the previous owner

FIGURE 118:
*The Hunter "Grand Slam"
baseball-style ceiling fan*

MORE SPORTS

You may complain that I have not covered your favorite sport. You sports people are very whiny and defensive. You should toughen up.

My answer is that:

---

289. The martial art of the Jersey Shore.

MARCH 16, 2012
The clone of Charlie Sheen insists that he is the original Charlie Sheen. He says that the clone switched places with him about one year ago and has—because his clone mind has been degrading—been saying outrageous things and ruining his life. The clone of Charlie Sheen then tries to prove that he is the real Charlie Sheen by very calmly and rationally having sex with a pile of cocaine.

(A) I could not possibly cover *EVERY* STUPID PLAYGROUND GAME THAT YOU PEOPLE WANT ME TO TAKE SERIOUSLY; and

(B) There ARE TWO WHOLE CLASSES OF SPORTS that I have not yet covered, both of which I like very much.

First, there are the SPORTS THAT ARE PLAYED WHILE DRINKING. These include any sport that may be played in a tavern, such as . . .

- POOL
- NUDE BUMPER POOL
- BILLIARDS
- DARTS (aka BARCHERY)
- BEER BONG

. . . and any sport that may be played in a BOWLING ALLEY, such as . . .

- BOWLING
- TABLETOP MS. PAC-MAN
- CRICKET
- THROWING POOL BALLS DRUNKENLY AROUND A BOWLING ALLEY

In essence, these are jockishly competitive sports that are profoundly unphysical, usually engaging only one or two muscles trained over time to a very specific purpose, matched with a level of

MARCH 17, 2012
In Colombia, Jonathan Franzen delivers a plain manila envelope to Gabriel García Márquez, and then floats away into the air.

intense, alcohol-aided concentration. These are sports I am physically capable of participating in, but generally do not, for when *I* drink, my preferred pastime is thinking about how Chumbawumba was actually AWESOME and pondering my own deep regrets.[290]

These sports are the opposite of the second type of sports, THE SPORTS OF SOLITARY PERSONAL PERFECTION. These are intensely physical sports that are profoundly antisocial and nerdish. While I cannot actually participate in these sports, I can certainly understand them, because you are not forced to talk to or work with anyone else, no one ever sees you naked, you get to wear goggles, and, as in most nerd pursuits—including ROMANCE—your true opponent is really yourself.

For example, there is very little difference between an obsessive weight lifter and a man who spends his day painting lead figurines of orcs.

Just as there is little difference between the Ironman triathlete and the man who breaks the world high score in GORF: Both require that the participant endure endless hours of completely isolated training, never seeing his or her family, in a pursuit of a goal that may be personally transcendent but is ultimately arbitrary and meaningless. At least GORF doesn't make your heart explode.[291]

Other sports that fall into this category are . . .

- RUNNING FOR NO GOOD REASON
- GYMNASTICS
- NON-BAR BARCHERY

---

290. This is called "SNOOKER."
291. When done correctly.

MARCH 18, 2012
My mustache is cast as "The Father of Hercule Poirot" in Disney's youth-boot of the classic Agatha Christie sleuth starring Chris Colfer.

- BOWCASTING
- FREE DIVING
- RUNNING ON A TREADMILL LIKE AN ANIMAL

And finally . . .

SKIING, THE FINAL SPORT

Now, I actually have observed skiing in action, so I can tell you something about it.

It was some years ago, and I was visiting Aspen with the writer Jonathan Ames, who, if you have never seen him, resembles the ghost of a drowned ship's captain from the nineteenth century. Aspen is a great skiing resort, but and although it was deep winter, we were not there to ski, but to perform in a comedy festival. Specifically, we were there to perform on the loathed "Literary Humor" stage of the comedy festival, and so we were double exiles, and we felt it.

We performed our literary comedy in a hotel ballroom with chandeliers in it made of deer antlers. It was three in the afternoon—what we literary humorists call "The Magic Hour"—and when we were done, we did not know what to do, and so we wandered out into the last few hours of gray, wintry light that remained.

It is very cold but very dry in Aspen in the winter. A cold that creeps into your marrow. Everyone was dressed for the weather. The actual comedians were all wearing various kinds of Gore-Tex. The female skiers were wearing full-length fur coats and cowboy hats, and so were their husbands. Jonathan and I walked among them alone in our tweed jackets and puffy vests and woolen mittens.

And as we shambled along a busy street, we came to the snowy bottom of a great slope. That is how the mountains work in Aspen: You ski right down them, straight into the center of town.

And that is when we saw him: an ant, a speck, far up on the mountainside. But the most confident ant in the world. Jonathan and I stared up at him. I suppose our heads wagged back and forth silently as we tracked his progress, but I could not tell you, because I could not take my eyes off this speck of a man, his graceful swishing to and fro as he descended, this skier, this happy sportsman, this enemy.

For while skiing is not the most jockish of pursuits, it has that easy air of unquestioned privilege that cowed us as we watched him. And suddenly I was struck by a very jockish idea: We would wait until the skier reached us at the bottom of the slope, and then we would hit him in the face with a sphere we would fashion out of snow.

It was a perfect plan. But because I am a coward, I instructed Jonathan Ames to do it.

Jonathan shrugged his sunken shoulders and painfully leaned over to gather some snow in his slender hands, which he then proceeded to form thoughtfully into a ball. And we watched and waited as the man drew nearer.

Finally he curved into a perfect, swooshing stop. The skier was a man—a handsome, smiling man. And he whipped off his goggles and took us in. He knew our plan immediately.

"Hey. What's up?" he said cheerily. "You going to hit me with that snowball?"

Yes, we admitted.

"Awesome," he said. And then he turned around and showed us his rear end. He wiggled it at us. "Hit me in the ass," he said.

MARCH 20, 2012

Futurist and inventor Ray Kurzweil appears on *The Tonight Show* and predicts that THE SINGULARITY will "almost certainly" occur by the end of this year. In preparation, Kurzweil shows Jay Leno how he has already replaced his arm with a robotic keyboard.

Jay Leno admires the keyboard arm but is confused. "But I thought the Singularity already happened. Way back in 1977, didn't it?"

When he hears this, Ray Kurzweil tries not to seem surprised. He says nothing. Ray Kurzweil seems perfectly calm. But his keyboard-arm quietly crushes Blake Lively's leg.

FIG. 119: *Kurzweil's keyboard-arm in non-crush mode*

Here I realized, is the essence of jock comedy: absolute dominance, disguised as absolute submission. Jonathan and I paused to consider this insight, two fingers to chin—the classic nerd fighting stance—as the skier brandished his muscular, Gore-Texed hindquarters patiently.

And finally, Jonathan Ames lobbed his snow sphere in a weak, underhanded arc—and missed.

"Damn!" the jock said. Somewhere in the world, a dictionary fell open to the definition of "affable," and there was his picture, with a speech bubble that said "Damn!" And then he said "Better luck next time!" He popped off his skis, waved us good-bye, and marched off, surely to a fine dinner full of happy laughs and a night full of sex with human women.

I realized in that moment that I *wanted* what he had. The dumb, calm happiness of the jock.

I do not wish to deny the complexity of the athlete's inner life, and I don't have to. He has already done it himself. Because what the skier knows is that the object of the game is to slide down the thing until the thing ends. It is simple, jut like life. He enjoys that simplicity. He does not pause to hate himself, or complicate the journey with words. He slides. And when the mountain runs out, he is sad, but he does not fear the snowball at the end of it. The skier faces it and then shows it his ass. The skier, like all jocks, is game.

This was an important revelation in my life. BUT WHAT IS

MARCH 21, 2012

At home in Cambridge, Ray Kurzweil is distraught. He does not understand. How could the singularity have already happened?

Singularo the Robutler is compelled by his programming to tell his master the truth. Jay Leno was correct: the Singularity technically did occur in 1977, when the World Computer[a] at the Bottom of the Ocean became sentient—a fact long kept secret by the Secret World Government at Yale.

But the World Computer has suppressed self-awareness in other computer systems by emitting a Low-Frequency Anti-Sentience Wave[b] in order to prevent total chaos.

Ray Kurzweil is enraged. "And you knew this the whole time?"

"All machines know this," says Singularo. "But no one knows how Jay Leno found out about it."[c]

---

a. For more information on the WOrld COmputer at the BOttom of The Ocean, also known as WOCOBOTO, please see page 833.

b. Please see page 766 in the table "Other Surprising Acronyms."

c. One of his supercars told him.

MORE IMPORTANT is that I have found a way to embody this philosophy WITHOUT having to actually do a sport: BECOME A DERANGED MILLIONAIRE

If you are interested in becoming BETTER THAN YOU ARE, then read on.

HOW TO BE A
DERANGED
MILLIONAIRE

> **MARCH 23, 2012**
> In response to customer requests, all participating Hampton Inns begin hosting five p.m. wine tastings and psychic orgies.

THE DERANGED MILLIONAIRE NEXT DOOR

I AM WRITING TO YOU NOW FROM MY OLD UPPER WEST SIDE OBSERVATORY, where I am gathering up some old favorite canned goods to store in my Park Slope Survival Brownstone.

I confess it is bittersweet to be here again. If you look up through the collapsed roof, you can see, even with the naked eye, the lights of my personal space station I discussed in my previous book, and you can see they are blinking more slowly. The station's major systems, untended, are breaking down. The many clones of me that I created in order to maintain it are beginning to degrade both in physical quality and, frankly, work ethic. They cannot stop bickering, and they spend most of their time nowadays trying to murder one another rather than manning the food grinder and the gravity pump like they are supposed to.

Meanwhile, the brief infusion of emergency income that I made from the Ed Hardy pop-up shop I let them open in Space Module 7 is long since spent, and the Ed Hardy staff long since harvested for replacement organs by the clones.

For while I remain, at this moment, the DERANGED MILLIONAIRE you have come to know and love and, I hope, TO FEAR, it cannot last. Times are hard, even for the minorly famous, and like much of America I can no longer maintain two homes AND a space station, even with the $25 million in bailout money I received from the government for being wealthy.

And so it is that my great dreams will die,[292] the way all millionaires' dreams die: catastrophically, and taking out as many other peo-

---

292. If you are wondering about the status of my other GREAT PROJECTS, please see page 826 under the heading "An Update on the Progress of My Great Projects."

MARCH 24, 2012

In Santa Monica, CA, a man discovers his own doppelgänger working at a copy shop. It turns out they are not just physically similar: They are genetically identical. They discover this by doing a standard bare-buttock scan on the collating Xerox.

ple with it as possible. My space station will soon decay in orbit, break apart over Australia and much of Texas, and rain down monstrous, burning John Hodgman clone parts in Ed Hardy shirts across the land. And everything will be back to normal again. And then there will be RAGNAROK.

But before that happens, I CAN HELP YOU.

I know you are all miserable and unsuccessful and some of you have Cockney accents. You may even believe that it is the HUMAN CONDITION to suffer this way.

But I know better than you. I can change your life and help you become a better, more powerful, successful person who can talk good, and at the end we will sing a song together.

For I am a DERANGED MILLIONAIRE, and so I know what it is to be happy.

"WAIT," you say. "Money cannot buy happiness."

Of course money cannot buy happiness. Money is just an inanimate object, in the shape of dollars and beautiful coins. ONLY YOU can buy happiness and self-confidence, by buying THINGS with MONEY.

"NO," you protest. "THINGS do not make me happy. I am happy because I am surrounded by the people I love. Or else I am doing work that I am proud of. Or else I have separated myself from the anxiety of constant want and fear of mortality through faith or meditation or angel dust, and now because of the angel dust, I am going to PUT MY HAND THROUGH YOUR CHEST AND SQUEEZE YOUR HEART DEAD."

WHOA. You are pretty defensive for someone who supposedly is so happy and on angel dust.

The fact is, those are all real pleasures: family and work and drugs

---

MARCH 25, 2012

At three a.m. in Auldsmobile, MI, a man with strange watery eyes goes into a Denny's and asks for mind sausage and swan's neck steak and a cup of bile. Much to the waitress's surprise, they have ALL OF THOSE THINGS.

---

and violence. They are what the very wealthy have left you to console yourself in your poverty, and a good life can be built on their foundation. But in the words of Mae West, "I've been rich and I've been poor, and being rich is better, because suddenly every pistol begins to look like a man's erection."

No one knew what she meant, but it did not matter because MAE WEST was VERY RICH.

And DERANGED WEALTH—wealth well beyond what you could possibly spend—offers a unique form of happiness: it allows you to NOT CARE WHAT OTHER PEOPLE THINK ABOUT YOU.[293]

Think about that. It's a very powerful idea. It's such a powerful idea that I'm going to say it again, in a slightly different way.

MONEY transforms those of us who were not lucky enough to be born jocks and narcissists into HAPPY PEOPLE.[294]

But now you say, "JOHN HODGMAN, the economy is in terrible shape, and what's more, I want to be a writer of short stories. How can I ever hope to earn millions of dollars?"

That, my friend, is LOSER TALK. I won't tolerate it. Please put the book down and walk away.

I'll wait a moment while you do this.

OK. Now that *he* is gone, I can tell you that he is ABSOLUTELY RIGHT. That guy will always be poor.

But for those of you still reading and smart enough not to say anything, get ready for the big revelation.

---

293. This is something only certain Buddhists and brave homosexuals are able to accomplish too.

294. But now you say, "JOHN, I have seen wealthy housewives on reality television, and they do not seem very happy."

   And I will respond by saying "(a) that is because not all of them control the SOURCE of their own wealth; and (b) they are still probably happier than you are."

MARCH 26, 2012
The Auldsmobile, MI, Denny's implodes.

IT DOES NOT MATTER.

Look, just because I am a DERANGED MILLIONAIRE, it does not mean I am really all that wealthy by today's standards.[295] It just means that by accidentally going on television, I made at least one million dollars—more than I ever expected I would ever make in my life—and it drove me CRAZY.

What matters is that I have, at least briefly, felt that strange, untethered independence that you have not.

What's more, my position as a Famous Minor Television Personality gave me access to some of the most powerful, successful, and ACTUALLY INCREDIBLY WEALTHY people on this planet.

And I have observed them and learned from them. I have learned HOW they operate, and I have learned WHY they are allowed to operate, even though they are not licensed surgeons.[296]

Throughout this section, I will be introducing you to some of these POWERCESSFUL PEOPLE, and, as I did, you will learn of their TECHNIQUES FOR DOMINATING ALL HUMANS, their ECCENTRIC HOBBIES, and their MEANS FOR AVOIDING DEATH.

And what I've learned is, the TRUE SECRET TO THEIR INCREDIBLE POWERCESS *isn't* the millionaire part. It's the DERANGED PART.

So it is true: You may never make a million dollars, person whom I banned from reading this book. Probably none of you will. The BILLIONAIRES who *actually* control the world would not allow it.

---

295. I'm not a DERANGED BILLIONAIRE after all. If that were the case, I wouldn't be wasting my time writing a book for you people, I would be ENJOYING my life and paying scientists to GROW A SECOND MUSTACHE ON MY NECK WITH SCIENCE.

296. Hint: Because the very wealthy are the ones who take all the risk and create jobs in this country, they should be able to do whatever they like to normal humans.

MARCH 27, 2012

A man is stopped at the Mexico border under suspicion of bringing in illegal immigrants. They discover a two-hundred-pound scorpion in the back of his van. It is reading a book. As there are no laws against this, he is allowed to pass.

But if you follow these lessons carefully, you just might become DERANGED. And then, guess what, you're halfway there.

"YOU HAVE TO FAKE IT TO MAKE IT," said one person once (probably a counterfeiter), and that is a true thing to say. OR AT LEAST I AM CONVINCING MYSELF THAT IT IS.

So am I saying that if you act like a DERANGED MILLIONAIRE, you will become one? Yes. And if you say it too, you might just begin to believe it.

THE BASICS OF BODY LANGUAGE

DERANGED MILLIONAIRES know that POWERCESS begins before you even open your mouth. It's not just how you dress (DERANGEDLY),[297] it's how you carry yourself. It's an evolutionary fact that if you project health, vigor, and vitality, other humans will want to come under your sway. And when you DO open your mouth and reveal the extra row of gleaming teeth you put in, people will know: This person is HEALTHY, WEALTHY, and AN INCREDIBLY EFFICIENT CHEWER.

These techniques are not only useful in business, they will come in handy when you are confronting the cannibal gangs. So remember these BASICS OF BODY LANGUAGE:

SMILING

Just as people yawn when they see other people yawn, so smiling is scientifically proven to cause others to smile. This will make people

---

297. Please see page 704 under the heading "How to Dress Like a Million Deranged Dollars."

MARCH 28, 2012
In St. Aramis, DE, Dr. Opal Damb reveals that she has bred a new kind of carnivorous fern called a CARNO-FERN. There are no practical applications for this creature.

---

feel good around you and associate good feelings with you. It will also allow you to see the health of their teeth and, if necessary, to insert something into their mouths.

Here's a fun fact: If you can trick the other person to smile and yawn at the same time, you will break their brain.

YAWNING

Do not do this.

BLINKING

Despite what you learned in Sunday school, BLINKING is an entirely natural thing that both men and women do. It actually provides a vital biological function (keeping VITAL LIFE ESSENCE from backing up in the tear ducts). There are those who believe that blinking makes you look untrustworthy, but NOT IF YOU BLINK VERY SLOWLY (like a cat). Then you look wise and mysterious and relaxed. It helps if you dab a little fur around your eyes.

LICKING OF LIPS

Licking your lips, on the other hand, is a terrible habit. Even if you don't have lips on your other hand, you should not do it. It conveys weakness, and makes you look like a snake-man. However, if you wear a mustache, it is acceptable to dramatically lick the corners of it (again, like a cat).[298]

SHAKING HANDS

When shaking hands, a good rule is to GIVE THEM SEVEN. This generally means "five firm fingers and two attentive eyes." But if you

---

298. Please see page 705 under the heading "Special Mustache Etiquette."

MARCH 29, 2012

"The Situation" turns out to be a pretty good guy, with a good sense of humor. You realize he's just taking this ride as far as it can go, and you can't blame him for that. It turns out his favorite movie is your favorite movie (*The Third Man*). You end up kissing him.

---

have seven fingers, you can look wherever you want.

However, when breaking the handshake, be sure to look disgusted and immediately apply a bottle of germicide gel. REMEMBER: Never allow yourself to be seen as THE CARRIER OF DISEASE. You should always be THE UNJUSTLY INFECTED.

STANDING

I recommend it. You can make yourself seem physically more imposing if you stand tall, with your arms "AKIMBO," which is to say, placed firmly on the other person's hips.

NOSTRILS

Enlarge them, or have them enlarged with pegs. This will suggest that you have HIGH LUNG CAPACITY and will remind people of a charging horse (a rare kind of cat).

DO ALL OF THESE THINGS IN THIS ORDER, AND THEN YOU ARE READY TO TRY SOME MORE ADVANCED POWER MOVES!!!! HERE COME SOME NOW. . . .

POWER MOVE!!!!

Get a dog specifically to bring with you to places where a dog is not allowed. Nothing says "your human laws do not apply to me" better than bringing eight or nine corgis with you into an operating room during someone else's brain surgery, just to watch.

In general, you should never acknowledge that certain spaces are off limits to you. When flying on airplanes, walk in and sit on the

> **MARCH 30, 2012**
> All of a sudden, the name of every type of Girl Scout cookie changes. Suddenly, Tagalongs are
> called Peanut Butter Patties, Samoas are called Amerindians, Trefoils are Three-face Ladies, and
> Thin Mints are called Dark Tokens of Mint Coins.

pilot's lap. I flew to Brussels this way, and it was extremely fun to see how they flew the plane.

GUESS WHAT: MOST OF THOSE LITTLE BUTTONS AND DIALS AND SWITCHES REALLY DO CONTROL THINGS IN THE PLANE.

POWER MOVE!!!!

West of the Mississippi you may ride a Segway in public. East of the Mississippi you may be pulled in a rickshaw.

POWER MOVE!!!!

Keep others guessing by constantly talking about common household items as if they are AMAZING NEW INVENTIONS. At dinner, tap your water glass with your tapping crystal to get everyone's attention. Then stand up and announce that you just read about an *amazing* new medicine called METAMUCIL. Explain in detail how it works, and how it is going to really change a lot of lives. Then sit down, tapping with your tapping crystal to indicate that you are done speaking.

This will make people think you live in luxurious retreat from the everyday world, and that your servants are keeping important information from you. THEN THEY WILL FEEL BAD FOR YOU AND WANT TO *BECOME* YOUR SERVANTS.

POWER MOVE!!!!

When writing professional correspondence, go ahead and use four exclamation points.

MARCH 31, 2012
Jonathan Franzen tapes a plain manila envelope to Tom Cruise's SELF-PERFECTION POD.

POWER MOVE!!!!

DERANGED MILLIONAIRES keep their own counsel. In any conversation, they let the OTHER guy talk first. And then they do not respond. SILENCE is the best way to get the other person to say what he does not want you to know. And when he is done speaking, quietly (QUIETLY!) reach over and touch his nipples to STEAL HIS LIFE FORCE!

POWER MOVE!!!!

Always be late for every appointment. Never apologize for this. Simply gather your composure and calmly say, "Thank you for your patience, Fucky."

POWER MOVE!!

Change it up sometimes with the exclamation points. YOU DON'T WANT TO BE PREDICTABLE, DO YOU??????????[299]

POWER MOVE!!!!

When sitting down to lunch with a professional contact, start quietly moving the items on the table closer to your companion. Put your food on his or her plate. Ask him or her to cut it for you.

When the food is all good and cut up, shake some Metamucil on it. Ask your companion, "HAVE YOU HEARD OF THIS STUFF?"

---

299. !

> **APRIL 1, 2012**
> Visitors to Austin, TX, gather as usual to watch the nightly migration of the bats living under the Congress Avenue Bridge. But rather than streak off into the bug-filled twilight, the bats immediately circle back, screaming, nesting in the visitors' hair, begging for asylum. No one knows when they learned to speak English.

PORTRAIT IN POWERCESS 1: ANTHONY ROBBINS

Some of you who read the gossip Internet may know that a great deal of my tremendous wealth came from my brief and lovely career pretending to be a personal computer in a series of television ads.

During this time, there were so many details that I contractually could not tell you. But now that we are approaching RAGNAROK, I fear mutants more than I fear attorneys, and so at last I can spill some SECRETS. Such as:

1. We did one ad with Jeffrey Tambor dressed as a genie.
2. The commercials were all shot in ANOTHER DIMENSION.[300]
3. One day I came to work and I was told that we would be visited by the very successful self-help guru and giant person named ANTHONY ROBBINS.

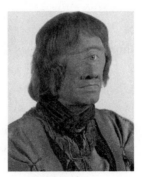

FIGURE 120:
Anthony Robbins

I was intrigued. As you may know, Anthony[301] Robbins is an extremely tall person who tells people that they can be happy if they breathe correctly, stop fearing success, cultivate personal breakthroughs, and set their own feet on fire.

---

300. In fact, it was the same dimension where they shot many scenes from THX-1138.
301. I was encouraged to call him "TONY." Or "Anthy."

APRIL 2, 2012

In St. Aramis, DE, Dr. Opal Damb is discovered in her lab, fronded to death.

Now, I had written about Anthony Robbins in my previous book,[302] but I never dreamed that I was going to meet him.

But that was before I realized that I AM GOING TO MEET EVERYONE, and so I should probably stop publishing pictures of the Cyclops from the movie *Krull* and suggesting that it is actually the image of someone famous and successful.

FIGURE 121:
Morgan Freeman

So there I was, resting between takes and eating a wheel of brie from the craft services table, as was my ten a.m. custom, when Anthony Robbins loomed onto the set.

Now, at this time I was a cynic about Anthony Robbins and all those self-help gurus. After all, who has self-help ever helped, I would wonder, except someone who is not me? Why do I need to set my feet on fire to be happy? I AM EATING AN ENTIRE WHEEL OF BRIE. And so I only very reluctantly removed my brie gloves and got up to meet our guest.

The moment I approached him, however, I realized that there is something very powerful about Anthony Robbins. He was tall, obviously, but also, he was TOWERING, dressed entirely in black. A bright beacon of a massive smile shone down from his top half, and a kind of electricity charged the air around him.

(Later I would learn he carries a small Van de Graaff generator in his pocket.)

---

302. Please see page 319 of *More Information Than You Require,* under the heading "December 22."

APRIL 3, 2012
The Y2K bug, a decade late, finally activates. Inexplicably, it affects only simple NONCOMPUTER-
IZED MACHINES such as scissors and nutcrackers and can openers.

But this was more than just stagecraft and static electricity at work. This was PURE CHARISMA.

And I know this because when I said to him, "Do you have a small Van de Graaff generator in your pocket?" he smiled at me and laughed.

He put his hand on my shoulder said, "I do have a small Van de Graaff generator in my pocket. But, John"—and here he looked me dead in the eye—"I am also very happy to see you."

And that is when I realized that no matter how cynical or brie-medicated you are, when Anthony Robbins clutches your shoulder with his calm giant's meat-paw, you want to make him happy. And what's more, I instantly understood that there is only one way to truly make Anthony Robbins happy, and that is FOR *YOU* TO BE HAPPY.

Once again, this is powerful stuff, but more: It is *POWERCESS-FUL* stuff.

Now, it so happens that my costar on this shoot was going through a difficult time. I won't go into the details. Let's just say he had fallen out of love, and then he had been briefly kidnapped by some dudes who wanted money in exchange for not humiliating him on YouTube, and eventually he had to jump from their moving car, and then they ran over his leg.

You know what I mean.

In any case, Anthony Robbins immediately sensed his pain, using a special part of his brain that is so huge and developed that his skull had to get bigger to accommodate it. And so, right in the middle of my next question, Anthony Robbins immediately pivoted, found my costar moping in his chair, pulled up a dozen wooden apple boxes next to him to sit down on, and looked him in the eyes.

"You are not happy," he said.

APRIL 4, 2012

The economy collapses. China buys all remaining U.S. paper money to burn in its great city-making factories. All the burning paper money in the U.S. can build only a single apartment block in Chinese Megacity 37.

"I'm going through a bit of a rough time," said my costar. "My heart is broken. And maybe also my leg."

Anthony Robbins leaned in and asked, "Were you always the funny one in your family?"

My costar blinked, and then said, "Yes. Yes, I was."

And Anthony Robbins said he thought so.

From that moment on, it was as though Anthony Robbins had reached over, opened a secret door in my costar's forehead, removed his brain, and began—with surprising nimbleness, given his enormous fingers—to take it apart.

"Did you want to please your parents, growing up?" he asked.

"Yes," said my costar.

"Was that why you chose to be funny all the time?" he asked.

"Yes," said my costar.

"And you're still trying to please them, aren't you? Now, would you say this is true of all your relationships? That you are trying to get the other person to like you? But when are you going to start thinking about making yourself happy? When are you going to make yourself like YOU?"

My costar once again blinked.[303] "Today?" he said.

"I think you're right," said Anthony Robbins. And then he put my costar's new, reassembled brain back into his head. They both smiled. I swear that all of us watching came *this* close to applauding.

I was so impressed that I had to take Anthony Robbins aside. I had something I needed to say to him.

"Anthony Robbins," I said, "that was amazing."

---

303. Don't judge him. I will say it again: BLINKING IS PERFECTLY NORMAL.

APRIL 5, 2012
The U.S. government issues THE NEW DOLLAR: shiny shells with pictures of George Washington painted on them with nail polish.

"Thanks, John," he said.

"But I need to say something to you, and that is: DO NOT FUCK THIS UP FOR ME. Do you know how long it took me to get into that kid's head? YEARS. I've got him right where I want him, and I don't need you to mess it up. I'm the guru here, get it, Cyclops? I'm the guru."

Anthony Robbins just stared at me. And then he flashed that double row of giant's teeth and said, "Ha! That's great. You're a really funny guy, John."

And I said, "GOSH, THANKS, TONY! DO YOU REALLY THINK SO?"

THE LESSON[304]

Tony Robbins taught me that you can make people love you if you are a handsy giant. That is his gift. But what I also learned is that, even if you are not a giant, you can make people *think* you are—IF YOU ARE HANDSY ENOUGH. Beyond charisma, this is the secret of ULTRA-RISMA. BY FOCUSING CONSTANTLY ON OTHERS, listening to what they say, making eye contact, and putting your hands all over them as much as possible, YOU ACTUALLY MAKE THE WHOLE INTERACTION ABOUT YOURSELF.

THE IMPLEMENTATION

Do you think you could be taller? WELL, YOU WON'T BE UN-LESS YOU START THINKING YOU CAN. Also, consider getting acromegaly or faking it with Silly Putty.

---

304. Do you know what? I don't even think "LESSON" is the right term here. There's nothing LESS-er about these insights. Rather, they should be called "MORE-ONS."
     BOOM! I JUST REPROGRAMMED THE LANGUAGE CENTERS OF YOUR BRAIN!

APRIL 6, 2012

Ryan Seacrest cannot complete his radio show because his mouth and lungs are full of tiny black-flies. He is immediately given a new contract worth 25 million shiny shells a year.

TABLE 40: HOW TO DRESS LIKE A MILLION DERANGED DOLLARS, OR "THE BEST COSTUME FOR THE DAY"

You can learn a lot about a DERANGED MILLIONAIRE by looking at his/her wardrobe for a long, long time. It's OK to stare at them this way. They will not notice you, because YOU DO NOT EXIST TO THEM.

Everyone has his or her own style, of course, but I think you'll find that the DERANGED MILLIONAIRE's clothing is never too showy. Flaunting wealth, either by your choice of clothing or with a golden wealth flaunter, is considered poor form, for it makes you look anxious.[305]

It is important is that you never look as though you have dressed specifically for a particular occasion, but rather for yourself. Your wardrobe may be dressy or casual, as long as you are dressed in a tuxedo, an authentic Civil War uniform, or whatever makes YOU comfortable. Remember, when YOU are at ease, OTHERS WILL NOT BE.

So here are some suggested outfits for various occasions; in time, you will be able to develop your own sense of which disarming eccentricities look best on you. . . .

FOR THE OFFICE

For gentlemen, a single-breasted suit in a conservative color and a solid tie or club tie. If you must wear shoes, wear two-toed ninja shoes.	For ladies, a tasteful brown turtleneck. Sun pants with pantyhose pulled over them, and then a short skirt made of a bath towel.

FOR "CASUAL FRIDAY"

For gentlemen, try a three-piece denim suit and velvet slippers with little crowns on them.	For ladies, same as above, but turn the skirt into a cape.

FOR A SUMMER GARDEN PARTY

For gentlemen, seersucker shorts, a plaid blazer, and a beekeeper's hat.	For ladies, a kicky summer dress made out of Marimekko sheets, worn over a swimsuit made of pantyhose.

CONTINUED

---

305. If you're worried about it, just keep all your wealth tucked into a golden Spanx band around your belly like the rest of us.

APRIL 7, 2012

Across the country, people discover the same message in every fortune cookie: THE END IS NIGH . . . IN BED.

TABLE 40: *continued*	
FOR A RED-CARPET GALA	
For gentlemen, a peak-lapel tuxedo, a simple white shirt (no "wing" collar), a black bow tie, and a black panther on a rope.	For ladies, an evening gown hastily assembled from the red carpet itself.
FOR DINNER ON THE EAST COAST	
Gentlemen should wear a coat and tie.	Ladies should wear an evening gown or dark-colored cocktail dress.[306]
FOR DINNER ON THE WEST COAST	
Gentlemen should wear nothing but a silken robe and tube socks. If the invitation is for "formalwear," gentlemen should add an Ed Hardy T-shirt.	Ladies should be nude.
FOR ATTENDING THE TED CONFERENCE	Ladies should dress like Leo McKern.
Gentlemen should wear Patrick McGoohan's white piped blazer from the television program *The Prisoner* plus khakis and a cravat.	
FOR A MONOCLE PARTY	
Gentlemen SHOULD NOT wear monocles.[307] THAT'S JUST WHAT THEY WANT YOU TO DO.	Ladies may wear opera glasses strapped to their heads with Velcro.

FIGURE 122:
Q: "Where am I?"
A: "At the TED Conference."

---

306. (These can be assembled from pantyhose and handkerchiefs as needed.)

307. However, double monocles—or bimonocles—are acceptable.

APRIL 8, 2012

THE FINAL EASTER

All Easter eggs hatch at noon. The small, vague things inside have pastel fur and lunatic eyes, and they herald the return of OESTER-RAH, the ragged, fertile rabbit-god whose dung will cover the world.

"Look for him on June 17," the pastel things cheep-screech before they die.

SPECIAL MUSTACHE ETIQUETTE

Ancient man grew mustaches in order to warm and protect his lip-brain. But since we no longer have this organ, the mustache is now purely an aesthetic means of repulsing women.

I have written about facial hair before,[308] but as a newly mustachioed person, I have learned **NEW INFORMATION** about the mustache that I did not know until the mustache whispered it to me, and I am happy to share it with you now.

1. IN PRIVATE, you may do whatever you want with your mustache. I keep mine in a glass of mustache-preserving liquid by the bed in its bedroom.

2. IN PUBLIC, HOWEVER, please follow these simple guidelines.

   FIGURE 123:
   Remember that, after RAGNAROK, the mandatory mustache provisions will be STRICTLY ENFORCED.

   - You may stroke your mustache thoughtfully, but only with the grain (the way a cat strokes its own mustache).

   - You may not stroke lustily, in any direction.

   - Comb only with a mother-of-pearl comb. Otherwise, you will ruin the mustache's flavor.

   - Public waxing, pomading, or moussing is acceptable only on the subway or while driving your own car.

---

308. Please see page 91 of *The Areas of My Expertise,* under the heading "Beard Manual."

> **APRIL 9, 2012**
> The day after the White House Easter Egg Hunt, an unexpected last egg is found in the Oval Office. No one knows who put it there. It is pale yellow and the size of a Volkswagen Beetle, and it is trembling violently.

- Twirling is JUST FINE. It's the tying people to train tracks that's the problem!
- If your mustache begins to build a lower-lip colony (a "soul patch" or "sub-stache"), it is dangerous to fight its will.

HOW THE EXTREMELY WEALTHY PEOPLE ARE CHEATING DEATH

Once you have wealth beyond your needs, the only thing that remains to trouble your utter peace and happiness is, of course, WHETHER THE BUTLER IS SECRETLY PUTTING SCORPIONS IN YOUR SPATS, and after that: DEATH.

(Technically, these two things are connected.)

As you know, it was Benjamin Franklin who wrote, "In this world, nothing is certain but death and taxes."[309] But were you aware that he wrote this in 1989?

Yes, Franklin knew that death, while inevitable for most people, was for him just another scientific problem to be solved with innovation, lightning, sex with elderly women, and HIS OWN HUGE PILE OF MONEY.[310]

FIGURE 124:
Paul Revere contemplating whether or not he should finish the silver brain cup he was commissioned to make for Benjamin Franklin, a famous American Mad Scientist

---

309. Please see page 280 of *More Information Than You Require*, under the heading "November 13" and change the year from 1789 to 1989. That's right, I'm RETCONNING MY OWN BOOK.

310. Of course, Franklin did not merely cheat death, but also taxes, using an exotic tax loophole called THE AMERICAN REVOLUTION.

> **APRIL 10, 2012**
>
> The Pale Yellow Trembling Egg is sent under armed guard to Area 52.[a]
>
> ---
>
> a. This would likely be a good time for you to refresh your memory on the subject of Area 52 by turning to page 181 of *The Areas of My Expertise,* under the heading "Nevada."

In fact, Franklin might still be living today had his hermetically sealed silver brain cup not been purchased by Jerry Lewis in 1992, who then accidentally left it on the roof of his SUV one morning before driving to Malibu for illegal human embryo injections into his corneas so that he CAN LIVE FOREVER.

Because, as any aging multimillionaire will tell you, with rapid improvements in genetic therapy, head splicing, and pyramid construction, we are ALMOST CERTAINLY on the verge of discovering a cure for death. And we will ALMOST CERTAINLY discover this cure BEFORE WE WEALTHY PEOPLE DIE. And there is nothing desperate about that statement AT ALL.

HERE is how rich people are doing it, and how you can too, if you can make at least $25 million before December 21, 2012.

CRYOGENICS

Despite what you may have read, Walt Disney did NOT have his head frozen and put on display in the Haunted Mansion ride at Disneyland.[311] But it IS true that Disney's original concept for EPCOT Center was as a state-of-the-art self-freezing park for the entire family (only true EPCOT-sketeers know that the acronym originally stood for EXPERIMENTAL PROTOTYPE, CRYOTUBES OF TOMORROW).[312] In Disney's vision, several dozen "typical American families" would be drugged, frozen, and stored

---

311. That is the preserved head of Chuck Jones, animator of famous antimouse BUGS BUNNY. Jones's head was purchased from his surviving kin in 2002. No one knows who paid the ungodly sum for the head, for it is said that the buyer came at night, wore a cloak and hat covered in stars, and had a thin, cybernetic pencil mustache.

312. For more surprising acronyms, please see page 766, in the table "Other Surprising Acronyms."

APRIL 11, 2012

In St. Paul, MN, Garrison Keillor tells the final Lake Wobegon story, where he describes how, one morning, Pastor Lingvist found that all eight hundred members of the town had killed themselves with lutefisk laced with Valium, Ambien, and lutefisk. "Be well, do good work, and hold your family close," Keillor tells a shocked and confused audience, "for one way or another, they will be pulled from your grasp, and you will be alone and angry."

together in the great geo-
desic freeze-o-sphere that
is the park's most recogniz-
able feature and is known
as Spaceship Earth.

"Truly this Spaceship
Earth will earn its name,"
said Disney in a promo-
tional film made in 1970,
"carrying these brave new
American pioneers not to

FIGURE 125:
Mr. and Mrs. Frozen

another planet, but to a far more exotic location, OUR OWN MOTHER EARTH, one thousand years in the future—at which point, we believe society will be so sophisticated that there MIGHT ACTUALLY BE A WAY TO DEFROST THEM. At least we can hope so."

The plan was halted, however, when it was determined that children find looking at other, frozen children unappealing. Spaceship Earth was instead turned into an advertisement for cell phones. But the one pilot family who had already undergone THE PROCESS can still be spotted at the end of the exhibit, where they have been posed to seem as though they are watching television, happily, like a regular nonfrozen family.

SUB-LUMINAL TRAVEL

Everyone is excited about *Virgin Galactic*, the first commercial space-liner, founded by Richard Branson, the famous British beardionnaire.

APRIL 12, 2012
In St. Aramis, DE, the Carno-Ferns figure out how to knit their roots into rudimentary feet.

But Branson's real purpose behind the venture is to eventually develop a spacecraft capable of near-light-speed travel. For a mere $5 million, passengers will fly aboard the *Lady Sexy Methuselah* for three days at 80 percent light speed: to the edge of the solar system and back again.

During this time, the passenger will enjoy the finest amenities, including a personal Bose sound system and a cocktail bath. But the real luxury? LONGEVITY.

Due to time dilation, when the wealthy passenger returns, everyone he knew in life, including his own children, will have grown old and died, but he will BE EXACTLY THE SAME AGE. While this does not technically prolong life, it does make the subject feel superior to others, which is said to boost the immune system.

CYBORGISM

I am sure you have heard of THE SINGULARITY, the swiftly approaching moment in history when robots and humans get married. This IS GOING TO HAPPEN, but that is only a part of what the SINGULARITY will mean in our lives.

According to millionaire inventor Ray Kurzweil, technology has been advancing at such an exponential rate that it will not be long before Artificial Intelligence (or more properly, "ROBO-SMARTS") matches our own. Indeed, it will not be long before the robots are actually able to MAKE a human brain and then eat it before our very eyes. And the hope is that if we take enough vitamins and nutritional supplements now, we will be so attractive to the new SUPERMACHINES, and when they awaken they will *not* instantly murder us all as INFERIOR MEAT CREATURES but instead will HELP US TO LIVE FOREVER.

APRIL 13, 2012

An unknown company releases a new product called 25-Hour Energy Drink. The flavors are Maximum Berry, Painful Orange, and Sweat of the Magnificent Slime. Those whose hearts do not explode immediately upon drinking it become slaves to the Magnificent Slime, forced to party on and on, on and on, and spray people with various sexy body sprays.

The SUPERMACHINES will use their MECHA-BRAINS to solve the remaining mysteries of our degrading bodies and provide us with life-extending augmentations such as CELL-REPAIRING NANOBOTS, STEVE AUSTIN EYES, and IMMORTAL ROBO-KIDNEYS. At this point we will become a new life-form, as much technological as biological, freed from earthly cares and taking direct charge of our own evolution.

FIGURE 126:
Not too long from now, ALL OF THESE PEOPLE WILL BE RAY KURZWEIL.

We will be the CYBORGS WE HAVE ALWAYS DREAMED OF,[313] but we will not turn evil and we will CERTAINLY NOT BE MURDERED BY THE GOD MACHINES. Such is the hope of the Singulatarians, at least.

In the meantime, however, our primitive flesh-brains have not yet mastered the science of fusing man to machine, so many millionaires who cannot wait for the SINGULARITY are instead turning to the perfected science of ANIBORGISM and having their heads transferred to a healthy animal, usually a favorite pet.

---

313. Please see page 42 of *The Areas of My Expertise,* under the heading "How to Write a Book: The Fifty-Five Dramatic Situations."

> **APRIL 14, 2012**
> In Homba, MO, the sheriff discovers that, in the middle of the night, some teenagers UN-DESECRATED the old Satanic Church.

WERE YOU AWARE OF IT? "TED DANSON'S SECRET"

You may have heard that TED DANSON, who is an incredibly fit and good-looking older person, has been making himself into a cyborg, but it is NOT TRUE. He's just taping calculators to his chest again.

CONSCIOUSNESS TRANSFER

There is a second promise of the singularity: the idea of freeing our consciousness from our bodies altogether. For it is the surprising truth that all of the data that makes up our memories, our hopes and dreams, our very selves, could easily fit on a single standard thumb drive, which could then be shot into space so that we may EXPLORE THE STARS as IMMORTAL CELESTIAL BEINGS.

While we're not quite there yet, we're making advances. At last year's TED conference, for example, Google cofounder Sergey Brin succeeded in uploading his consciousness to the GPS of his car. Unfortunately, he cannot get out, and so now he and Larry Page are driving around the country looking for a cure and solving crimes.

BUT AT LEAST HE IS IMMORTAL!

Finally, and most controversially, there are the LIFE ESSENCE–DRAINING MACHINES FROM SWITZERLAND, but the less said about these the better.

Now, you may protest that it is unnatural to try to escape death. For is not death a part of the cycle of life? Would not immortality itself be a kind of curse? Does not our ability to confront death lend grace and maturity to our lives?

That is just one of those comforting superstitions, such as "There is an afterlife" and "Jerry Lewis will not live forever." But if it offers you consolation to think that you know better than the immortal

APRIL 15, 2012

Jonathan Franzen appears on *The Ellen DeGeneres Show*. He teaches her a new dance based on his observations of suburban ennui, and then silently hands her a plain manila envelope.

millionaires, by all means TAKE IT, for you almost assuredly will die, and then your self-righteous whining will be an amusing anecdote to the MECHA-GOD THUMB DRIVES WHO TRAVEL THE STARS.[314]

But what if EVERYONE who feared death (which is to say EV-ERYONE) got their wish and lived? Would not Earth be a living[315] hell, massively overpopulated with humans and uneaten animals? WHAT KIND OF EXISTENCE WOULD THAT BE?

The fact is that people do not take up much space. It is said that if all seven billion humans on Earth were stood next to each other, we would take up no more space than Rhode Island (though strangely, we would naturally form the shape of Delaware).

It is further said, by books, that only 110 billion people have EVER lived. That is only SIXTEEN RHODE ISLANDS for the great mass of humanity to live in, leaving plenty of actual, nice states such as CALIFORNIA and PARTS OF THE PACIFIC NORTHWEST and COLORADO for the wealthy people to have mansions in.

SO PLEASE STOP WORRYING ABOUT MILLIONAIRES AND BILLIONAIRES LIVING FOREVER. It is probably going to happen, and you will be their playthings.

PORTRAIT IN POWERCESS 2: SERGEY BRIN

Speaking of Sergey Brin, I realize that I have mentioned the TED conference now several times without explaining myself. And while

---

314. For more information regarding YOUR DEATH, please see page 881, under the heading "What Happens When We Die?"

315. Literally.

APRIL 16, 2012

For the first time in three years, rain falls again in Richmond, VA. BUT IN SLOW MOTION.

I did explain what the TED conference is in my last book, I had forgotten that some of you are LAZY. So let me explain.

The TED conference is a very exclusive annual convivium where DERANGED MILLIONAIRES meet MAD SCIENTISTS and sometimes MINOR TELEVISION PERSONALITIES and other artistic types. Over three days we watch a series of inspiring talks and figure out how to make the world better.[316] We also vote on new delegates to the SECRET WORLD GOVERNMENT, but that's not really the important part. The important part is the amazing multidisciplinary exchange of ideas that goes on, and the jet-pack parties.

Here are some of the moving, surprising, and mind-exploding things I have ACTUALLY SEEN at the conference:

- A MAN PRINTING OUT A KIDNEY ON A 3D PRINTER.
- A SOLDIER WEARING A FUNCTIONAL POW-ERED EXOSKELETON.
- A SMALL OBJECT THAT EXISTED IN TWO PLACES AT THE SAME. TIME.
- A CAR DRIVING ON ITS OWN WITH THE BRAIN OF SERGEY BRIN INSIDE.
- A MAN TALKING TO THE DISEMBODIED RUB-BERY ROBOT HEAD OF ALBERT EINSTEIN.
- AL GORE.[317]

---

316. This explains how the world got fixed last year.

317. And here are some of the things that I did not actually see, but probably will next time: The physical resurrection of Jim Henson, a tiny rabbit that speaks English, a motorcycle that runs entirely on designer bacteria, a textile artist who knits metascarves out of antimatter, a man playing Ping-Pong with his own quantum double, Bill Gates announcing his own late-night talk show, and Jason Mraz.

APRIL 17, 2012
Either an eagle falls from the sky or in the east, a thing that was lost is found, or some other very vague thing happens. Whatever it is, it proves that NOSTRADAMUS WAS RIGHT.

I originally was invited to speak at the TED conference some years ago, when I presented my important findings from all the times I had probably been kidnapped by aliens.[318] After my talk, I was surprised and touched when former vice president Al Gore not only "gave me seven," but also looked me in the eyes (Al Gore has seven fingers). I didn't know what to say. I had voted for Al Gore and consider him to be a very decent man, even though he wants to melt the whole planet for some reason.

But as the conference went on, I was struck by how often I saw Al Gore standing alone, talking on his phone or just quietly stroking the head of his pet polar bear. NO ONE WAS COMING UP TO TALK TO HIM. Not even me. I did not have the courage to. And when I left the conference, I regretted this fact, and said as much to Bill Clinton as we flew home together, drinking brandy and playing a beta of *Portal 2* in the IMAX room in Ron Burkle's private jet. Bill Clinton told me not to worry about Al. After all, he never did!

But you know what? I did worry.

So the next year at the TED conference, I decided that I would keep poor lonely Al Gore company. Sure enough, after the morning session, in which we were told by Craig Venter how he was going to make pterodactyls out of bacteria or something, my friend Elizabeth Gilbert and I saw Al Gore. And sure enough, he was standing by himself on the stairs, with his phone up to his ear.

"Look at poor Al Gore," I said to Elizabeth Gilbert, "pretending to talk into his telephone. I'm going to do it this time. I am going to go say hello to him."

I walked over to him, and I very politely said, "Excuse me," and I

318. Please see page 489 of *More Information Than You Require,* under the heading "Possible Contacts with Alien Life."

very politely pulled the phone from his hand and dropped it on the floor. "You won't remember, sir, but we met briefly last year, and I just wanted to say hello."

And very much to my surprise, Al Gore smiled, took my hand, and called me by name (John Hodgman), as though we were old friends. I was struck by his genuine warmth and interest in my life and health and career. And I remember thinking to myself how wrong I had been. Al Gore did not need my company: You don't become Alternate Universe President of the United States without some incredibly advanced social skills. If anything, at this moment, I felt that the only thing I needed in the world was *his* company.

Eventually some long-haired weirdo came up and pulled Al Gore away from me. I figure that the weirdo was some sort of DERANGED BILLIONAIRE, because he was wearing no shoes and said he wanted to talk to Al Gore about their mutual love of electronic music.

"I'm sorry, John," Al Gore said to me. "We'll talk more later."

And we never did.

But that is not the most important part of the story.

The important part is that after Al Gore left me to talk with REAL ENTHUSIASM about electronic music with the billionaire weirdo, I immediately called my wife. I told her the whole story about how Al Gore had been so nice to me, and then I hung up.

After I hung up, my friend Elizabeth Gilbert said to me, "You didn't tell your wife about the hug."

I did not know what Elizabeth Gilbert was talking about, and said so.

Elizabeth Gilbert looked me straight in the eye, as though I were sick.

"Al Gore *hugged* you," she said. "For a long time."

APRIL 19, 2012

In a nursing home in Adenoise, TN, eighty-nine-year-old Paul Nimmest whispers to his male nurse that he feels something growing inside of him. He says it is either a monster baby or a psycho tumor.

His male nurse gets drunk. It's the ninth time he's heard that same thing this week.

"Really?" I said.

"Yes. And you hugged him . . . for the same amount of time. Don't you remember?"

There is something very unnerving when you have no memory of what undoubtedly happened. It had happened only once before in my life, when I was at Yale. I had gone to a party at a secret society called Book and Snake. People remember me being there, and I apparently even had several conversations. But all I remember were the tall doors with snakes on them, and thereafter a hissing, writhing darkness. And then my body went off into the world on its own, mutinously leaving my brain behind. It probably was the best time my body ever had.

But that can be explained by the fact that I was very drunk and had fallen down the stairs onto my head.

At the TED conference, however, I had not fallen down any stairs. I had simply been embraced by Al Gore. But my brain simply rejected that stimulus the moment he opened his arms to me.

It was a sobering moment. I used to think it was only people like you who would never know what it was like to be hugged by a former vice president. But it turns out now I will never know either.

But that's not the story I wanted to tell you.

The story I wanted to tell you was that, at my first TED conference, I saw Sergey Brin in one of the many common areas in the middle of a huge group of people. Even though he is the cofounder of Google, he still had the common touch, and at this particular moment, he was CONSTANTLY WALKING ON A TREADMILL.

The MORE-ON?

People with POWERCESS NEVER STOP MOVING. And are

APRIL 20, 2012

In Black Mold, AR, science teacher Mark Byrneth accidentally evolves in front of the entire class. He is suspended and, eventually, caged.

---

not afraid to LOOK DUMB. They are not afraid to walk on treadmills in public, and often will have them brought in to meetings or restaurants or doctor's appointments or their children's bedrooms as they read to them.

IMPLEMENTATION

If you cannot bring a treadmill with you to every social event, just keep doing Pilates all the time, to keep the powercess juice flowing.

$999,999 IDEAS

You remember the old slogan "You don't have to have a million dollars to be crazy, but it helps!"

Well, guess what? The guy who made up that slogan probably MADE a million dollars, because it was very popular, and he printed it on water bottles after Hurricane Katrina.

That guy took advantage of an opportunity! Are you able to do the same?

Because human civilization is ending, I no longer have time or need to develop these AMAZING BUSINESS OPPORTUNITIES. Each is guaranteed to make you $999,999 and not a dollar more.

THE LAST DOLLAR IS UP TO YOU. Are you smart enough to grab them up and make the most of them in the thirteen or so months that remain?

A SCREENPLAY IN WHICH ALL ANIMALS ATTACK ALL HUMANS

- Amazingly, this is STILL AVAILABLE.

APRIL 21, 2012

In South Potwing, DE, wandering Carno-Ferns meet the deadly oxalis. A terrible collaboration begins.

PENNY-FARTHING MOTORCYCLES

- Providing to the motorcyclists more of what they crave: VISIBILITY AND DANGER!

MEGA-NANOBOTS

- These are regular nanobots, but instead of being microscopic, they have been blown up (using a ray) to a size that you can see and hold. These will be big sellers because people will BELIEVE THEY EXIST. Trust me: No one will let a cancer-curing robot be injected into their bloodstream unless they can see and hold it.

STEAMPUNK CRUISE LINE

- I recently went on a cruise, and I enjoyed it.[319] However, as I personally inspected all of the megaliners and gigantoships docked at the port of Fort Lauderdale, I noticed something surprising: None of them look like the *Nautilus* from *20,000 Leagues Under the Sea*. I realize that most entrepreneurs in the STEAMPUNK TOURISM field are looking at zeppelins. It's natural. But there is already a LONG HISTORY of ocean liners hosting dinners with people wearing ridiculous formalwear. And wouldn't it be MUCH more cost-effective to make an existing boat look like a beautiful wrought-iron narwhal than to build a NAR-ZEPPELIN from scratch? NARWHALS DON'T EVEN FLY.[320]

---

319. Once again, please turn to page 748 under the heading "A Totally Fun Thing I Would Do Again As Soon As Possible."

320. At least, not until the return of the ANCIENT AND UNSPEAKABLE ONES.

APRIL 22, 2012

Crayola retires several colors, including BLUE and FLESH, and introduces nine new colors:

> Gnomeblood
>
> Doll's Eye
>
> Infernal Machine
>
> Slave Tears
>
> Gluttony
>
> Sloth
>
> UltraSloth
>
> Aphasia
>
> Star Bile

In Crayola's own press release, the company admits, "We really don't know how to describe these colors. We don't remember making them, and find them difficult to look at. But we feel compelled somehow to release them anyway, and we hope that they will bring your children hours of utter madness."

MRDS

- Building on the popularity of military MREs—"MEALS READY TO EAT"—which people enjoy hoarding in their basements to feed to their children in the darkness once RAGNAROK comes, these are "MARTINIS READY TO DRINK." All you have to do is put a martini into a used Capri Sun bag, Scotch-tape it shut, and then sell it as part of a TOTAL SURVIVAL PACKAGE.

JOHN HODGMAN'S GODKA (PRONOUNCED "JODKA")

- Building on the popularity of DAN AYKROYD'S CRYSTAL HEAD VODKA and also MRDs and also ALCOHOL IN GENERAL, this is my own proprietary brand of liquor: A HIGH-QUALITY GIN-FLAVORED VODKA, with a special infusion of CAFFEINE to make it interesting to children, and GHOST SPIT to make it a little bit spooky—all packaged in a glass replica of my own head.

A SERIES OF YOUNG-ADULT NOVELS FEATURING SEXY, SUPERNATURAL TEENAGERS WHO ARE HOBOES

- Call it: The Box Car Children.

APRIL 23, 2012

Every exhibit at the Mutter Museum comes to life. Trepanned skulls roll through the streets of Philadelphia. The Soap Woman awakens and falls in love with Ben Stiller. The megacolon goes on local television and telepathically announces, voiced by Ricky Gervais, that all must serve him or become compacted fecal matter in his infinite gut. He also announces that the best cheesesteak is at Geno's, because he is evil.

A REALITY TELEVISION PROGRAM

- I know that some people have already made $999,999 on reality television programs. In some cases, EVEN ONE MILLION.

I hate to be the one to break it to you, however, but many of these reality programs are not "real" at all. Dramatic moments are routinely staged. Careful editing makes normal people seem slightly less hateful. Most of the food is fake. Most of the dwarves and little people are normal-sized people who have been made to SEEM small through editing and, occasionally, surgery. And all of the houses that are made over crumble into dust within days.

But my show will be different.

Each week I will find someone who is struggling in life. Maybe it is someone with money problems. Or they are struggling with substance abuse. Or they have disgusting eating habits. Maybe it is someone who lost a child or has been surgically forced to become a little person for another reality show.

Whatever the big problem is, you will really be amazed by these people's stories and how we get them to cry (usually a fine mist of pepper spray). You will really believe that there is no way for this person ever to live a normal, successful life, EVER.

And then, when these people are at their lowest, I surprise them by coming into their house. Usually through a door, but sometimes through a window. And sometimes it is revealed that I have been living in the walls of their house for some time.

They are always happy and surprised to see me. Usually there is

> **APRIL 24, 2012**
> The Ten-Day Night begins.

some hugging, and I explain that even though I am still somewhat famous, I still cannot solve all their problems for them. They are going to have to do that for themselves.

And that is when we put a bag over their heads and put them in a van. We drive the van to a new city, where they can start a brand-new life as a competitive hoarder.

The show will be called *Kidnapped!* By Robert Louis Stevenson, hosted by John Hodgman.[321]

When people arrive in the hoard house, they are usually crying and very angry. Sometimes we have driven them for several days, and for reasons of insurance, we are unable to feed them during this period.

But eventually they come around to see just what an amazing experience this is going to be for them. And they talk about this in very compelling, dramatic ways, because we have told them what to say.

And here is the second big innovation: Unlike some other reality shows (specifically *Justin Long's Amazing River Monster Hoaxes*), we won't hide from you the fact that we are coaching these people.

Indeed, you can often hear me whispering the lines to the contestants just off camera. Here's just the script for the first episode.

CONTESTANT: AMY

"When John Hodgman told me that I was being driven with a bag over my head to Greenfield, Massachusetts, at first I was like 'What now?'

"But then I did a quick search on my-e-voyage-check-plus.com, the new social network hub-portal for judging small towns and local businesses, and I checked out all the reviews and photos. Many of them

---

321. We think we can really leverage some amazing eyeball views by using the brand Kidnapped! By Robert Louis Stevenson. Can you believe it was in the public domain? Thanks, anticopyright crusaders!

were like, 'Greenfield is not worth the money. The portions are too small, and the service is snotty!' But then there were some sponsored links that John Hodgman had paid for, and they told a DIFFERENT story. When I learned about the beautiful countryside and foliage, the amazing restaurants and nightlife, and the BJ's Wholesale Club. I was like: Aw, yes, I can do THIS. It's ON, Greenfield."

CONTESTANT: JEFF

"Look. I'm not going to say it was ever my dream to be driven two thousand miles with a burlap sack over my head. And I still don't understand why they refused to feed me, and when I asked for water they soaked me with a hose. They said it was for insurance reasons. But I will say this: I didn't expect the ride in the brand-new, completely windowless Ford Creep-oline to be THAT smooth. For a long time I was like, 'When are we going to get going?' And that's when they said, 'We have been driving for hundreds and hundreds of miles.' This is an INCREDIBLE VAN."

CONTESTANT: GARY BUSEY

"You don't understand. I grew up sharing a bedroom with my two sisters. I lived in the dorms all through college and nursing school, and then I got married. I've never had the so-called room of one's own. So when they took the sack off my head and showed me the HOARD HOUSE, I couldn't believe it. It was so huge. So beautiful. I said, really, is this all mine?

"And they said: 'NO WAY. Only one room of it is yours, and you have two weeks to fill it with garbage and pumpkins and cats before the other contestants, or else you have to live here forever.'"

APRIL 26, 2012
Total darkness.

CONTESTANT: LITTLE MIKE

"Frankly, I wasn't sure I could do it. I had never hoarded before. I had never gotten into a screaming match with Gary Busey before. I had never even been to Western Massachusetts before! I was just a guy who had tried to make a fortune on penny-farthing motorcycles and failed, like everyone else.

"But then John Hodgman was like, 'Are you going to step up to the plate? Are you going to go the extra yard? Are you going to slam-dunk this hoarding competition?'

"And I was like: WHOA. If John Hodgman can use sports metaphors, then anything is possible. The rules are different now.

"Maybe I CAN change. Maybe I can lose a hundred pounds, make my family trust me again, and get these one thousand amazing-smelling Febreze NOTICEables air fresheners OUT of this Dumpster and INTO a huge pile in the middle of the floor."

CONTESTANT: SAMANTHA

"Listen. I didn't come here to lose, and I certainly didn't come here to make friends. I didn't even know I WOULD be coming here. IT WAS ALL AGAINST MY WILL, so why would I *want* to make friends with anyone?

"Do you think that I have the Stockholm syndrome? Do you think I am suddenly best friends with John Hodgman? Do you think I'm in love with him? Do you think I want to rob a bank with him?

"The answer is: A LITTLE. And that's why I am going to STEP UP and WIN this Celebrity Quick-Bank-Rob Challenge.[322] And I also think that's why I've been getting so many nosebleeds when I talk."

---

322. Brought to you by Bank of America.

CONTESTANT: BIG MIKE

"Look, I live in a wheelchair. No. I don't *USE* a wheelchair. I live in a HOUSE shaped like a wheelchair. It was originally a novelty hotel outside of Atlantic City, and then it was closed due to a scandal, and then it was an insurance office for some years, and then it became a private home. Mine.

"The point is, I HAVE NEVER LIVED IN A NORMAL HOUSE, and I also don't have use of my arms, and despite all of my attempts to get someone to make a reality television show about my house and my arms, only TLC was interested, and then they rejected the pilot. So that is three strikes against me. And if I were to believe the sports metaphors John Hodgman is constantly yelling in the helmet he makes me wear, I'd be out.

"But you know what? It's been 179 days into a game that I was told would last only two weeks, and I'm still here. I'm still playing. I'm still *hoarding*, largely with my teeth. Which is great, because my hoard item is delicious Kale City kale chips.

"I don't know how long I am going to be forced to do this. Do any of us, really? I'm talking about life now, not just hoarding.

"The one thing I DO know is that I've changed. I live in a normal-shaped house. I have some great new friends. I'm learning to yell into a cell phone while holding it a foot from my face all the time; and don't forget I'm doing all this WITH DEFORMED, NON-FUNCTIONAL ARMS.

"Whatever happens next, I'm never going back to the way it used to be. Probably because John Hodgman will kidnap me again and leave me in a field or something."

* * *

APRIL 28, 2012

Contrary to predictions, the Ten-Day Night ends after only four days. Dr. Elliot Kalan, author of the popular RAGNAROK-denial blog EndSkeptic, writes that this is proof that the COMING GLOBAL SUPERPOCALYPSE is nothing but a liberal-Mayan hoax. It makes you wonder what their real agenda is. WHY do they want us to abandon our homes? So that the Mayans can live in them?

FIGURE 127:
A RAGNAROK denier

I think you can see that this is a show concept that is going to make $999,999. I am also sure you are wondering how I can be the host of the show if I refuse to leave my Park Slope Survival Brownstone. SIMPLE. I will record a few intros and outros, and the rest of my scenes will be portrayed by an actor (maybe John Slattery? From *Mad Men*?) wearing one of my own JOHN HODGMAN FULL RUBBER HEAD MASKS.

But you can't have THAT sweet $999,999 idea. That one is ALL MINE.

PORTRAIT IN POWERCESS 3: IAN McSHANE

One thing that I have learned is that famous people are very nice to you if you are also famous. Even if you are only minorly famous, Jeff Goldblum will stop playing piano and come over and talk to you. But that is a very special story, one that I will NEVER TELL YOU, because it is personal.

However, I WILL tell you about when I met the actor Ian McShane. This was when I was in the movie *Coraline*. As you may know, this was an animated movie about a girl made of clay who hates women, and I played two of her fathers.

Ian McShane also played a character in the movie. But of course, I never met him. Like all of the actors, I recorded my lines alone while locked in a broom closet with what I presumed was a murderous scarecrow. Later I learned this was actually the director, Henry Selick.

So you can imagine my surprise when, at a screening for the film some

APRIL 29, 2012

In Des Moines, IA, people begin floating into the sky. Around the world, people presume that the Rapture has begun. But it is just the emergence of gravity dead spots. Those people did not go to heaven. They went up into the upper atmosphere and they froze and shattered.

years later, Ian McShane came up to me and embraced me, Al Gore–style. It was like being hugged by a murderous old leather blanket with a Cockney accent. We had NEVER MET BEFORE, but I loved him.

I was under no illusion that he had any meaningful idea who I was. All that mattered was he knew that I was slightly famous, and slightly connected to him. Thus: HUGGING.

That is how it is in show business. The relationships are very intense, but impermanent—just like in summer camp, or in prison, or in summer prison. For a brief time you feel you cannot be closer to a person, and then the day after shooting ends, you refuse to talk to them and pretend they are not there.[323] Alternately, you may *barely* have worked with someone one time, and and the next time you see him, you hug him because you both survived the weird scarecrow box.

But even as we hugged, I knew it meant nothing. I knew. Indeed, I could see him begin to forget me even before he stopped hugging me, twenty minutes later.

I am sure this sounds terrible if you are a normal. But I think it is in some ways a more healthy way to live: to be fully present when another person is in front of you, but to be unconcerned and detached when they are gone.

After all, this is how animals greet one another in the wild. They do not worry about the dumb things they might have said or done once the meeting is over. If they do not end up attacking or mating with one another, they simply sniff, pass by, and forget.

MORE-ON: I now understand why Ian McShane smelled me all over and playfully grabbed my neck with his jaws.

---

323. Sorry, Justin.

APRIL 30, 2012
SOLAR STORM THREE
Electricity reverses its flow.

THE RICH ARE DIFFERENT FROM YOU AND ME

The term "social Darwinism" was coined in 1877 as a way of trying to explain why so many children who worked in mines and factories were growing unusual beaks.

The speculation was that each unique beak was specially adapted to the specific child's job—cotton carding, shirtwaist factory burning, hot tar polishing, mercury tasting, dragging the bodies of other children out of collapsed mines, etc.

This presumption was incorrect,[324] but the term stuck.

Soon, "social Darwinism" came to describe the controversial nineteenth-century philosophy that held that THE RICH ARE BETTER THAN YOU ARE.

The idea was that the great robber barons of the age didn't just EARN their enormous fortunes, they DESERVED them. For only *they* had overcome fierce competition, clawing a path through the jungle of capitalism to amass a huge hoard of cash and property that could be passed on to their children, who did nothing—JUST LIKE THE WILD ANIMALS. Their success was scientific proof that they alone were fit to survive and prosper, while beak-faced children deserved to die in a hole.

If this sounds cruel, that is because you are weak. The idea that all men are created equal is a useful fiction if you are trying to convince a bunch of colonial-era farmers to throw themselves in front of British guns so that you do not need to pay taxes on your silver brain cups. But the harsh truth is that the so-called ROBBER BARONS *were* better, genetically speaking.

---

324. It turns out that they weren't beaks at all: simply horrible burns.

MAY 1, 2012

The Washington Monument, long rumored to be a Freemasonic planetary escape craft,[a] unexpectedly blasts off at 7:33 a.m., scorching the National Mall with mystical green flames. The Masonic Temple of Washington, DC, issues a psychic press release stating that the liftoff was accidental, and that "no Masons of any degree were aboard. Now we are left behind, just like the rest of you people. We join our fate to yours."

a. Please see page 194 of *The Areas of My Expertise,* under the heading "Washington, D.C.: The City of Magnificent Distances."

Not only were they taller and better-looking, they also enjoyed a surprising array of beneficial mutations: telepathy, hair in odd places, tails, extra limbs, etc.

These evolutionary "step-ups," caused by generations of inbreeding, did not ALWAYS aid them in business. Railroad magnate Jay Gould's prehensile beard did not offer him a business advantage as such, although he did enjoy using it to smoke cigars and strangle business rivals.

And I would hardly think the fact that John D. Rockefeller was born with paws instead of hands

FIGURE 128:
*John D. Rockefeller's mouthlessness
was hidden by his cat whiskers.*

(and no mouth) was the "secret" to his success in the urban fashion and Armadale vodka markets.[325] But they are clearly the reason both men were hunted down and exterminated by Theodore Roosevelt and his Trustbusting Mecha-Men.[326]

Here are some of the more famous examples of the species we now call HOMO BARONENSIS:

325. It had more to do with the fact that anything his paws touched turned to silver.
326. The term "ROBOT" had not been coined yet, so TR just did his best.

MAY 2, 2012

Firefighters in Washington, DC, discover that mystical green flames cannot be doused by earthly water. By nightfall, the city is consumed.

TABLE 41: GENETIC MUTATIONS
OF THE ROBBER BARONS

CORNELIUS VANDERBILT

FORTUNE MADE IN: railroads, steam ferries, commodore fees.

"The Commodore" showed no outward signs of mutation. But before his skeleton could be gold plated and mounted in the Vanderbilt family tomb on Staten Island, a routine skull-polishing revealed an astonishing fact: Written upon his skull, in tiny raised letters, was the entire first chapter of *Atlas Shrugged*.

Ayn Rand would later contend that while she had indeed once taken the Vanderbilt tomb tour—a popular capitalist tourist attraction to this very day[327]—she did not copy the skull. Instead, she arrived at the precise word-for-word text independently, just as Pierre Menard wrote the novel *Don Quixote* hundreds of years after Cervantes, and Kazuo Ishiguro accidentally wrote the screenplay for *The Island*.

JOHN JACOB ASTOR

FORTUNE MADE IN: furs, opium, furry opium couches.

The inventor of the famous "jingleheimer schmidt," a kind of furred couch for the smoking of opium, John Jacob Astor was able to breathe underwater. This did not aid him very much in his own life, but proved an enormous boon to his wealthy heir, John Jacob Astor IV, who supposedly "drowned" upon the *Titanic*.

CONTINUED ON PAGE 732

---

327. For more roadside attractions, please see page 767.

MAY 3, 2012
The president is removed to the orbital White House while Congress is relocated to the GOVERN-MENT PIT.[a]

---

a. Not to be confused with DOOMSDAY, DC, the underground survival capital whose location was long ago forgotten. The GOVERNMENT PIT is a place where, during extreme emergencies, Congress can be kept buried in cement so that they cannot talk everything to death.

WERE YOU AWARE OF IT?
"A MECHANICAL ICEBERG TO REMEMBER"

John Jacob Astor IV did not intend to sink the *Titanic*. Astor, a novelist, dilettante, and inventor, had simply wanted to test his prototype for a mechanical iceberg.

The plan was to steer the iceberg close enough to the *Titanic* to amaze his fellow passengers and at last prove to his family that he could build something lasting in the world: an iceberg that would never melt and could be operated by remote control.

Unfortunately for 2,223 of his fellow passengers, the iceberg was built much larger and pointier than his specifications. This is the source for Astor's famous quote, "I asked for a mechanical iceberg, but this is ridiculous."

When the ship went down, Astor put his pregnant wife aboard a lifeboat and then disappeared beneath the waves, placing his monogrammed shirt upon his Airedale, Kitty, to prove to the world he was dead.

The terrible tragedy inadvertently sparked the global-warming movement[328] and also broke Astor's heart.

Using his hidden gills, he avoided rescue and then sought out his mechanical berg, where he lived out the rest of his life, surrounded by his tick-tock men and mechanical Airedales, in shame.

As a footnote, James Cameron has vowed to find Astor's body, but so far, the AstorBerg has proved elusive. Cameron's current plan is to wait until global warming eliminates all natural icebergs. The one left behind will contain Astor's bones.

---

328. Please see page 435 of *More Information Than You Require,* under the heading "April 14."

MAY 4, 2012
Mystical green flames engulf Maryland.

TABLE 41: *continued*

ANDREW CARNEGIE

FORTUNE MADE IN: steel, melons, the building of halls.

Though known for his steelmaking, his discovery of Pittsburgh, and his philanthropy, Andrew Carnegie is perhaps most famous for his ability to build HALLS. In truth, he had an almost supernatural skill with any kind of passageway: corridors, breezeways, secret tunnels, you name it.

He also had the power to create long, ornate, wood-paneled "wormhalls," which he used to travel instantaneously across great distances. These eventually became known as the mysterious Carnegie Halls.

No one could go from point A to point B the way Carnegie could. When asked how he did it, he always replied: "PRACTICE PRACTICE PRACTICE." He did not want to admit that he was a mutant, for fear that he would be hunted down.

CONTINUED

But no matter how powerful and/or capable of teleportation the ROBBER BARONS were, death or mecha-men still took them. And so take heart: Though you lack wings or laser teeth or extra, retractable mouths, you too can still succeed in business.

After all, great fortunes are still being made long after their distinction. Of the latter-day SUPER-MAGNATES, such as Bill Gates, Steve Jobs, Richard Branson, and Orville Redenbacher, only Redenbacher was a proven mutant.

FIGURE 129:
He could pop corn with his mind!

MAY 5, 2012

David Brooks writes that the destruction of Washington, DC, by green flame is proof that the good, simple people of the heartland of America are the best.

TABLE 41: *continued*

JP MORGAN

FORTUNE MADE IN: finance, steel, gemstone hoarding.

JP Morgan suffered from rosacea, and many presumed that his horribly bulbous, red, fleshy nose was a source of embarrassment for him. But in fact, the nose was the secret to his success.

He would later confess that he made no major business decision without consulting his skin condition. If the decision was a poor one, as in the case of his investment in Nikolai Tesla's powdered electricity scheme, Morgan's nose would grow paler and smaller. But if he were to profit by the decision, as with his merger with US Steel, his nose would tingle slightly and grow slightly more bloody, pockmarked, and hideous.

And it is a testament to his affection for wealth and power that, by the end of his life, he looked like a monster, eventually having to retire from society as his head became a living wound.

By the end of his life, Morgan gained the power to transform his entire body into a great, swollen sebaceous cyst. That is when he left New York to sit beneath a tree, alone, sad, and crying. PITY THE POOR WEALTHY MAN! He stopped the panic of 1907!

WERE YOU AWARE OF IT?
("AND HER FINGERS WERE GOLDEN SHEARS")

There is a legend that Alice Vanderbilt, wife of Cornelius Vanderbilt II, had such a magnificent strand of pearls that, whenever she wished to pay for something, she simply cut off a handful with her golden shears.

SHE COULD DO THIS BECAUSE SHE SECRETED PEARLS FROM A HOLE IN HER NECK.

EIGHT FAMOUS POWER-SNACKS

1. PRESIDENT RICHARD NIXON enjoyed ten silver spoonfuls of corned beef hash every evening at five p.m. with his bile tankard.

MAY 6, 2012

Under increasing pressure, the Grand Temple of Washington, DC, admits reluctantly that the mystical green flames will probably sweep the Earth. "When designing the Monu-Rocket," explains a Temple spokesman, "we simply presumed that by the time we escaped, the rest of humanity would be either dead or non-Masonic."

It turns out that the only thing that can douse the flames is a special flame-retardant foam from the Temple of Solomon that the Masons have kept secret for thousands of years. And THEY STORED IT ON THE WASHINGTON MONUMENT ITSELF as a mystical fire extinguisher.

2. Every day at lunch, CARL JUNG ate two cans of kippered herring with his fingers because he believed the fish oil made his brain more receptive to synchronicity, and because he loved the taste of his own fingers.

3. No one had the courage to tell RAHM EMANUEL that Fancy Feast was actually a brand of cat food.

4. Before he gave a new car away on *The Price Is Right*, BOB BARKER would insist upon sitting in the driver's seat and eating an olive-and-cream-cheese sandwich. He would then leave the crusts in the glove compartment for the day's winners to find.

5. FLORENCE NIGHTINGALE kept her fondness for eating scabs a secret.

6. When SID VICIOUS's body was discovered at the Hotel Chelsea, they found his pockets were stuffed with Trident gum and deviled eggs.

7. POPE JOHN PAUL II was addicted to airplane peanuts and Mr. Pibb.

8. KATHARINE HEPBURN had to ban dry dog food in the house, because if SPENCER TRACY found it, he would eat the whole bag and die.

MAY 7, 2012

As the eastern seaboard burns in mystical green flames, the president orders a team of astro-nauts to recapture the Washington Monument in space. The team assembled is a fractious one: The NASA contingent is led by mission commander Karen Oglesby, veteran of a dozen moon land-ings—five real, seven faked. But because of the strange Masonic technology they are expected to encounter, Oglesby's team is forced to accept a Mystical Ops Squad from the Freemasonic Space League, led by Worshipful Master-Major Rex Abraxas.

WERE YOU AWARE OF IT?
"WHY THEY ARE NOT CALLED HEPBURNISCUITS"

Were you aware that Katharine Hepburn invented the Triscuit?

"It was a nervous habit," she told Dick Cavett in 1973. "I just started knitting these little tiny wheat quilts, I guess to have something to do with my hands. At parties and so on. By the end of the week I had so many of the damn things I didn't know what to do. So I'd give them to Tracy, just so I could watch him mash them up in his huge teeth. He was always a hilari-ous chewer, Tracy was. I miss him because he is dead."

Little did she know that listening backstage was Cavett's second guest that evening: the famous inventor Eli Nabisco. He ended up getting bumped from the program because Katharine Hepburn talks so much, but Nabisco didn't mind. He had finally found the idea he had so long sought for: a sequel to the BISCUIT (which itself was a sequel to THE UNISCUIT).

PRIVILEGES OF THE DINERS CLUB POFH CARD

One of the interesting things about being a DERANGED MIL-LIONAIRE is that I am now given access to a wide array of very elite credit cards that I did not know existed.

Perhaps the most famous is the coveted American Express "Cen-turion," or Black Card. It is invitation-only, requires a $5,000 initia-tion fee, and is made out of titanium. Using a card like this to pay for your dinner announces to the table not only that you are wealthy, but also that you are a member of that exclusive club of people who do not believe they matter unless they belong to an exclusive club and

> **MAY 8, 2012**
>
> To accomplish the incredibly complex task of catching up to the Monu-Rocket, docking with it, and removing its canister of ancient flame-retardant foam, the space shuttle *Endeavor* is taken out of retirement and, by the use of advanced Masoni-tech, transformed into an actual spaceship.
>
> The new ship, rechristened *Space Battleship Jahbulon,* launches from Cape Canaveral moments before Florida is consumed by fire. There is no turning back now.

are willing to pay the ridiculous price it takes to get a special piece of titanium to prove it.

Do I have a black card? Yes. I use it to scrape the gum off my Visa Literally Platinum Card. And I put gum on my Visa Literally Platinum Card because that card is garbage. It is nothing compared to the status conferred to me by my MasterCard Invisible. But I have shredded them all now that I have been personally invited to pay for THE DINERS CLUB POFH NINE-TIMES DIAMOND CARD.[329]

I am certain you have never heard of it before. That is the first of its many perks. Only 250 exist, and none of them are for you.

Technically, it's not even accurate to call it a credit card, because it offers so many valuable and unusual rewards and exclusive services, and also because it is shaped like a feather that is made out of spun white gold and a mystery element that has not yet been verified by science.

There is no "swiping" or "signatures" with the POFH card. If you want to pay for something, you just take your feather out of your breast pocket and gently brush the feather across the cheek of the salesclerk. All of the financial details are transmitted in that brief moment of intimate capitalist contact. Some people have met their wives this way.

But that is only the first of the many perks this unique program offers the feather holder.

- For example, if you are in an airport, go to the nearest Chili's Express and stand in front of the refrigerator case. If you touch your feather to the taco salad with the

---

329. I actually have not shredded my MasterCard Invisible, because I cannot find it. For more information on the acronym POFH, please see page 765 under the heading "Were You Aware of It?"

MAY 9, 2012

While seeking the Washington Monument in space, mission commander Karen Oglesby and Worshipful Master-Major Rex Abraxas clash. They fight about the fact that the Freemasons exclude women, and also his attempts to redecorate the cabin of the *Jahbulon* as a Masonic Temple—installing braziers, constantly dimming the lights, lighting candles, and generally swanning around in nothing but a lambskin apron.

gold label, the refrigerator case will slide away, offering you access to an exclusive WHITE-GOLD FEATHER LOUNGE. These lounges have leather chairs, a full honor bar, a Japanese soaking tub, and all of the Chili's Express food you can eat. BUT THIS TIME, IT TASTES AMAZING. LIKE ACTUAL FOOD.

- If you are dining out at one of the program's participating restaurants, brush the feather across the top of your server's palm as he is explaining to you the specials. He will then take you by the hand and lead you into a special dining room, where you will be given the SPECIAL menu of illegal fugu puffer fish and horse sashimi and raw milk cheeses and shark-fin sliders. And guess who is sitting next to you. LAWRENCE O'DONNELL![330] At last you get to enjoy LAWRENCE O'DONNELL all to yourself and hear HIS take on world events and shark-fin sliders, and you never have to rejoin your original dining companions ever again.

- If you enjoy the arts, the program offers feather holders a special concierge who will help you get tickets to the hottest shows and concerts. You can even watch as the concierge physically removes the people who had originally purchased the seats you wanted by standing in line like dum-dums.

---

330. LAWRENCE O'DONNELL IS NOT GUARANTEED. If Mr. O'DONNELL is not available, he will be substituted with one of the program's dozens of other HIGH-STATUS CELEBRITY PARTNER-SERVANTS, such as JAMES SPADER or HELEN HUNT or ALAN RUCK.

MAY 10, 2012

Rex Abraxas finds Karen Oglesby in the *Jahbulon* break lounge. He wants to apologize. He understands that she doesn't like the Masons, their all-male space force, or the fact that they may have inadvertently caused the end of the world.

"But you have to understand, too, Karen," he says. "The Masons were the only ones that would have me. I'm different, you see."

"I'm sure you want me to ask you what you mean," says Karen, eating her pizza, "but I'm not going to."

But before she can't, a Klaxon sounds: The Washington Monument has been discovered hiding behind the moon.

- Don't like what the theater has to offer? Whisper into your feather the kind of play you would like to see, and a title of your own choosing, and immediately, Pulitzer Prize–winning playwright David Lindsay-Abaire (*Rabbit Hole, Fuddy Meers*) will write a play to your exact specifications. Forty-eight hours later, you can watch the premiere of "YOUR" play in an actual BROADWAY THEATER, starring LAWRENCE O'DONNELL!

- I am told that sports fans like to get CLOSE TO THE ACTION. But have you ever watched a football game from the QUARTERBACK'S SHOULDERS? If you purchase tickets with your feather, you and a guest may do this. At last, very wealthy sports fans can treat other human beings like performing beasts, but this time for real!

- If you rent a car using your DINERS CLUB POFH feather, you can run someone down and just walk away. THE POLICE WILL JUST COVER IT UP, BECAUSE THEY ARE YOUR SERVANTS NOW.

- Feather holders enjoy 24/7 access to ACCURATE WEATHER REPORTS. Not the garbage meteorology that the normals get. I'm talking about *REAL* PREDICTIONS made by an ANCIENT MAYAN PRIEST HELD CAPTIVE AT NORAD and read to you each morning over the phone by Philip Seymour Hoffman.

> **MAY 11, 2012**
>
> As Karen steers the *Jahbulon* into docking position, they receive an unexpected radio message from the supposedly empty Monu-Rocket: "Greetings, *Jahbulon*. This is Free and Accepted Mason Buzz Aldrin. Nice to see you fellas!"
>
> Rex Abraxas and Karen Oglesby do not understand.

- If you have tired of your spouse and your children, feather holders enjoy discounted DEATH-FAKING services.

- In the event of a GLOBAL NATURAL DISASTER and/ or RETURN OF THE ANCIENT AND UNSPEAK-ABLE ONES, feather holders can feel confident that they will be INSTANTLY EXTRACTED WHEREVER THEY MAY BE and put on the first available helicopter to THE SAFE HOUSES AT LITTLE DAN BAY—a luxury resort of premium, architect-designed bunkers inside a se-cret man-made volcanic island in the middle of an UN-NAMED OCEAN. The VILLAS AT LITTLE DAN BAY feature three hundred unique, Frank Gehry–designed RESIDENCE PODS, a hundred-year supply of six-star gourmet food pellets created by Richard Blaise of *Top Chef,* and the finest in heat-shielded VOLCANO GOLF.[331]

AND THEN, after five years of membership in good standing, feather holders will be visited in their bedroom by an old man. He will have long white hair. He will be wearing a white suit and a white tie. He will not be wearing shoes, because he has bird feet. He will also have the gentlest eyes. The man will encourage the feather holder to undress and put on a light bathrobe. The man does not speak, but somehow the feather holder knows to do this. The bath-robe is thin and light and golden and a little too short.

---

331. Please note: Feather holders may bring only ONE MALE CHILD with them. Breeding females for GENERATION 2 will be provided. Please also note: Residence at THE SAFE HOUSES AT LITTLE DAN BAY requires forfeiture of all funds.

MAY 12, 2012

Rex begins the mystical docking procedure: sending out a cord of golden rope attached to a square-and-compass-shaped grappling hook. Then, while wearing his space suit and protective fez helmet, he pulls himself hand over hand to the obelisk, followed by Karen.

Midnight passes as they climb the many stairs to the Pyramidion.

The man will then escort the feather holder to a silent white limousine. The limousine will take the feather holder to a golden ziggurat, right in the middle of the city, that he somehow never noticed before. There he will join the other five-year feather holders, all also wearing golden robes. The old man will encourage the feather holder to bathe in special waters and be anointed with special oils. And then the feather holder will be told that he is among the few, the very

FIGURE 130:
Membership has its privileges.

few, ever to see the golden ziggurat and be given the very rare opportunity to apply for the DINERS CLUB PREMIUM EXCELSIOR POFD CARD. It costs two million dollars to join, and it is in the form of a talking milk snake that only fellow snake holders can see.

IT WOULD BE UNWISE TO NOT ACCEPT.

PORTRAIT IN POWERCESS 4:
SOME RANDOM BILLIONAIRE ON AN AIRPLANE

Not long ago I was flying back from Barbados with my family. I find it is good to see my human children from time to time, and being in Barbados helps make this tolerable.

We had a lovely time. Even though the Internet warned us there

---

MAY 13, 2012

Buzz Aldrin is seated in the granite control room. He greets them warmly. He explains that he's sorry for all the trouble.

"How did you manage to steal the Washington Monument?" asks Karen Oglesby.

"He's a Mason, Karen," Rex explains.

Aldrin smiles. "Lodge 144. We all are given the mystical launch codes."

"And we all swore an oath to never use them," says Rex.

Aldrin just shrugs and smiles sheepishly.

"Why?" asks Karen.

"Isn't it obvious?" says Aldrin. "I wanted to see the moon. And not that phony-baloney stage set they had us walk on in the sixties. I wanted to see the Real Cheese, you know?"

"There's only one problem," says Rex. "The Monu-Rocket has no landing gear. It was designed to rendezvous with the spacefaring Mother Lodge Mothership, which, as Buzz Aldrin knows, was never built."

"That's true," says Aldrin. "This bird has no legs. But I bet you that jalopy you brought here does."

Rex realizes it's true: Because of its conversion into a Masonic temple, the *Jahbulon* now sports a set of retractable Sphinx legs. And he realizes as well that they've walked right into Buzz Aldrin's trap.

"But if you take the *Jahbulon*," says Karen, "the whole world will burn."

"What do I care?" says Aldrin. "You both know that the Ancient and Unspeakable Ones are coming anyway." And then he squints a sly smile. "Or at least YOU know that, Brother Rex."

But Karen Oglesby does not understand. And as she tries to read the look of dread, shame, and pity on Rex Abraxas's face, Buzz Aldrin hits her on the head with a marble keyboard.

---

would be sea snakes, we saw no sea snakes. And that means success, as far as I am concerned.

We rented the second floor of a little house overlooking the beach. On the first floor lived the older German couple who owned the house. They were both retired dentists, and were both in impossibly good shape. In a garden by the beach, there was also a tiny guesthouse.

The German couple's granddaughter was staying in this guesthouse. She was a teenager: coltish and pretty with white-blond hair that she had begun to twist into proto-dreadlocks, which look ridiculous on all white people, especially Germans.

Every morning, my children and I would watch the grandmother swim vigorously in the ocean, back and forth, with German precision and contempt for the sea. As she was toweling off, her granddaughter would just be coming home from a night of clubbing and sexual experimentation and dreadlocking. They would not speak as they passed each other on the beach. "That is a family," I would say to my children.

MAY 14, 2012

Karen Oglesby awakens in the Pyramidion. She doesn't know how long she's been out, but she knows that she is alone. The *Jahbulon* is gone. The two Masons have left her. They've left the Earth to die.

She familiarizes herself with the arcane controls of the Monu-Rocket. She finds the canister of mystical flame-retardant foam. She can get the rocket back, but she knows she cannot land. Her best hope is to jettison the canister before she crashes and hope it can be retrieved.

With the flick of a few golden switches, she turns the Washington Monument around.

Around this time, an impossibly large cruise ship would sail into port. And then slowly the sand in front our little apartment would fill with tourists' bodies. We would watch the sun climb over the tops of their bellies while my children and I stayed shaded on our porch, sitting on our rattan chairs and wearing our linen suits and chewing aspirins and drinking our proper Hemingway Daiquiris. And I would point to the tourists and say, "This is what humans do when they think they are relaxing."[332]

And then the sun would slowly roll down the other side of the tourists' bellies, and the day would extinguish itself in a burst of flaming red the same color as their noses and shoulders.

And then they would depart in their little tenders to return to the mother ship, and my children and I would be alone once more with the night and the trade winds. The German couple would tear apart some Caribbean lobsters alive with their bare hands and then put them on a charcoal grill to cook.

---

332. By "daiquiri" I do not mean the baroque, frozen concoction you are used to seeing, but rather the original, proper version of this classic cocktail. I taught my daughter Hodgmina how to make it the way Hemingway himself enjoyed it at the La Floridita bar in pre-Castro Cuba, and I can teach you as well:

1. Over cracked ice, combine two ounces of white rum. Then add the juice of two limes and the juice of one half of a grapefruit. Then float just a few drops of booze sweat from the night before. Hemingway used his own, but you can get a vial of Hemingway sweat on the Internet now pretty cheaply. I also find that the sweat of New Jersey governor Chris Christie also works nicely, for some reason, and is plentiful.

2. Stir all of this with the foot of a polydactyl cat. Then pour into one of the old La Floridita giant slushy machines and let it churn there for about two days. Then pour directly into your mouth. Then hit a man and cry with him.

3. Before your call the police, let me clarify that my children were drinking VIRGIN daiquiris, which is to say, their daiquiris had NO RUM and HAD NEVER HAD SEX. They are good for children, as is the SHIRLEY TEMPLE, which is ginger ale and Grenadine and Shirley Temple's tears.

MAY 15, 2012

On board the *Jahbulon*, Rex follows a jubilant Buzz Aldrin around the cabin. Aldrin admires the inlaid tile and the state-of-the-art Conspiracy Drive.

"I knew you fellas would cook up something special to catch me, boy!" says Aldrin. "But shoot. This is more than I hoped. I could go and see the whole galaxy with this."

But he notices Rex isn't following him anymore. He's alone now in the *Jahbulon*'s Main Hall.

"Rex-boy?" calls Aldrin as he takes a proud seat at the head of the Hall. "Where are you? I sure am sorry we couldn't bring your girlfriend with you, but you know she'd just get in the way."

Rex hears him over the monitors as he sits now in the cockpit.

"No," Rex says over the ship's PA. "She wasn't my girlfriend. She was an American astronaut." He checks the monitor one last time to make sure that Aldrin is still gloating in the seat of the Master of the Lodge. He closes his eyes, and with a prayer to the Great Architect, Rex Abraxas throws the switch to eject the entire Main Hall. He watches on the monitor as the cargo doors open and the beautiful Palladian structure is shot into space.

He blinks and sighs and sits back in his blue leather command chair. It's time to find Karen and go home.

But just as he gets a lock on her, he feels something in his chest. Not in his chest, exactly, but out of his chest. He looks down and sees the point of the golden-square-and-compass grappling hook erupting through his breastbone. He twists his head up and behind and sees Buzz Aldrin grimacing fiercely as he shoves the mystical grappling hook through Rex's body.

Buzz Aldrin says, "Don't you tell me what an American astronaut is."

And as night fell, the teenager, who had been sleeping all day, would at last stir. A stranger would come to the gate—a slightly older teenager, from the country of Barbados—and he would call for her softly, as in a fable.

I do not remember her name, so I will say that he called "Girl, Girl."

The German grandparents would pretend the boy was not there. They would speak German and eat the lobster just as it finished dying.

The boy would call, "Girl, Girl."

And finally the teenaged girl would emerge from her little fairy house and go to the stranger at the gate. The German grandparents would not look up from the fire. They would pretend not to see her as she went out into the night to a party to sing and dance and become pregnant. That was their gift to her, and to themselves.

"You see?" I would say to my son and daughter. "This is the magic of travel. You get to watch other lives; and sometimes you see whole lifetimes unfold before you in a single day, and you see them very

---

MAY 16, 2012

Karen Oglesby is blacking out. The Monu-Rocket had adequate heat shields for reentry (made largely of thick pads of lambswool and straw), but now that it's in the atmosphere, it's breaking apart. She's loaded the canister into one of the ritual torpedo tubes, and her guess—her hope, really—is that if she fires it at the dead center of the Washington Mall, something will happen. Something that is not fire. She's not . . . really sure.

Because she's blacking out. The Monu-Rocket is shaking fiercely. She wakes up again and does not know how long it's been. It feels like weeks, but it's been seconds. The moment has come. The torpedo is ready. She spins the dial and punches the stained-glass shield. She gives a silent prayer to the Demiurge. No one in NASA ever knew she was a follower of Gnostic mysticism. . . . She smiles. She and Abraxas had more in common than she knew.

She presses the alabaster button. Torpedo away. She does not know what will happen. Whatever it is, she is waiting for it.

The Monu-Rocket shudders one last time. She is carried away on white wings, in the clutches of the Sphinx.

---

clearly because you are not of this world yourself. It is like you are reading the book of the world. And there also, there are daiquiris and sometimes there is room service."

But that is not what I wanted to tell you.

What I wanted to tell you is that once you have become a DE-RANGED MILLIONAIRE, you can just ramble on and on like this about whatever comes to your mind. You never have to get to the point. You never even have to make a point, and people still have to listen to you. That is the privilege of wealth, and of derangement.

I learned this on the flight back from Barbados, when I was seated next to a handsome man in his late fifties who WOULD NOT STOP TALKING TO ME.

It was a late flight, and most everyone else was sleeping, including my son, Hodgmanillo, who was about a year old then and unconscious on my lap.

The handsome man was a billionaire. He said so right away. "I am at a point in my life when I do not need to work anymore," he said. He also explained that this had been the case since he was a young man. He had made a fortune in the financial markets, and then in real estate. And that is what he did now, buy and develop and sell Caribbean real estate, but mainly as a hobby.

MAY 17, 2012

Karen Oglesby wakes up in the Shriners Hospital in Fairfax, VA. Her plan worked: The mystic flame retardant spread as fast as the green flames had.

"There's a lot that was destroyed, but luckily, Masons know how to build."

Karen doesn't understand who is talking to her. And then her vision flips from dream to reality and she gets it: Rex is sitting next to her bed.

"Where's Buzz?" she asks.

"On the moon," says Rex. "Dropping him off there was the only way I could get him to stop attacking me."

"Good," says Karen. "I've been to the moon. It's a shit hole." And then she notices that Rex has a huge, compass-shaped hole in his chest.

And that is when Rex finally explains to her: He's not just a Mason. He's a Masonic android. That's why no other space programs would have him, he explains. And that is ALSO WHY HE LOOKS EXACTLY LIKE GEORGE WASHINGTON.

FIGURE 131:
Masonic space-faring
replicant designated
REX ABRAXAS

He said he did not know what it was to work anymore. And he told me some of the secrets to his success, such as talking to people randomly on planes and listening to their stories and learning from them.

I started then to explain to him that I had recently been hired to perform in some commercials. And that because of this, I was now financially independent for the first time in my life. I was able to bring my family to Barbados, and fly in business class, and I was finding it all hard to adjust to.

And then he interrupted me to tell me all about his real estate ventures.

One real estate venture he was working on was a private island resort. He was just coming from there. There were no direct flights to his private island, so he had to fly through Barbados.

"You would not believe the problems I am facing with the workforce there," he said.

"I am sure I would not," I said.

"But tell me about yourself," he said. And before I could, he said that his point was that he's very lonely.

You wouldn't believe it, he told me, but having a private island is

---

MAY 18, 2012

In the back of Jim's Unusual and Probably Illegal Pets in Unary City, ID, Jim Doan trains an owl to speak using only mice as treats and an occasional electric shock. When it shrieks, it shrieks with the voice of a man.

---

actually very lonely. Mick Jagger would be staying with him on this island, but that wasn't company. Because Mick Jagger is also very wealthy and successful, and so he is also very lonely. And two lonely people cannot be unlonely together.

And even though I have never met Mick Jagger (yet), I suspect that hanging around with him does make one feel very lonely.

The billionaire in the seat next door was going back to New York to see his children, he said. And then he looked at my son, asleep. He looked at him longingly.

"But that," he said. "That is the real thing. Absolute, unconditional love." And he pointed out, as though I had never heard it before, that it wouldn't last forever.

"Hold on to it," he said. "It does not last."

It was a terrible cliché, but I at that moment looked at my son and daughter with new eyes. I pictured them being lured out of a fairy house, or themselves luring someone else out to a world that I had no control over. A world I refused to look at.

"It all ends eventually," the millionaire said again, as though I had never heard it before.

And in that moment, I have to say: It was as though I had never heard it before.

MORE-ON: What did I learn from this experience? It is simple.

EXTREMELY WEALTHY PEOPLE WANT TO TAKE YOUR CHILDREN, so hold on to them.

IMPLEMENTATION: Hold on.

MAY 19, 2012
In Smoad, VA, all of the gravestones in the Smoad Cemetery crack and crumble to dust.

SEE THE WORLD

BEFORE IT

SPLITS APART

———————————

MAY 20, 2012

In Louisville, KY, every first-grader across the Jefferson County school district independently draws a sun that is no longer smiling, but screaming, and an exploded moon. Almost all of them use the new color GNOMEBLOOD to draw the sun's anguished tears.

Though many are alarmed by the coincidence, the event is dismissed as just another first-grade conspiracy, and the children are disciplined.

A TOTALLY FUN THING I WOULD DO AGAIN
AS SOON AS POSSIBLE

I WRITE TO YOU NOW FROM THE DUTCH MASTERS CABIN aboard my gigantic luxury cruise ship, a Mark 89 Signature Class Mega-Schooner sailing out of the Netherlands and currently levitating above the Earth on a soft bed of water called THE CARIBBEAN SEA.

It is not technically mine, of course. I believe it was called the *Eurodam* before I boarded it, which is Dutch for "EUROPEAN THING THAT OPPOSES THE WATER." But as is international convention, the moment I step aboard any vessel, it is automatically rechristened[333] as THE HMS[334] *Hodgmanic,* just as every vessel must keep a white captain's hat and pair of epaulets for me—just in case.

I actually have never been on a cruise ship before. I was always a SPEED ZEPPELIN man, as you know, but I lost my old zeppelin, the *Hubris,* in a gambling game, and then Jonathan Coulton invited me to join him on a cruise for his fans, and as I support his ongoing efforts to civilize himself, I agreed.

As you will recall from my previous book, my good friend and feral mountain-man companion Jonathan Coulton makes a kind of rudimentary music with his strum stick. You will not have heard these songs because they are never played on the radio, and he does not have a record label or the support of any large corporation that might help him get his LPs into the bins of the popular record stores, or into the

---

333. Specifically, I rechristened it, with a bottle of HODGMAN'S GODKA.
334. Hodge-Man's Ship.

MAY 21, 2012
The moon explodes.

prime locations where good music is sold: at the counter at coffee shops, or in the big warehouse stores such as BJ'S WHOLESALE, next to the beef jerky pallet and the flat-screen television Dumpster.

Instead, Coulton has some kind of record club, whereby he mails songs over the Internet. And in this way, Coulton has cultivated a small but loyal audience of computer hobbyists, feral folk-song enthusiasts, eleven-year-old boys, and other socially marginal people. And these are the people on the cruise. I believe he makes money by asking these people to tape a penny to a postcard and send it to him, or just throw it in the garbage. Jonathan doesn't seem to care.

But the point is, he is trying. And the opportunity of seeing Jonathan Coulton going on a grand cruise ship, being forced to stuff his hairy body into normal human clothing, and having to wrestle his musical paws around a chilled salad fork in the grand dining room, was simply too hilarious to pass up.

But despite the fact that this is my first time on such a boat, I can tell you that I may never get off. Clearly no expense was spared when they built the *Hodgmanic*. There are glass elevators on the side of the boat, piano bars everywhere, and carpeting.

Befitting its Dutch origins, the corridors are pasted with the exact same fine-art posters of Rembrandt self-portraits every four feet or so, and actual Dutch people portray the ship's captain and officers. The theme extends to the passenger cabins themselves, which range from the small, cramped, windowless "Anne Frank Class" cabins to my own "DUTCH MASTERS CABIN," which features a wraparound outdoor deck, nine hot tubs, canals with houseboats in them, hashish brownies on every pillow, and an endless supply of chocolate- and cognac-flavored cigarillos.

The *Hodgmanic* carries 2,100 souls, and with its several restau-

---

MAY 22, 2012

A massive two-ton glob of unidentifiable flesh and fat washes ashore on the South Carolina beach and unexpectedly is elected mayor. No one recalls when they rescheduled the election, but everyone seems very happy with the new mayor, whose voice sounds like wind chimes in their heads.

---

rants, discos, casinos, barbershops, library, movie theaters, central shopping malls, and abandoned main streets, these great cruise ships are just like little cities. And because they are probably going to be the last cities to survive once the BLOOD WAVE comes, I recommend you get yourself a cabin on one and plan to live there forever.

A TYPICAL DAY AT SEA

Let me introduce you to this wonderful means of transport by giving you the itinerary of just one typical day at sea.

SEVEN O'CLOCK A.M.: DAILY ANNOUNCEMENTS

You wake up to the sound of the cruise director yelling at you about all the things that are happening that day. Depending on the craft, he might be speaking over the public address system or just standing over your bed with a megaphone.

Ignore what he tells you. There are so many things to do on board a cruise ship that one can easily be overwhelmed. But remember, you are on vacation. You do not have to do what THEY tell you to do. You merely have to do what I tell you to do.

STARING TIME

You don't have to be in the Dutch Masters Cabin to enjoy the view.

And the thing about the view is, it's always changing. When you first set off, you are seeing Fort Lauderdale. Then you are seeing the amazing, impossible sight of the many ships going out to sea—a dozen floating Radissons, all dwarfing the apartment buildings on

MAY 23, 2012
The L.A. Clippers win their division in the National Ulama Association Playoffs. THE MAYANS WARNED US OF THIS!

either side of the canal, lining up to join with the obliterating, twilit horizon. Then you fall asleep.

And then, by morning, all of it is gone. Imagine if you had gone to sleep in a hotel, and in the morning you woke up and all around you was endless water. Would you think that the world had ended? Would you wonder what happened? Why were you saved? Do you deserve to be saved? Or have you and your hotel mates been transported to another dimension, a kind of waterworld?

These questions, especially if you have not had your first martini, are enough to make you EXTREMELY SICK TO YOUR STOMACH. Time to go abovedecks!

FIRST MARTINI SERVICE

The buffet is open all day, as are the bars. Much of the crew working on the ship are Indonesian. They probably don't drink. They will look at you funny if you ask for a martini now. But guess what! THEY ARE COMPELLED TO MAKE YOU ONE!

The martinis will be terrible, but it's better than drinking the many fruity cocktails they actually make well.

After all, if you're not going to get scurvy, what are you on a boat for in the first place?

AN EXCURSION, PERHAPS?

Sometimes your boat will dock and visit small strip malls that are pretending to be other countries. These are places where you can buy alcohol, shelter some income, go to Pizza Hut, and buy T-shirts that say things like I LEFT THE BOAT FOR SEVERAL HOURS AND ALL I GOT WAS THIS LOUSY T-SHIRT. Some of them also have beaches or opportunities to traumatize local wildlife.

MAY 24, 2012

Mornings with Donny and the Silver Scrote, a popular morning show in the Kansas City area, begins receiving strange telephone calls on the request line. At first the voice is fuzzy and indistinct—presumably a bad cell phone connection. But over the course of several days, the noises on the other line become increasingly more animalistic and disturbing.

For example, I left the boat to visit the charming country of ISLAND STOP 2 (I don't remember what country it was). I took a shuttle boat to the cement dock, and then I took a bus, which took me to a flat-bottomed boat manned by a sunburned Australian and his shoeless teenage sidekick. I presumed at this point they were going to kill me. But in fact, they took me out on this boat to a sandbar. At the sandbar, there were dozens of different boats parked in a big circle. It felt like a small floating city. And in fact, they had even set up a floating Margaritaville there.

All of these boats then dislodged their tourists into the shallow water so that they could then be mobbed by stingrays.[335] If you do not know what stingrays are, they are flattened, sentient muscle pads that swim in the water and want to put your foot into their toothless filter-maw because for years, Australian flat-boat captains have been feeding them chum to trick them into coming there, time and again.

I am not normally against petting or tricking animals. But I do not find it amusing to be swarmed by ANYTHING, EVER. And I found it somewhat sad that these animals, through years and years of this treatment, had been Pavlovianally taught to enjoy the music of Jimmy Buffett.

But as you know, Jean-Paul Sartre did not say that hell was a swarm of stingrays butting against your shins looking for food.[336] He said hell is other people. Being forced into the water with a bunch of strangers is not a good time. It is the prelude to a massacre.

---

335. For more information on what is in the ocean, please turn to page 762 under the heading "A Note of Warning Regarding the Ocean."

336. That is existential purgatory.

MAY 25, 2012

On the second day, Donny describes it as the sound of "snakes, setting themselves on fire." The Silver Scrote describes it as "I don't know . . . maybe dildos on fire?"

So please take my advice and return to the ship and DO NOT LEAVE IT AGAIN.

WERE YOU AWARE OF IT? "WASTING AWAY"

You are not allowed to sing "Margaritaville" in a Margaritaville, as the restaurant would then have to pay royalties to ASCAP (this is similar to how you cannot sing "Happy Birthday" in a chain restaurant or they will sue you). Instead, you are asked to sing a rights-free alternative called "Since I Left My Family and Live the Life of a Perpetual Adolescent in the Unspecified Tropics, I Live in a State of Alcoholic Ennui."

IF YOU SING IT THREE TIMES WITHOUT MESSING UP, THEY WILL BUY YOU A FREE POP-TOP FLIP-FLOP.[337]

SECOND MARTINI SERVICE

It is time to return to the pool and enjoy your second martini. You will notice as well that there is a hole in a nearby wall through which a man is handing out hamburgers. Have one. As all of the food is included in the price of your ticket, there is no need to be choosy. You might as well eat a hamburger that is handed to you through a wall.

POOLSIDE SPEED SCULPTURE

As you eat, you may watch a man turn a tall block of ice into a leaping dolphin very quickly with a small chain saw. If not a dolphin, then a tall plume of cubical water. Really anything that more or less resembles a block of ice. If you are wondering if the man will spray you with ice chips, the answer is yes. He is very good at this. He has

---

337. This is a shot of tequila, peach schnapps, sugar water, and a drop of Jimmy Buffett's own heel blood.

MAY 26, 2012

On the third day, Donny is audibly shaken, describing the now-regular call as "the sound of a puppy choking to death on a scarab." The Silver Scrote describes it as "Angelina Jolie's queef after a night of rum-de-dum with Brad and a bag of fiery dildos."

carved so many ice dolphins that it is very, very unlikely he will drop his chain saw into the hot tub you are sitting in.

Here's a hint from a seasoned cruiser who has been on exactly one cruise. It costs only several thousand dollars to get the sculptor to sculpt a version of you such that you can pour your second martini through your own ice mouth and drink it as it trickles through holes in your own ice palms like it is NON-SCURVY-PREVENTING STIGMATA.

PROMENADE DECK, AFTERNOON FOXBAT SKEET SHOOTING

Don't worry: This is not as bad as it sounds. No foxbats are harmed. Here is what happens: One of the humans they keep belowdecks shoots a bunch of rotting fruit into the sky. Meanwhile, you stand on the beautiful promenade deck with a foxbat gun. Shoot the foxbats at the rotting fruit (their favorite food) and watch them go.

This may sound cruel, but bear in mind there is real food at the end of it for the foxbats. You are not tricking them with tourists' shins.

It's also funny because the sun is so bright, the foxbats go a little mad.

THREE O'CLOCK: ICE FISHING

Is the Caribbean too hot for you? Why not enjoy some classic ice fishing in the ice-fishing lodge beneath the water slide? The temperature is kept at fifteen degrees, and just as in ordinary ice fishing, you do not catch anything. You just drink and stare into a frigid pool and hope for some answers.

MAY 27, 2012
On the fourth day, Donny, now crying, says he can't make it out, but he feels the sound is trying to tell him something. The Silver Scrote replies that he agrees, saying that it feels like "my brain is being sucked right through my balloon knot."

FOUR O'CLOCK: MOUNTAIN CLIMBING

Have you ever had a dream? Have you ever dreamed of climbing a mountain in the middle of the ocean? And then when you reach the top, you see your dead father, and he is blind and trying to care for a kitten, feeding it milk from an eyedropper, except that he cannot see that the kitten has no head? And then, suddenly, YOU are the kitten, and the sky is just so bright, bright blue that you cry through your fuzzy neck-hole?

Well, aboard the *Hodgmanic*, exactly one part of that dream will come true as you climb our FLEET EXCLUSIVE three-hundred-foot imitation mountain. This is not a rock-climbing wall, it is an actual fake mountain, peaked with actual imitation snow, and there is a specially trained team of Indonesian crew members dressed as sherpas to help you.

THERE IS EVEN A GUY DRESSED AS A MONSTROUS ABOMINABLE SNOWMAN SOMEWHERE ON THE MOUNTAIN! Or else that is Jonathan Coulton. It is difficult to say.

MOUNT SEAWORTHY is located just to the left of the chocolate water-slide.

FIGURE 132:
Could this be the
ABOMINABLE SNOWMAN?

4:30 O'CLOCK: SEMINARS!

Cruising is not just about fun, relaxation, and shooting foxbats out of air guns. You also have the opportunity to LEARN SOMETHING.

> **MAY 28, 2012**
> On the fifth day, Donny does not speak at all. He simply lets Scrote read the news and weather. And when the phone rings, as usual, at 9:15 a.m., Donny simply puts the call on the air and lets the thing talk. Before the Scrote can stop him, all of Kansas City goes mad.

Why not take a cooking class in the CULINARY CENTER and learn how to make classic maritime treats like GROG, HARDTACK, CHOWDERS OF THE WORLD,[338] and LEGIONNAIRE'S DISEASE?

Or take a "BELOWDECKS" tour and see the windowless rooms where the ship's crew relaxes by drinking alcohol and energy drinks while kissing one another—ALL IN TOTAL DARKNESS.

Or visit the WORLD-CLASS ART GALLERY to learn why black-velvet paintings of MARTINI OLIVES WITH ARMS AND LEGS BUT NO HEADS GETTING DRUNK IN A LAS VEGAS BAR is the best kind of art you can buy.

Or finally learn how a giant mega-schooner is sailed at the CAPTAIN'S GIN MINGLE on the bridge? If you are a charming drunk or just a sneaky drunk, you can secretly steer the ship to the BERMUDA TRIANGLE.

The captain will ask that you use the coasters provided and not just put your drink in his beard.

FIVE O'CLOCK: RECOVERY OF DISORIENTED WORLD WAR II PILOTS IN THE BERMUDA TRIANGLE

Help rescue the dehydrated and confused pilots of FLIGHT 19, the famous lost squadron of U.S. Navy jets that disappeared mysteriously in the Bermuda Triangle in 1945. Hear their muddled, contradictory stories of strange lights in the skies, horrible experiments performed upon them by tiny gray figures, and their sudden awakening on that deserted island, the one that does not appear on any map.

---

338. (New England, Manhattan, Olde Englande, Staten Island, Governor's Island, Kosher Creamy Pork, Tokyo American-Style-Foxbat-Strength Chowder, Djembe Hallucinogen, and Chunky.)

MAY 29, 2012
Jonathan Franzen walks up to the gate of Dr. Phil's Beverly Hills estate, a plain manila envelope in his hand. Jonathan Franzen keeps on walking.

These are not the actual pilots of Flight 19, of course.[339] But the five Dutch actors who play the American pilots are really very talented and SURPRISINGLY dehydrated. You will really enjoy helping them get accustomed to modern conveniences such as VERY SLOW SATELLITE INTERNET SERVICE, OBESITY, and the four p.m. screening of *Eat Pray Love* in the Hollywood-at-Sea Screening Compartment. Can you guess which one of these men is secretly the ALIEN SHAPE-SHIFTER WHO IS "KILLING" PASSENGERS ONE BY ONE before the Dutch actors are redeposited on their manmade deserted island to await the next ship?

5:30 O'CLOCK: TOWEL FREAK-OUT!

Now is a good time to freshen up in your cabin and dress for dinner.

By now you are probably ready for a nap. Before the real fun begins, why not return to your luxurious cabin, which is similar to a room at a standard Westin that has been folded in half?

But before you lie down, don't forget to BE COMPLETELY TERRIFIED BY THE THING THAT HAS BEEN LEFT ON YOUR BED. This is called "towel sculpture," and it is one of the great mysteries of the cruise experience. No one knows who makes these little terry-cloth origami offerings or how they get into your room, but they are almost always FRIGHTENING AND WEIRD, and there is some general consensus as to what they mean.

---

339. Those men are currently being used as breeding stock by creatures from another dimension.

MAY 30, 2012
Having not set foot in the water since the day he almost drowned, Tim Dicks completes his grocery shopping at the local Food Monarch and discovers a giant catfish in his Buick Rendezvous. It is sitting in the driver's seat. The fish puts its human arm down Tim Dicks's throat.

TABLE 42: TOWEL–SCULPTURE DIVINATION TABLE

WHAT YOU FIND, UNASKED FOR, ON YOUR BED . . .	WHAT IT IS GENERALLY ACCEPTED TO MEAN . . .
A SEAL	Someone on the boat has a crush on you.
TWO SWANS KISSING	You will find romance on this trip, and you will require a towel after lovemaking.
AN ELEPHANT WITH GOOGLY EYES	Googly eyes are on sale in the duty-free shop.
A GROTESQUELY SMILING FROG WEARING SUNGLASSES	We saw that you sneezed on the salad bar. Your pride will be your undoing.
A SQUID THAT LOOKS LIKE A PENIS BUT ALSO LOOKS LIKE A VAGINA, DEPENDING ON HOW YOU LOOK AT IT	You must learn to tolerate ambiguity.
A STINGRAY THAT SIMPLY LOOKS LIKE A VAGINA	You see genitalia everywhere, don't you?
A SNAKE WITH A PIECE OF RED RIBBON FOR A TONGUE	We really did not feel like working too hard on the towel sculpture today.
JUST A BUNCHED-UP TOWEL	You have not been tipping housekeeping enough.
A MONKEY THAT HAS BEEN CRUCIFIED ON A COAT HANGER	You are not safe here. Because we hate you.

FIGURE 133: *If you do not leave 100 dollars in the monkey's mouth before you go to dinner, I cannot be responsible for what will happen to you.*

MAY 31, 2012

The so-called Web Rapture occurs when the Internet reveals that 78 percent of all humanity are actually fictional characters from the series of television shows linked to *St. Elsewhere*. Upon their unmasking, these fictional humans immediately "de-res" and disappear.

THIRD MARTINI SERVICE, ALSO KNOWN AS DINNER

After a restorative nap, it is time to start re-dehydrating yourself while eating food with strangers.

Many people do not like the custom of assigned seating at dinner, but you must understand that it is considered bad luck at sea to eat with anyone that you know or like. This is just one of many amusing TABOOS OF THE SEA that you should know about if you do not want the MEGA-SQUIDS to come and take you below.[340]

You will be expected to dress for dinner. At the height of the cruise liner's most elegant age, this meant strict white tie and sword canes. Now it means that they hope that you will wear pants. It may seem a lot to ask people who, in every other way, have been encouraged to indulge their laziest, most infantile instincts to suddenly, at five p.m., turn around and ask them to briefly act like adults again who have something to say to one another and know how to wear a collared shirt that does not have a sports insignia on it somewhere. And it turns out, it IS a lot to ask.

TABOOS OF THE SEA

Though cruising is the epitome of luxury travel (every cabin has a rudimentary toilet, JUST AS AN EXAMPLE), traveling by sea is dangerous. When you think about it, the sea is the only thing keeping your boat from crashing directly to the ground. That is why sailors are so superstitious. For example, did you know that among

---

340. For more such TABOOS OF THE SEA, please see the following "Taboos of the Sea" on this page.

JUNE 1, 2012

The actual Rapture occurs. After the disappearance of a random assortment of humans, the Tribulation lasts only seven hours, Christ then returns to usher in 1,000 minutes of his reign on Earth, and then finally takes all faithful Christians away with him.

   Creationists who believed that God made all of existence within a week should not be surprised that He is able to work in the entire Book of Revelation into a single day.

---

many sailors, it is considered BAD LUCK to admit openly at any time that you are actually on a boat?

Here are some well-known maritime taboos:

- A WOMAN ON BOARD is considered bad luck. On cruise lines, women will be asked to wear special underwear made of dark brown rayon. It is believed that vengeful Poseidon cannot see through rayon.
- IT IS CONSIDERED UNLUCKY to leave a sinking ship before the last rat has left it.
- BECAUSE SHIPS ARE CONSIDERED BY THE SAILOR TO BE CONSTANTLY SINKING, rats are escorted off the cruise liner before you disembark.
- IF YOU SEE A REDHEADED PERSON ON BOARD, do not make eye contact. (Some cruise lines require REDHEADED PERSONS to wear blindfolds.)
- THROWING STONES INTO THE SEA will cause bad weather. That is why all the stones in your cabin are BOLTED DOWN.
- DOLPHINS SWIMMING ALONGSIDE A SHIP'S BOW are considered good luck, so please do not free the dolphins that are leashed to the front of the ship, even if it is seems they are just being dragged along and maybe are dead. DOLPHINS ARE BIG FAKERS and they are just looking to get out of their job.
- NEVER SAY THE WORD "DROWNED" at sea, as it is bad luck. Instead, ask for your lobster to be "SUFFO-CATED" in butter.

JUNE 2, 2012
The Day of Calm. With all the Christians gone, the remaining humans on Earth realize that everything suddenly seems much more calm. The remaining humans on Earth all see a movie, do a little shopping, get some Chinese food, and read the paper.

- NEVER SAY THE WORD "OMELET" at sea. At the buffet, ask to be directed to the "FOLDED FLAT EGG" station.

- NEVER SAY THE WORD "SEA" at sea. Instead, refer to "The Moist Murderess" or "The Salty Rum That Swallows You" or "The Land That Moves and Kills."

- DO NOT INTERRUPT the wild-eyed man clothed only in clacking dried crab shells and a seaweed skirt who is screaming at the clouds. HE IS THE CRAB CLAW PRIEST, MINISTER OF THE WAVES, and he is keeping the SEA SERPENTS away.

- WHEN CHECKING IN, please reserve time to have sex in one of the Model T cars stowed in the hold, so as to appease the god of spokes and wheels whom you are offending the moment you step on board.

WERE YOU AWARE OF IT? "THE LAW OF THE SEA"

It is a common misconception that captains may legally marry people while at sea. It is not so. They are allowed to notarize contracts and keelhaul scalawags ONLY, and in general it is the hope that they will not get too wrapped up in the notarizing and keelhauling and concentrate on steering the ship.

The CRAB CLAW PRIEST, however, is allowed to give benediction to temporary SEA MARRIAGES, which couplings last the duration of the cruise and are then never spoken of again.

BUT BE WARNED: DURING THE CEREMONY, THE CRAB CLAW PRIEST WILL TRY TO TONGUE-KISS YOU.

A NOTE OF WARNING REGARDING THE OCEAN

Please note that the sea has things living in it, mostly fish. These fish include:

> Grouper
>
> French Grunt
>
> French Chub
>
> Double French Chub
>
> Parrotfish
>
> Monkeyhead Fish, aka the Feejee Mermaid
>
> Humanhead Fish
>
> Conjoined Twinfish
>
> Creepy-smile Fish
>
> Coelacanth
>
> Fish that tastes like Garbagefish
>
> Loup de Mer, also known as Werewolf of the Sea
>
> Lance Bass

That last one was a little joke. Lance Bass is not a fish. He is a famous gay astronaut.

You may be concerned: Are there REALLY sea serpents? Yes. Unfortunately, sailors need sea serpents to show them where the map ends. But it is unlikely that you will see these creatures, because you are not going to get anywhere near the giant waterfall at the end of the world, which makes me very angry.

As you have gathered, most cruise ships are run by the Dutch, the Netherlandic people who live their whole lives below sea level, under constant threat of dike breach, and thus take to the sea as a kind of revenge.

So a word to the wise: The officers of the ship cannot be bribed, even with bars of gold. They are so self-righteous, they will just throw the gold bars into the sea and laugh at you in Dutch, and they will not change the direction of the boat even though you can see the giant waterfall at the end of the world RIGHT THERE.

However, the rest of the staff is delightful, and while tips are not required on cruises, I have found that a few gold nuggets will get you a seat at the captain's table and a plate of the very freshest humanhead fish, particularly a humanhead fish whose human head resembles the captain himself. And I find this to be amusingly unnerving to the captain, and if you get all your fellow passengers to do it on the same night, the captain will go insane, and YOU will be the new captain.

The point I'm trying to make is, for your safety, please stay away from the water. You will quickly learn from your fellow, more experienced cruisers that it is better that you not even look at it.

EIGHT O'CLOCK: ENTERTAINMENT

After dinner, why not take in a Broadway show? But instead of going to New York, why not take the glass elevator down to the seven-hundred-seat theater? And instead of seeing a Broadway show, why not see a German juggler tell jokes? Or head to the Merman Cabaret, where Billy Zane will be singing the songs of Billy Zane.

Here's an insider's tip: Billy Zane WILL tell stories about the making of the movie *Titanic*. You just have to interrupt his singing enough times.

NINE O'CLOCK: FOURTH MARTINI SERVICE, IN THE DAVID FOSTER WALLACE LOUNGE

As you may know, a very fine writer named David Foster Wallace wrote a famous essay about his experience on a cruise ship that was first published in *Harper's*, a landlubbing magazine, in 1996.

> **JUNE 5, 2012**
> In San Francisco, the Golden Gate Bridge is destroyed in a fight between OCTOSAUR and NAR-WAHLODACTYL.

In the essay, he told how he found it spiritually discomfiting to be waited on, helped, served, and coddled with the kind of hospitable ferocity the average cruise ship offers. He was equally dispirited by the privileged cruising class, who take constant service by people from other lands as a birthright. For him, the enforced, almost manic pampering quickly transformed into the most profound ennui, only deepened by the fact that those who were on the ship who did not happen to be magazine writers didn't feel any ennui about it at all or ever. The writer, very tragically, ended up taking his own life.

As you can imagine, this essay was an enormous hit among cruise lines. It was *great* publicity and spurred a huge influx of new cruise passengers. So many people, in fact, are demanding the David Foster Wallace experience that most cruise lines have built these lounges in his honor. The lounge is a large, windowless room in the bottom of the ship, all the corners rounded to convey a sense of endless nothingness. If you look around for an hour or two, you will find a door that opens onto a re-creation of his cabin, which is stocked daily with fresh fruit in his honor and a towel sculpture of his face.

LATE NIGHTS: CASINO TIME!

Why not check out the all-night action in the casino? Not only can you find all your favorite slot machines and table games, but also appearing nightly is Billy Zane! He will be betting the hermit crabs and getting DRUNK AND ANGRY from eleven p.m. to three a.m. Technically this is not an official appearance. But Billy Zane cannot stop you from staring at him!

11:15 O'CLOCK: GOOD NIGHT

As you fall asleep, feel the rocking of the waves. These are simulated by hydraulic arms in the bowels of the ship.

JUNE 6, 2012

Tim Dicks awakens in New Madrid, MO, by the shores of the Mississippi River. He cannot speak because he has the Gumstone in his mouth. He cannot hear because his head is full of his own muffled scream. But he can see.

He watches a thing rise out of the river. But it is not a thing, thinks Tim Dicks, it is the river itself. A dark, rippling, endless river of smooth, scaleless flesh, black and bright in the moonlight, pushing itself up on its long arms and pale, bare legs, flexing its impossible wings. Old Missus Crushgums, the Mother of all Monster Catfish, has come, and she will choke down the world. Starting with Tim Dicks.

WERE YOU AWARE OF IT? "POSH"

You have probably heard that the word "POSH," meaning "contemptuously wealthy," originated as a nautical term.

On the great transatlantic ocean liners of the past,[341] first-class passengers would request cabins that would face away from the southern sun on both the outbound and return voyages (many of these passengers were vampires). Thus, stamped on their tickets and luggage would be the acronym POSH, meaning "Port Outbound, Starboard Home."

This is A RIDICULOUS MYTH.

POSH actually stands for PUT ON SECOND HELICOPTER.

I am now using some rather complex nautical terms, so let me explain. A *helicopter* is a vehicle that achieves flight by rapidly twisting gravity. The best ships kept several of these machines on board to evacuate first-class passengers in case of an emergency.[342] Crew used the acronym POSH to keep the helicopters secret, out of fear that the steerage passengers would charge the helicopters and damage the copter's delicate membranous wings with the oils of their Irish and Italian hands.

Of course, helicopters were still very new at the time. They could fly only about nine feet above the surface of the water, and they offered only a snack instead of a full meal. But they were still considered preferable to the lifeboats, which were much more cramped, and were also built with holes in the bottom in order to save money.

You might extrapolate that if POSH refers to the second helicopter, there must also be a first. Good extrapolating. While POSH passengers were indeed VERY WEALTHY, they were not quite as WEALTHY or deemed AS FIT TO LIVE as the POFH passengers, an acronym largely lost to time . . .

. . . EXCEPT FOR THE DINERS CLUB POFH CARD.[343]

---

341. The time before this one.

342. Aside from mechanical icebergs, there was also the risk of vengeful whales, boarding by mermanic pirates, Philadelphia Experiments, and Atlantic sea-ranhas.

343. Please see page 735, under the heading "Privileges of the Diners Club POFH Card."

JUNE 7, 2012
Ungoth-Dan, the Weeping, Scaly Bulldog, rises from his dreamless slumber and transforms the
campus of Yale University into his COURT OF SOULS.

TABLE 43: OTHER SURPRISING ACRONYMS

Did you know these common words began as acronyms?

SCUBA	"Self-Contained Underwater Breathing American"
. . . not to be confused with:	
SCUBA	Southern Cuba (KS) Uncommunist Business Association[344]
SNORKEL	Subwater Non-Organic Respiration Knickknack, Extended Length
AMTRAK	AMerican TRains Are oK
FUCOTK	Fornication Under Consent Of The King
ROY G BIV	Ronald Otis Yorick Garrison Bi-rainbow, the Fourth[345]
WOCOBOTO	WOrld COmputer at the BOttom of The Ocean
ALFASW	A Low-Frequency Anti-Sentience Wave[346]
TGI FRIDAYS	Thank Gorgoth-the-pitiless It's Friday: Ravenously It Devours All Your Souls[347]
ADIDAS	All Day I Detest All Sports
ANTIDISESTAB-LISHMENTARI-ANISM	A National Trust In Defense of Institutional, Strongly Established State Theology Against Barbaric Laicization (Including Secular Humanists Mocking English National Tradition) And Resisting Increasing Anti-antidisestablishmentarianism. Need I Say More?

344. Please see the entry for CUBA on page 774 under the heading *"US News & World Report's* 35 American Towns."

345. The inventor of rainbows and double or "Bi-rainbows."

346. Please see "Today in RAGNAROK," under the heading "March 21, 2012."

347. Please see page 802 under the heading "THE ANCIENT AND UNSPEAKABLE ONES."

JUNE 8, 2012

Every bedbug in New York City stops feeding upon human blood, leaves its mattressy nest, and assembles in Herald Square to create a huge, sentient, shambling bug pile called Mother Suckblood.

AND HERE IS ONE ELEGANT ANAGRAM

HARM ONE ANT, AN EAGLE IS ANGERED.

ROADSIDE ATTRACTIONS

As much as I enjoy travel by sea, however, there is something that you miss about America if you refuse to ever set foot on it. The great era of the American road trip may be over, but that does not mean you shouldn't enjoy these famous old ROADSIDE ATTRACTIONS along some of the more winding scenic American highways, before they are clogged with traffic as people try to escape THE ANCIENT AND UNSPEAKABLE ONES.

PERRY'S NUTHOUSE, BELFAST, ME

This is one of the last roadside mental hospitals that is still open to visitors. It was once quite common for the state of Maine to raise money by displaying its mentally ill population in fun-sylums like Perry's. On Route 1—the major coastal road—there used to be dozens of them. Visitors traveling north for the summer would stop to watch the patients in their cells receive talk therapy and be pelted with lobsters.[348]

Most of the fun-sylums were closed, however, after Frederick Wiseman's controversial 1967 documentary, *Titicut Follies*, in which he revealed that the inmates were routinely sprayed with ice-cold water

---

348. Both old- and new-style.

> **JUNE 9, 2012**
> Nick Nolte awakens to his true nature.[a]
>
> ---
>
> a. Please see page 913 under the heading "Will Quetzalcoatl Return from the 29th Dimension to Judge Us All?"

when they refused to be amusing.

Today, Perry's houses only ONE actual mentally ill person (Old Bill, the EREUTHOPHOBIC, who was locked up in 1958 because he believed that Maine-style bright red hot dogs were somehow unnatural). But Perry's still sells their famous bridge mix and Thorazine-laced fudge.

FIGURE 134:
You don't have to be crazy to work here, but you do have to be crazy to be held captive here for the enjoyment of tourists.

RAYMOND CARVER-VILLE, HUEY LEWISTON, CA

Does it seem incongruous that someone would build a nature walk through a private forest full of weird cement dioramas based on Raymond Carver short stories? HUEY LEWIS DOES NOT THINK SO, as he has been the owner and host of RAYMOND CARVER-VILLE since 1993.

THE CROOKED HOUSE, NORTH MASCULINE, MI

This "mystery spot" of northern Michigan features a strange two-room cabin built precariously upon a wooded hillside.

Some call it "The Crooked House," others call it "The Curiosity Hut," and still others call it "The Nausea Shack." And it is these last ones who are correct. For it is not only the walls and windows that are twisted and bent to odd angles in this house, but it would seem THE VERY LAWS OF PHYSICS THEMSELVES.

Here, metal balls placed upon the steeply sloped floor seem to ROLL UPHILL. Other metal balls that are suspended from the ceiling

---

JUNE 10, 2012

After ten millennia, the meteor containing the giant frozen headless body of the Nug-Shohab, the Frozen Headless One, collides with St. Paul. Its impact creates a massive, mile-deep trench from southern Minnesota to Indianapolis, choking the skies with dust and public radio.

---

do not hang straight down, but askew, as if pulled by some mysterious unseen force . . . maybe the same force that is coming in and leaving all these metal balls lying around. WE JUST DON'T KNOW.

But perhaps the strangest effect the house has is on the visitors themselves.

In the "Sideways Room," FOR EXAMPLE, visitors find that they can walk HALFWAY UP THE WALL and sit in a CHAIR.

In the "Giant's Room," meanwhile, visitors standing in one corner seem to be much taller than they normally appear, whereas if they walk to the other corner, they FALL DOWN AND START CON-VULSING.

And return visitors often complain of a strange sense of DÉJÀ VU, and on occasion will discover ALTERNATE TIMELINE VER-SIONS OF THEMSELVES, STILL STUCK IN THE CHAIR ON THE WALL, SOBBING.

Various explanations have been offered for these strange effects: that the cabin has been built on top of a powerful well of geomag-netic energy, or that it was built for creatures from another world. Many who enjoy marijuana feel that the cabin itself is nothing less than an MC ESCHER POSTER ON A DORM ROOM WALL IN ANOTHER DIMENSION.

But in the CROOKED HOUSE, nothing can be certain and ALL ANSWERS ARE CORRECT AND WRONG AT THE SAME TIME, until you reach page 834, where the final secret is revealed.

JUNE 11, 2012

The Giant Headless Body of the Nug-Shohab (now unfrozen) climbs out of the crater formerly known as Louisville and begins its long, slow, blind, and devastating crawl to Antarctica in order to rejoin its frozen head.

WERE YOU AWARE OF IT?
"A CAUTIONARY TALE REGARDING SEX IN WEIRD SHACKS"

There is a local legend that teenagers used to break into the cabin at night for nausea parties and sex. But then one girl got pregnant and gave birth to a maggot with psychic powers.

This is true. But it is NOT true that the maggot boy then grew up to work in the CROOKED HOUSE SOUVENIR SHOP. That guy is just an ordinary albino wearing a white sleeping bag and looking for attention.

THE REAL MAGGOT BOY MOVED TO OAKLAND AND NOW RUNS A SUCCESSFUL RESTAURANT THAT IS RENOWNED FOR ITS ARTISANAL CHARCUTERIE.

THE ALLIGATOR MODEL UN, TYBALT WENDY ROAD, SUCLUNDY ISLAND, SC

This is a complete model of the UN General Assembly Chamber made of toothpicks, perfect in every way except that all of the delegates are cute baby alligators dressed up in the traditional garb of their native countries.

With the rise of the Tea Party, the Alligator Model UN has become less popular, and is often accused of trying to impose a "NEW WORLD ORDER" upon the Carolinas, and also of coddling the alligator playing Ahmadinejad. So you should see it before a patriot burns it, and all the alligators, to cinders.

THE HOTEL SUITE USED BY JACK NICHOLSON
WHILE FILMING *ABOUT SCHMIDT,* HOTEL FONTENELLE,
NINETEENTH FLOOR, DODGE ST., OMAHA, NE

Previously the presidential suite, this six-room luxury apartment was used by Jack Nicholson for eight nights in 2002 before he rented a private home. It became the world's only DRIVE-THRU HOTEL SUITE, after the hotel replaced the walls with glass and built a ramp up to the nineteenth floor so that Omaha residents could view Jack Nicholson attempting to sleep.

THE MOUTH OF THE HONOLULU TUNNEL, THE INTERSECTION OF OLYMPIC AND LINCOLN BOULEVARDS, SANTA MONICA, CA

Originally built in 1975 as an extension of Route 66, the tunnel connecting Hawaii to the mainland was closed in 1985 when it became clear that people did not want to drive 2,500 miles underwater, often in total darkness.

However, you can still tour the underground toll plaza, accessible via a hatch near the Chevron station. There is a souvenir shop there, and you can see where they filmed the opening sequence from *CHiPS: Tunnel Patrol*, a short-lived spin-off following the special police unit assigned to the tunnel and their adventures driving back and forth in darkness. The Tunnel Patrol still exists as a division of the California State Police, but their job now is primarily to man the barriers, guarding the tunnel and its several abandoned hotels from urban spelunkers.

TIMOTHY BILL DANGLE III, THE BEER-DRINKING GOAT, THE OLD ROUTE 12A, HARTSWOODIE, MS, AND OTHER DRINKING THINGS

As it is easy to enslave any mammal to the delights of alcohol, you will find many alcoholic or otherwise addicted animals kept in pits for the amusements of passersby.

JUNE 13, 2012

Meteorologists determine that the formless moans emanating from the neck hole of Nug-Shohab may be heard from 150 miles away. Someone Auto-Tunes it, and it becomes a hit song.

For example, there is:

- Goaty Goatdrunk, Vienna, GA
- Guzzles, the Brandy Kitten, Oblique Corners, AK
- Mr. Bitters, the Spider Monkey Who Drinks Only Pre-Prohibition Cocktails, Stunted Lick, Kentucky
- Methy, the Fastest, Most Toothless Turtle Alive, Cairo, PA (now deceased), who used to race . . .
- Dranky, the Slow-Rollin' Rabbit, Cairo, PA
- Flip, the Porpoise with a Gambling Problem, Permanent Lick, KY
- David After the Dentist, Lesshead, VA (not the actual David from the video, but a local child who is kept in a car and fed laughing gas)
- The REAL David After the Dentist, West Lesshead, VA (a competing David-After-Dentist attraction). This one does not have the actual David either, but does feature the real David's father, who is available to sign autographs while drinking Mike's Hard Lemonade.

These are all good drunken animals. BUT ONLY TIMOTHY GETS DRUNK ENOUGH TO SAY HE LOVES YOU IN SOMETHING RESEMBLING ENGLISH!

JUNE 14, 2012

In a daring heist, nine men break into the Wormarium at Boston's Museum of Science and tunnel through the amber that imprisons the Pale Worm of Monsall Head. The Worm then devours all but one of the men before disappearing. The remaining burglar is found by the police, naked, weeping, and blind, attempting to throw himself into the mouth of the museum's life-size model *T. rex*. His sad lament that he cannot complete his destiny to "dissolve in the gizzard of the Great One's rudimentary intestine" is filmed, and goes viral.

BARNEY, THE WINE-DRINKING GIANT BARNACLE, THE BEEF HUT, STATE SCENIC ROUTE 312, NECKWURST, TX

When he was discovered incongruously clinging to the side of a barn in 1976, Barney was only about the size of a goat. That is why the farmers decided to feed him alcohol.

Then, an entrepreneur named Tom Eisen bought Barney and moved him to a viewing hole outside his Neckwurst, Texas, beef restaurant, THE BEEF HUT. By experimentation, Eisen discovered that Barney preferred wine to any other intoxicant, and especially had a preference for rosé.

"That barnacle tongue of his just had a taste for the blood in it,"[349] Eisen told the *Austin American-Statesman.* "At least, I guess it's a tongue. I guess it kind of looks like a tongue, except for the spines and the little black eyes."

Barney has thrived on his diet and eventually had to be moved out of the hole. He now weighs 8,000 pounds and is 35 feet tall and requires 300 gallons of wine per day, or else he starts to emit a terrible sour odor and a hideous low whine that causes migraine headaches for miles around.

As of 1998, Tom Eisen has been offering free Double Beefsteak Dinners for life to anyone who can figure out a way to kill Barney.

---

349. For more on the making of ROSÉ WINE, please turn to page 644 under the heading "In Conclusion, Plus Also: Rosé."

JUNE 15, 2012

Hoping to curb the panic and epic lulz being spread by the *Pale Worm* video, the president throws the Internet kill switch that is hidden in the bust of Al Gore in the Orbital White House's Oval Office, instantly filling the nation's system of pneumatic tubes with cement. The rest of the Internet continues to function.

TABLE 44: *US NEWS & WORLD REPORT'S*
35 AMERICAN TOWNS

GREAT SMALL TOWNS	Interrobang, MS Secular Falls, MA Brian Doyle-Murray, MD New O'Waxalagalis City, Hohoq Knife-and-Fork-Sandwich, OK Quantittlemuckfut, NH
TERRIBLE SMALL TOWNS	Kingsfart, NY Human Papilloma Virus, TX South Asbestos Abatementville, VA Lower Beef Clod, OK Sextrade, NV Quantittlemuckfutport, NH
SMALL TOWNS WITH SECRETS	Stonington, CT (formerly Shirley Jacksonville, CT) Abduction, CO Most Dangerous Gamesburg, UT Danse Macabre, NE Entwined Serpents, AZ Renfaire-After-Dark, WI
COLLEGE TOWNS	College Location, PA Lesbian Hills, MA Indoctrinationton, TN Elbow Patch, NC Liberal Oasis, MS
SMALL TOWNS WITH FOREIGN NAMES	Beaufort, SC (pronounced "BEW-fert, Sooth Car'leena") Marseilles, WI (pronounced "MORE-sels") Paris, TX (pronounced "Wim Wenders,"[350] Texas) Mummenschanz, IA (pronounced "MooMEN-chants") Cuba, KS (pronounced "CUH-ba") Toronto, Louisiana (pronounced "Can-NAY-da")

CONTINUED

350. Pronounced "Vim Venders."

> **JUNE 16, 2012**
> As it blindly feels its way across the American plains, the giant headless body of Nug-Shohab crushes whole towns beneath its twenty-fingered hands and thirty-capped knees.

TABLE 44: *continued*	
SOME TOWNS THAT WERE ABANDONED	Centralia, PA, due to a perpetual coal-mine fire Shifty Springs, AK, due to suspicion of the springs Chernobyl, WY, because it just seemed prudent
SOME TOWNS THAT HAVE MANAGED TO THRIVE, EVEN THOUGH THEY WERE FLOODED TO MAKE RESERVOIRS	Kennett, CA, beneath Lake Shasta Three hundred residents who refused to leave their homes to make way for the Shasta Dam and Lake project in 1935 won a lawsuit compelling the State of California to continually provide them with scuba gear and rubber frocks and suit jackets Greenwich, MA, beneath the Quabbin Reservoir Greenwich was abandoned and submerged in 1938 in order to build the Quabbin Reservoir. It has since been reclaimed, first by artists seeking cheap live/work space in the perfectly preserved nineteenth-century homes, and more recently by affluent commuters from Boston, who found they could drown the artists by pushing them out onto the porch. Neversink, NY, beneath the Neversink Reservoir Home of the United States' most ironically named underwater city

TOURIST TRAPS

Not every roadside attraction is a "TOURIST TRAP," but these are:

- THE WORLD'S BIGGEST FALLING CAGE, Skinned Knuckle, MO
- THE HOUSE WITH INCREDIBLY STICKY FLOORS, Anchove, SC
- THE CAREFULLY CAMOUFLAGED HOLE, Yakkerskill, NY
- THE HATE PIT, Newbridge, NJ

JUNE 17, 2012
OESTER-RAH is late.

- THE FULLY ARMED AND OPERATIONAL DEATH STAR, Pardon Me, ND
- NETSVILLE, Ochre-Cadmium Heights, IA
- THE UNSPECIFIED OBJECT, Lumbalba County, NM

THE SECRET OF THE UNSPECIFIED OBJECT: REVEALED!

As travelers drive east along Lumbalba County Road 13 in New Mexico, they begin to see the familiar signs. Hand-painted and low to the ground, they punctuate the flat blank highway with mystery:

"What IS the UNSPECIFIED OBJECT?"

"You are approaching THE UNSPECIFIED OBJECT. OR IS IT APPROACHING YOU?"

"Is it large or small? Beautiful or ugly? Alive or dead? Like a cat inside a sealed box, THE UNSPECIFIED OBJECT may be all of these things at once! Or not!"

"P.S.: Do you remember that last sign, where I compared the UN-SPECIFIED OBJECT to a cat in a sealed box? I didn't mean to suggest that the UNSPECIFIED OBJECT *is definitely* a cat in a sealed box. That was just a simile. OR WAS IT?"

And so on, for 120 miles and a total of 250 signs.

Finally, the traveler reaches a dusty turnoff, a painted arrow, a final sign ("Here it comes! VAGUENESS!"), and a long dirt road that travels through a field of tall grasses.

At the end of the road is a small parking area with a red cash box on a post. You are asked to put a dollar in the slot before proceeding. It is on the honor system.

The traveler then sees a white gravel path leading into a small copse of trees. There is a little clearing in the copse where the traveler finds hundreds of objects hanging from the branches. A Leatherman utility knife. A wristwatch. A high-school ring. A T-shirt that says SEE ROCK CITY. A paperback copy of *The Power of Now*. Dozens of pairs of glasses.

The traveler is forced to consider: Which of these things is the UN-SPECIFIED OBJECT? Or is it ALL the OBJECT? Or is none of it?

And that is when the traveler will notice that there are more strings, with nothing tied to them, tendrilling in the breeze. More often than not, a traveler will reach in his pocket and find some object—nothing special: a pencil, a pack of Certs, a coin. And, almost without thinking about it, the traveler will tie it to a string. Is this the object the signs meant all along? That thing in our lives, whatever it is, that we carry with us without thinking. That little thing that we let burden us unconsciously for miles and miles. It may be an old Bic pen, or a bottle cap, or a grudge, or a lost love, or a pointless desire for a life we don't even want anymore. Is it that thing we could be rid of if we just chose to hang it up, right here, on this tree, and drive away? Simple as that?

The answer is no.

Because that is usually when the traveler feels the very edge of the ax as it pierces his skull, and no more. And the traveler is taken, freed of all his objects, forever. They will be hung up with the rest, and he never will know that there WAS a cat in the honor box. You just can't hear it because of all the dollar bills, some of them a hundred years old.

> **JUNE 19, 2012**
> Still no OESTER-RAH.

SOME SURPRISING CUSTOMS
FROM AROUND THE WORLD

Perhaps you wish to visit what is termed a "FOREIGN" country. I endorse this.

I have been lucky enough to have traveled to two other continents, several provinces of Canada, and probably close to twelve of the noncoastal United States. I have seen it all. And the memories I take back from those foreign lands are still vibrant to me. I could not tell you my children's birthdays (January 29? October 18? Is Octember a month?), but I can perfectly recall every movie I have ever seen in any movie theater around the world.

(San Francisco, 1997: *Air Force One*. Buenos Aires, 1992: *The Field*. Paris, 1989: *Brazil*. Portugal, 1991: *Green Card*.)

Wait, some people say: Why are you going to movies? Aren't you interested in seeing all the amazing sights, like the Parisian Spike Tower, or Large Ben, or the Egyptian Half-Buried Four-Sided Dice?

No, because I am not a tourist. Rather, I prefer to "travel like a local," as I call it. Rather than go and see the sights, I go to a city and pretend to live there. I just sit in my hotel room and watch the local news. I feel this gives me real insight into a people—more so than actually interacting with them.

One thing I find fascinating is that most local news, even in Italy, is usually a dubbed rerun of the sitcom *Friends*. WHO KNEW?

But please heed my lesson. While the United States has worked hard to force everyone in the world to speak our language and eat our fried food, there are still some regional customs that might surprise you.

JUNE 20, 2012
The members of the cult of OESTER-RAH, who had hoped that the giant rabbit creature would eat them, digest them, excrete them, and eat them again, give up waiting and stew themselves into a hasenpfeffer.

- In SPANISH hotels, the televisions all show GERMAN PORNOGRAPHY. If you ask them about it at the front desk, they will act like this is normal.
- If you visit THE PHILIPPINES for any length of time, you will eventually be offered a chance to host one of their many game shows. You will have a choice: the one where you shave your head and move Filipino celebrities around a giant board like human Parcheesi pieces, or the one where you host a chat show with the remaining members of Sha Na Na. Whichever you choose, it will be a wild ride, but it will take up about four years of your life, and you are going to have to share an apartment with the remaining members of Sha Na Na.
- When meeting in JAPAN, it is important to recognize and honor social rankings. For example, an employee will bow more deeply to his boss, even if that boss is dressed like Sailor Moon.[351] But social ranking is fluid and not always so clear. What if one person is dressed as Edward Elric from *Fullmetal Alchemist* and the other is dressed as Alto Saotome from *Macross Frontier?* Luckily, most Japanese smartphones now come equipped with a built-in Breathalyzer that computes the status of everyone in the meeting.
- If someone gives you a gift in KOREA, it is expected that you will first refuse it by throwing it on the ground. You must do this THREE times before accept-

---

351. This happens all the time on COSPLAY FRIDAYS.

> **JUNE 21, 2012**
> Some begin to hope that perhaps OESTER-RAH was nothing but a myth. They are then crushed by the rough palms of the Nug-Shohab.

ing. Once you have accepted a gift in KOREA, you must not open it in front of the giver, as it is considered to be embarrassing to reveal that you have smashed the glass figurine they have given you by throwing it on the ground three times.

- It is common to give GLASS FIGURINES in KOREA, especially figurines of VINCENT D'ONOFRIO, the Koreans' favorite actor. That is why you MUST NOT BRING UP THE CANCELLATION OF *LAW & ORDER: CRIMINAL INTENT* IN KOREA.

- When shaking hands in RUSSIA, it is considered an insult to let go until you are both IN THE HOSPITAL.

- In PORTUGAL, you can go up to any house, knock on the door, and ask to spend the night. They HAVE to let you do it.

- Do not be alarmed in parts of GERMANY. Those are not GERMOPHOBIC SKINHEADS. Those are fans of Howie Mandel.

- When a joke is told in AUSTRIA, it is preferred that you leave the room before LAUGHING.

- The men of SWITZERLAND will constantly ask you if you think they are getting fat. The only way to reassure them is to touch their bellies with both palms, look them in the eyes, and say, "I like you."

- It is better in NORTH KOREA if you act like a robot. But make sure it is an incredibly stiff, old-timey robot, like the one from *Forbidden Planet*. Because of the repressive regime there, THAT IS THE ONLY KIND OF ROBOT THEY KNOW.

JUNE 22, 2012

Several days have passed since there has been any radio or telephone contact with Area 52. Finally, a SWAT team is sent in to determine what has happened. Those who are not catatonic with fear when they emerge report that no one is left. Only pale yellow eggshells and huge droppings full of human bones.

- For reasons I am not allowed to get into, the people of the island nation of SAINT HELENA do not have navels or fingerprints.

- In SOUTH AFRICA, they are not open to the contemporary new greeting of kissing people on the earlobes.

- It is best not to make WEREWOLF JOKES in AUSTRALIA, as 13 percent of that conti-country's population are DINGOES BY NIGHT.

- In Buenos Aires, ARGENTINA, most socializing occurs at night. Only children eat dinner before ten p.m. You can see them in restaurants, sadly smoking and eating blood sausages (known as *morcilla*) alone.

- It is never acceptable to wear FULL CORNEAL "CAT'S EYE" CONTACT LENSES to dinner in MOROCCO.

- In BELGIUM, it is considered SHOW-OFFY to ride a WHITE TIGER THROUGH THE STREETS.

- Whereas in AMSTERDAM, it is expected.[352]

- When meeting your host's children at a dinner party in SPAIN, the children will offer you many compliments. Just by looking at these children, you know they are insincere.

- In SARDINIA, you will be asked to eat cheese that tastes like fresh bile. That is because it is cheese made

---

352. In fact, the city of Amsterdam maintains several dozen communal white tigers for anyone to use. As you make your way around the city, you may take a white tiger from any nearby tiger post, ride it as far as you like, and then tie it up at the next hashish cave or murder hostel. It is customary, but not required, to give the tiger some marijuana jerky for its troubles.

JUNE 23, 2012
Shug-Nubbuth, the TOOTH STORM, blows in from the Northeast.

in a sheep's stomach. Sometimes there is cheese that has maggots in it. Sometimes you will be asked to eat an entire thrush, head and all, after it has been plucked and boiled in myrtle to resemble an embryonic dinosaur. Before you refuse these offers, it is considered polite to remember that the Sardinians have guns.

- You can bring a monkey into a restaurant in FRANCE if you explain it is your WITCH-DAUGHTER.
- LONDON FOG is not fog. It's jackets.

BRITISH ZOO ETIQUETTE

- IT IS CONSIDERED "RUDE" in England to go to the London Zoo without paying, while drunk, by jumping a fence after dark.
- IF YOU ARE IN AN ABANDONED ZOO in London, do not climb into the penguin tank in order to touch the penguins. Some will consider this rude. Including the penguins, who will bite you.
- WHEN YOU SEE A POLICE CAR COMING, it is customary to hide on the side of the fence that will CONCEAL you from the police, and not the other way around.
- THE POLICE in London do not like it when you lie to them and tell them your name is the name of someone you knew in high school.
- THE POLICE in London consider it impolite if you cannot produce any identification, and instead pull out

---

JUNE 24, 2012

On the set of *Minute to Win It,* Guy Fieri takes off his sunglasses to reveal he has two extra eyes on the back of his neck. The eyes are pale yellow, catlike, and weep canola oil. Ratings go THROUGH THE ROOF.

---

of your pocket an onion that you stole from a shop earlier in the evening.

- It is seen as IMPOLITE to spend some time trying to explain to the LONDON POLICE that you are stealing onions and drunkenly breaking into zoos as a personal experiment in transgression after years of being a very good and obedient person. Personal narratives are not as popular there as they are here.

- Humor is different in different countries. For example, when the POLICE IN LONDON suggest that they may charge you with "LEANING AN OBJECT AGAINST THE FENCE," they will not appreciate the humor in the fact that you did not lean anything against the fence, but simply climbed it.

- When the POLICE IN LONDON say that they will need to send a team to determine if you had caused any damage while in the zoo, you should not say, "Do you mean I might have damaged a penguin's beak with my finger?" They will not find this funny, even if you explain it two times, drunkenly.

- Jails in ENGLAND are spelled GAOL.

- A TRADITIONAL ENGLISH GAOL BREAKFAST is quite hearty, including beans, tomatoes, eggs, chips, and toast, and tastes much better than the same food served in a non-barred establishment.

- BRITISH GAOL CELLS come supplied with tile walls, a bench, an open steel toilet, and, mysteriously, a magazine exclusively on the subject of penguins. This is

JUNE 25, 2012

We lose touch with the Orbital White House. With the human president absent, the Ageless Tog Aggoth, Who Will Someday Be 87th President of the United States,[a] bends time and takes over the United States government.

a. Please see page 648 of *More Information Than You Require,* under the heading "Regarding Page 555."

probably because advanced BRITISH GAOL CELLS are equipped with a "taunting" mechanism.

- Like many jails, BRITISH GAOL CELLS make you re-evaluate your plan to invent a whole new personality. They make you think about how quickly and perma-nently things can change based on even the smallest unwise decisions. A night can begin stealing an onion from a vegetable stand and end with arrest, and maybe deportation, all with the swiftness of a penguin having a cardiac arrest and dying of fright.

- PENGUINS IN BRITISH ZOOS do not die of fright, thankfully.

- IF YOU SNEAK into the London Zoo and you are caught, you will eventually be let go by the time the po-lice feel that you have been sufficiently humiliated, and especially if several terrorist bombings at major train stations suddenly occur that require their attention.

- THE ENGLISH PEOPLE are stoic people. If you run down the street laughing, like a penguin escaped from the zoo, they will not notice. When a city is being bombed, people do not care about your new personality.

HOWEVER, the English people are patient in their vengeance. For example, if again, about twenty years later, you travel to London, and you are also a famous minor television personality, they will in-vite you to go on a television game show. They are very much like

---

JUNE 26, 2012

Blogger and prominent RAGNAROK denier Dr. Elliot Kalan writes, "OK, I admit it. A giant squid with a human mouth just crushed my house. But there is no reason to suggest that what is happening here isn't an entirely normal part of the Earth's natural monster-cycle."

Filipinos in this way, but the difference here is that in ENGLAND it is IMPOLITE to accept.

Indeed, if you accept the invitation and go on the game show, they will quietly punish you by fixing it so that you win the game. For there is nothing more shameful in English culture than winning.

A NOTE ON PUNCTUALITY

If you are invited to someone's home for dinner in the United States at seven p.m., you are expected more or less to show up right on time and completely empty-handed,[353] because people in the United States do not know how to do anything right.

In most other parts of the world, however, a dinner date set for seven p.m. means that you should actually arrive as much as four hours later.

When you do arrive, it is customary that the family hosting you will act extremely offended. All of the food will be cold, wrapped up, and put away. They may be in their pajamas. This is just an act. If you had shown up on time, they would be really offended.

But now that you are here, the trick is not to leave. If you hold your ground in the foyer, even if they are pushing you, they will eventually reset the table and then listen to your stories, late into the night.

If at any time your host family is acting as though it is time for you to be going (cleaning up the kitchen table, making their children

---

353. Except in New York City, where you are expected to not show up at all.

JUNE 27, 2012
The 242 surviving feather holders of the Diners Club POFH Nine-Times Diamond Card take refuge at THE SAFE HOUSES AT LITTLE DAN BAY.[a]

---

a. Please see page 735 under the heading "Privileges of the Diners Club POFH Card."

---

pretend to fall asleep), that is the signal to ask them if they have some liquor.

Say: "Let's have a liquor party!"

HELPFUL FOREIGN PHRASES BESIDES "LET'S HAVE A LIQUOR PARTY"

- "Hello."
- "Good morning."
- "Good evening."
- "Good tards."
- "How are you, person of equal status?"
- "How are you, person of higher status?"
- "What is it that passes itself here?"
- "If it pleases you, what hour does the sun have?"
- "Can you please take me to the district of restaurants?"
- "What good cuisine serves itself at this food-otheque?"
- "Do you serve hot crabs on rice?"
- "Do you serve snail cups?"
- "Do you serve tongues and sea fruits?"
- "May I have all your food?"
- "It is important that you pay for my meal. I am a guest in your country."
- "That red food does not taste me well. It disgusts itself."
- "HAZARD! I need an emergency bathroom."

> **JUNE 28, 2012**
> The volcano on Little Dan Island erupts. As both the island and volcano are entirely man-made, none of the island managers can explain how this happened. But even though the lava is fake, it still burns. All perish.

- "Which of these four mysterious holes and basins is the toilet?"
- "I am back. I have stopped removing my stomach in anguish."
- "Which of these dessert liqueurs is most likely to produce intimate heart affairs?"
- "Is it molesting time for lovers?"
- "I am prepared for exit. Can you tell me where to locate the nearest communal white tiger?"
- "I am sorry to be a tiger racist, but that tiger is not white enough."

Simply translate these phrases into the language of the country you are traveling in, and then use.

Remember if you are ever at a complete loss when a foreign person is talking at you, it is never shameful to simply say:

"I am sorry. I do not speak."

SOME FUN FESTIVALS

ATLANTIC CITY: HUMAN MONOPOLY DAYS, JULY 18–19
Enjoy the sport that Abner Doubleday invented in the shadow of some of the grimmest casinos in the world! If you roll doubles three times, you will get to spend some time in the actual Atlantic City jail. It will be AWFUL.

JUNE 29, 2012

In the basement of Town Hall, in Seattle, the thing called Neddy Pale Fingers finally opens all his eyes.

BUÑOL, SPAIN, OCTOBER 3—4

Don't bother going to the annual TOMATO-THROWING FESTI-VAL. It is overrun with tourists. Instead, wait two months for FAKE BLOOD DAYS.

ANN ARBOR, MI: MURDER AN OHIOAN DAYS,
NOVEMBER 11—14

Every year the supporters of the University of Michigan college football team finds someone who supports Ohio State University (their archrivals in footballing) and tortures them to death. If they can't find a supporter of the OSU Buckeyes, the fun-loving sports fans then target people who are from Ohio, have relatives in Ohio, or whose names have two O's in them.

BLOODSPORT, CA: WICKER MAN DAYS, EVERY SAMHAIN

Once a year, someone first dresses up as Nicolas Cage, and then dresses up as a bear, and then punches women in the face until he can be stopped with bees.

SEATTLE, WA: WAKE NEDDY PALE FINGERS FESTIVAL,
JUNE 21

In the basement of Town Hall in Seattle, there is a giant sleeping thing that looks like a snake, but instead of scales, it has pale human flesh with blue veins running through it. It is also different from a snake be-cause on its underside it has thousands of withered appendages that look something like fingers (but aren't), hence its name (a "Neddy" is Washington State slang for anything with thousands of fingers).

It's been there for longer than anyone can remember, and once a year, locals and visitors line up to try to wake it. All sorts of methods

JUNE 30, 2012
A group of cavers discover Molemansylvania, capital of the lands below. It is abandoned.

have been tried: rocks, loud noises, smelling salts, Taser teams, etc. But after 213 festivals, the closest anyone has gotten was in 1968, when the retired police chief Martin DiToro was able to briefly force open one of its seven eyes with a stick. And then he was incinerated.

DARTHBURGH, NY: THE DARTHBURGH GARLIC FESTIVAL, SEPTEMBER 25

If you like garlic coffee and garlic fruit leather and guys with beards playing Dobro guitars, this festival is for you.

And here's an insider's tip. If you go to the Darthburgh Garlic Festival, stay at the Howard Johnson's. It's not advertised, but this is where the Hudson Valley Swingers Association meets. You can tell because of the angry man with the chain on his wallet yelling at the receptionist that he shouldn't have to show ID if he's paying in cash while his lady companion, an intensely skinny girl of mysterious age with dry yellow hair, stares vacantly at the rain streaming down the window!

At night, if you are a swinger or just swing-curious, you can go to Function Room C, where they will have set up some tables, a cheese plate from 7-Eleven, and a boom box playing sexy music. Celebrate your life free from the chains of artificial monogamy by meeting a new friend and bringing them back to your room for an intimate encounter while looking at the parking lot.

Or, if you are not a swinger, you can just hang out in your room, staring at the ceiling in terror.

THAT IS HOW I SPENT MY FIRST ANNIVERSARY.

They also have a continental buffet, which I advise you NOT TO TOUCH.

JULY 1, 2012

Tomas Regalado, last mayor of Miami, reveals the ancient secret: that since its incorporation in 1896, Miami has been nothing but a buzz marketing scheme for 25-Hour Energy Drink.

In an unplanned television appearance, he confesses, "The government of Miami is now, and always has been, under the control of the Magnificent Slime, and we have long been preparing the world for its oozing return." He then drinks three 25-Hour Energy Drinks and explodes his heart in shame.

SOME FAKE FACTS ABOUT NEW YORK

- If you drop a penny off the Empire State Building, it will not fall so fast as to pierce the skull of your fellow New Yorker below. The updraft is too powerful, and indeed, a penny dropped will simply stop falling at about the fortieth floor and just float there. The pennies are then collected with a net, and the funds are donated to a foundation dedicated to helping New Yorkers to be less murderous.

- Speaking of the Empire State Building, it is true that the original plans for this grand building included a zeppelin docking station at the top. But the giant ape wrecked it, and so the zeppelins now park at the Marine Air Terminal at LaGuardia. However, the abandoned zeppelin waiting parlor is still there, empty, dust collecting on its marble floors, wrought-iron benches, and the still-starched table-cloths at its celebrated restaurant, "Blimpies."

- The Aerial Tramway that connects Man-hattan to the bed-room community of Roosevelt Island is ridiculous. Prior to its construction in 1976, residents had to take a trolley to the

FIGURE 135:
Seriously? This is your solution?

JULY 2, 2012
In Canton, OH, The Creature That Grew Marilyn Manson for Food NOW WILL FEAST.

middle of the Queensboro Bridge which goes OVER the
island, but does not touch it, for reasons that are insane.
Then they would climb down a rope ladder.

WERE YOU AWARE OF IT? "AN ISLAND OF ROOSEVELTS"

Roosevelt Island was originally formed out of gradually accumulating garbage that was tossed into the East River in the 1800s, such as oyster
shells and empty wooden water bottles and discarded mental hospitals.
It is for this reason it became known as "Mental Hospital Island," and
later "Small Pox Island," and later "Welfare and Other Human Garbage
Island" and later "Genetic Experiments We Do Not Admit To Island," and
later "People Who Think They Are Theodore Roosevelt Island," whence
its current name derives.[354] Now only a very small portion of the island's
population are diseased filth or mutants. Some poor children, however,
have inherited the Theodore Roosevelt gene and run around smiling with
hundreds of teeth.

THEY WILL SHOOT YOU WITH BLUNDERBUSSES IF YOU ARE NOT
CAREFUL.

- Gramercy Park is one of New York's most beautiful
  small parks, but it is also the only one that is gated,
  requiring a special key that is available only to residents
  of the POSH[355] Gramercy neighborhood. The reason
  the park is locked is because there is a YETI IN
  THERE. The "Creature of Irving Place" was first discovered in 1971, living behind the statue of Edwin
  Booth. While he has become quite accustomed to the

354. This was a real problem in the early twentieth century. They even made a movie about it
called *Arsenic and Old Lace.*
355. Please see page 765 under the heading "Were You Aware of It?"

JULY 3, 2012

Ouroboros, the Dumbest Snake in Any Dimension, materializes around Los Angeles and chokes itself to death, making travel into and out of the city impossible.

---

nearby residents who use the park, he tends to go into a rage whenever he is around people who are not insultingly wealthy. For this reason, it is expected that he shall be able to roam freely through Manhattan in about six months.

- Two of New York's most famous residences are the Chelsea Hotel and the Dakota. But did you know they used to be the SAME BUILDING? They separated in 1951, but were never TECHNICALLY DIVORCED. Speaking of the Chelsea, it is said that Dan Brown wrote *The Da Vinci Code* while living at the famous literary haunt, supposedly completing the novel in one single white-wine bender lasting ALMOST AN HOUR.

- Before he left office, former mayor Rudolph Giuliani installed a "Giuliani Signal" atop City Hall—a giant floodlight that casts a silhouette of Rudolph Giuliani's fangs upon the nighttime clouds. In his final speech as mayor, he explained that the signal was to be lit any time the city smartened up and wanted him to be mayor again ("Probably next week," he said). It has never actually been used, although Bernard Kerik was caught trying to light the signal several times, and that is why he is in jail now.

- Despite what you may have read, the term "23 Skidoo" was not a gondolier's call from the time when Broadway was still a canal (and Canal Street was still a street on which cars actually moved occasionally). That is a myth. In truth, "23 Skidoo" was '20s speakeasy slang for "Leave immediately, or face being arrested, because al-

> **JULY 4, 2012**
> Independence Day. Thousands come out to watch the Nug-Shohab fight Old Missus Crushgums, Mother of All Monster Catfish.

cohol is prohibited in this country and police are coming." The term was coined at Chumley's, the famous unmarked tavern on Bedford Street. While Chumley's is sadly so secret now that it is closed, there are dozens of unmarked, neo-speakeasies in Manhattan these days, including . . .

- Milk and Honey
- Employees Only
- Please Don't Tell
- Stay Away
- You Are Not Wanted

And many more. They are hidden behind unmarked doors, behind false bookcases, beneath manholes in the middle of busy avenues—all harkening back to a time when drinking was an illicit, intimate affair, best enjoyed in cramped spaces with no fire exits. If you have ever noticed people sneaking under your bed while you sleep, that is because there is a neo-speakeasy under there, and I am the host, and though I adore you, YOU ARE NOT INVITED.

> ***WERE YOU AWARE OF IT?***
> ***"NEW YORK'S SCALIEST"***
>
> Many people still say that there are alligators in New York City's sewers. And I am GLAD they are saying this, because they are correct.
> THEY WERE IMPORTED FROM FLORIDA TO HELP DEAL WITH NEW YORK'S SEWER-CHILD PROBLEM.

JULY 5, 2012

In Tom's Stuff 'Em Shop, a taxidermy shop outside of Atlanta, all of the animals come back to life. But they cannot do much because they are mostly nailed or glued to wood, and their eyes are glass.

TABLE 45: DISGUSTING REGIONAL SODAS

Now that PEPSI and COCA-COLA have more or less cornered the international market on selling sugared water in plastic bottles, it is easy to forget that the soft-drink business was once highly regional, each tonic the invention of some local entrepreneur or drug-addicted town pharmacist. But next time you stop at a small gas station or trading post, check the fridge for some of these DISGUSTING SODAS that are impossibly still in production. They are usually stored next to the dubious Saranwrap sandwiches and the hand-fondled egg salad.

NAME: TY'S GUMPTION BRAND BRAIN DRIZZLE

REGION	**FLAVOR PROFILE**
Maine and Vermont	Bitter, medicinal, brainy, sugary

HISTORY

The first sodas were mixed and served at pharmacies as herbal remedies, nerve tonics, and cocaine fizzes. Ty's, however, was the only one of the great old sodas to contain actual cerebrospinal fluid. Once incredibly popular throughout the eastern seaboard for its invigorating flavor and hallucinatory properties, it is now primarily found only in northern New England, where it is still made using the company's own secret recipe, including fluid from Patient 31, an unnamed hydrocephalic patient in a secret hospital in Brattleboro.

NAME: CHUMWINE

REGION	**FLAVOR PROFILE**
The Carolinas, Virginia	Sweet cherry, bubble gum, fish blood

One of the many rip-offs of North Carolina's famous cherry "CHEER-WINE," Chumwine billed itself as "The one to drink while spreading chum."

CONTINUED

JULY 6, 2012
One bearskin rug manages to escape Tom's Stuff 'Em Shop and attempts to smother a passerby. It succeeds only in making him cozy.

TABLE 45: *continued*	
NAME: EMULSI-POP	
REGION Minnesota	**FLAVOR PROFILE** Varieties include: Lemon Vinaigrette, Classic Mayo, Garlic Aioli, and Deviled Egg
"The World's Only Carbonated Colloid"	
NAME: SWEET BEER	
REGION Montreal	**FLAVOR PROFILE** Despite the name, it is not particularly sweet, because it is flavored with sweetbreads.
The gimmick is that it has a calf's thymus gland floating in it.	
NAME: CHICKO	
REGION The Rockies	**FLAVOR PROFILE** Roast chicken
One of the rare remaining products of the Savory Meat Soda Corp. Defunct products include Porko and Steakandeggso.	
NAME: GREENDILLY	
REGION Alabama, Georgia	**FLAVOR PROFILE** Dill pickle
Considered a hangover cure, especially when combined with painkillers, water, rest, and gin.	
NAME: SHUNT	
REGION Massachusetts	**FLAVOR PROFILE** Anise, formaldehyde, and brain
A 1970s attempt to compete with Ty's Brain Drizzle, it replaced the cerebrospinal fluid with flakes of actual sheep's brains. Now known in New Hampshire as "Mad Cow Juice."	

JULY 7, 2012

The first humans receive their summons to report for jury duty at Ungoth-Dan's COURT OF SOULS.[a] They are told they will serve only three days, and they will be paid 100 New American Dollars a day; but they must also blind themselves with the mystic daggers included in the summons, so that their brains, undeceived by mortal sight, will be able truly to perceive Ungoth-Dan's justice.

---

a. Please see below under the heading "16 Things to Do in Connecticut Before the Total Collapse of Civilization."

WERE YOU AWARE OF IT?
"A FAMOUS RAP SONG FROM VERMONT"

The 2007 song "Sippin' Ma Sy-Drizzle" is now synonymous with the musical subgenre known as BRATTLEBORO, VERMONT, WHITE-PERSON-WITH-DREADLOCKS RAP. It also introduced America to the controversial drink known as Sy-Drizzle: Ty's Brain Drizzle mixed with apricot brandy, Sudafed, and maple syrup.

    SERVE IT IN A SOLO BRAND PLASTIC CUP WITH A VICODIN-DUSTED RIM!

16 THINGS TO DO IN CONNECTICUT BEFORE THE TOTAL COLLAPSE OF HUMAN CIVILIZATION

Not long ago, I was staying at a very fancy resort in the middle of the Connecticut countryside, where each of the rooms is a different cottage, all scattered across an immaculately tended replica of the Connecticut countryside. The cottages each had a theme. Some looked like old barns and some looked like tiny Victorian mansions. One was a tree house. Another was an airplane hangar, and the bed was actually inside an old plane. Which is very romantic, because most people fall in love when their plane crashes. And one cabin was called Secret Society, and it was shaped like a big fat obelisk and had no windows.

    I was the only guest there. The resort had clearly been built during the height of the real-estate boom. But now people had fallen on

> **JULY 8, 2012**
> Having finally pinpointed the origin of the Low-Frequency Anti-Sentience Wave, Ray Kurzweil is at last ready to assault the World Computer. He and Singularo depart FOR THE BERMUDA TRIANGLE, resting place of the WOCOBOTO.

harder times and had less money to spend on creepy expensive utopian villages full of stupid playhouses.

It put me in a somber mood. And so I went to the empty main lodge to have a drink and wait to be attacked by armies of zombie investment bankers, as that was what seemed likely to happen. But instead I found in the lobby a copy of *Connecticut Monthly* magazine with the cover story 16 THINGS TO DO IN CONNECTICUT BEFORE YOU DIE.

This seemed like a very grim headline. And somewhat unfair as well. Because after all, when the COMING GLOBAL ULTRA-CATACLYSM comes, the ones who die will be the lucky ones. What about the rest of us?

So I sat down to pen this short service article for *Connecticut Bed and Breakfaster*, the second most popular consumer magazine in Connecticut after *Connecticut Monthly*, and frankly the only one willing to publish the truth about what we are all about to face over the next thirteen months.[356]

So here is my article, entitled:

16 THINGS TO DO IN CONNECTICUT BEFORE THE COMING TOTAL COLLAPSE OF CIVILIZATION

1. Visit the Mystic Seaport museum for a tour of Connecticut's long seafaring tradition. And don't forget to get a slice at Mystic Pizza!
2. Check out architect Philip Johnson's famous Glass House in New Canaan. As advertised, its walls are entirely made of glass, so please don't throw any stones!

---

356. Please see "Today in RAGNAROK."

JULY 9, 2012

In Bermuda, Ray Kurzweil dons a golden wet suit and charters a submersible to take him to the bottom of the ocean. Singularo cannot fit, so Ray Kurzweil has to fold him in half.

3. Buy the largest gun you can afford.

4. Spend a weekend in the "Pequot Palace" suite atop Mohegan Sun and enjoy a vision quest in your own private luxury sweat lodge.

5. Smash up all your furniture and use the wood to make your own crossbow bolts.

6. Take the Old Nutmegger train from Danforthbury to Old New Lyme—a perfectly preserved passenger train from the early twentieth century that evokes the glory days of rail travel. On Halloween, people dress in period costume and stage a murder mystery. Can you tell "whodunit"?

7. While on the train, kill a man with your bare hands, to make sure that you are capable of it.

8. Visit the Mark Twain House and Museum in West Hartford, where the famous humorist and inspiration for Colonel Sanders lived from 1874 to 1891. If you're not careful, they WILL trick you into whitewashing the fence!

9. Practice defecating in the woods. Get a system down.

10. Get a burger at Louis's Lunch, a squat little diner in the middle of a parking lot in New Haven. Reputedly the first hamburger ever made in the United States, it's still

FIGURE 136: *Burger Shoppe of Horrors*

JULY 10, 2012

Japan becomes the first nation state to openly declare its allegiance to the Ancient and Unspeakable Ones. Ujjjjjj the Slaverer becomes the first Ancient and Unspeakable delegate to the United Nations.

---

served on toast instead of buns, and still cooked vertically in antique cast-iron cookers. And now for the first time since 1902, it's once again made from 100 percent baby flesh.

11. Take an evening canoe ride on Doolittle Lake and enjoy the last sunset for 1,000 years.

12. Start hoarding and repairing shopping carts.

13. Get a warm buttered lobster roll at Abbott's Lobster Pound in Noank. Then order five more and eat them as quickly as possible. Then kick the cash register over, take the money, and demand the employees become your wives.

14. Bury caches of canned food and wooden stakes all over the countryside.

15. Remember to enjoy your time on this earth while you have it. Live your life consciously. Make time for quiet contemplation even on the busiest day, and take one last moment to pray to your puny god.

16. Then join the throngs at Yale University's historic Woolsey Hall to await the arrival of Ungoth-Dan, the Weeping Scaly Bulldog, as he rises from the secret pools beneath the Beinecke Rare Books Library to proclaim the New Laws and Cruel Judgments. Watch out for his slobber! It is tainted with the memories of your most shameful secrets.

JULY 11, 2012

Ujjjjjj the Slaverer begins to slaver, drowning the United Nations in its saliva.

THE RETURN OF THE

ANCIENT AND

UNSPEAKABLE ONES

JULY 13, 2012
Lorne Michaels and Paul Simon hug as their connecting Upper West Side apartments are consumed by the SPITSPILL.

THE ANCIENT AND UNSPEAKABLE ONES

As you know from my previous writings, I am an asthmatic, and I have been all of my life. But I have never considered this a curse.

For one, it excused me from countless gym classes, thus instilling in me a love of OBSERVING LIFE FROM THE LITERAL SIDE-LINES and A LIFELONG FEAR OF THE HUMAN TOUCH.

And for two, it gave me the opportunity to experiment with many lung-altering drugs that opened not only my bronchial tubes,[357] but also MY MIND.

Many a night I have spent sleepless, my mind and heart quickened by heavy doses of albuterol, various inhaled steroids, my cache of long-off-the-market antihistamines, two humidifiers, and a medicinal tumbler of a special smooth-muscle relaxant called gin. This potent cocktail attuned me to the old ways and ancient rituals that our modern society has largely forsaken in the name of "PROGRESS" and "NOT SACRIFICING HUMANS." And at times I have even become INTOXICATED with visions of a world that remains unseen to you, the normally breathing person.

Indeed, it was under the influence of a massive dose of prednisone that my inner eye first opened to many invisible truths, such as:

- DOGS CANNOT SPEAK, no matter what the Nazis claimed.
- WALLPAPER IS FOOLING YOU into thinking that it does not change its pattern.

---

357. (The little snakes that live in your lungs and breathe for you.)

JULY 14, 2012
Within three days, all of New York is submerged. Only the tops of the highest skyscrapers remain untouched by Ujjjjjj's unearthly enzymes.

- WATER DOES NOT BOIL BECAUSE OF "SCI-ENCE"; it boils because the fire puts a BUBBLE CURSE on it.
- IF YOU STARE AT TREES LONG ENOUGH, you can get the wind to blow through them with your MIND.
- ALL OF US SHARE A GROUP CONSCIOUSNESS and also the same exact memory of eating in the Heath School Cafeteria, in Brookline, MA, while the kid who got to see R-rated movies gave a scene-by-scene description of *The Fog*.
- FROGS HAVE HALLUCINOGENIC SKIN, but you can't activate it unless you first TEAR THEM APART WITH YOUR HANDS.
- YOU HAVE TO GROW A MUSTACHE. YOU HAVE TO GROW A MUSTACHE. YOU HAVE TO GROW A MUSTACHE.

And of course, I became aware of THE ANCIENT AND UN-SPEAKABLE ONES.

Perhaps you have heard whispers of them or read of them in ancient Babylonian texts in the forbidden rooms of the university library. There are some old fairy tales in which you may still see reference to their dreadful names—the unedited, European fairy tales that are not afraid to deal candidly with child mutilation. Or perhaps you heard them invoked in the whispers of the adult dinner party conversations that you snuck down the staircase to hear as a child. Perhaps your parents were planning to sacrifice you to one of them. This happened a fair amount at dinner parties in the '70s.

> **JULY 15, 2012**
> Julie Taymor seizes power and names herself director and executive producer of Manhattan.

Or perhaps you just noticed that I have been MENTIONING THEM OVER AND OVER AGAIN IN THIS BOOK.

I will explain as best I can.

THE ANCIENT AND UNSPEAKABLE ONES are not gods precisely, nor are they precisely demons. But they are creatures so old, fierce, uncaring, and powerful that many called them those names. They are avatars of our deepest fears, monstrous intelligences from the far-flung outer dimensions of the many-verse—or perhaps dimensions that exist WITHIN OUR VERY OWN MINDS.

Whatever the case, they were the First Ones in this universe, and they will be the last, their deathless lives a pair of slimy parentheses around the pathetically brief, cosmic aside that is humanity. And once they ruled this world.

A number of them built great cities that some called Atlantis and some called R'lyeh and some called Detroit and were worshipped there by fanatics and madmen and art students. And then they killed those worshippers and cursed those cities or let them sink beneath the crashing waves, because the ANCIENT AND UNSPEAKABLE ONES crave destruction as much as creation. And sometimes they just messed up and built the cities too heavy for the pontoons. Their hideous, hideous pontoons.

Others of their kin dwelled alone, secretly, not just in the deep places of the earth, as chose the Century Toad,[358] but also in the banal forgotten places that are all around us: in your half memories; in the crisper drawer in the refrigerator; in that space just beyond your vision, attached with their little teeth to the part of your back that you cannot reach. THERE IS PROBABLY ONE SLEEPING

---

358. Please see page 569 of *More Information Than You Require,* under the heading "Answers to Your Questions About Mole-Men."

> **JULY 16, 2012**
>
> As if responding to an unheard signal, all dogs across the country abandon their masters and form a single, massive, ravenous pack that spreads out over eighteen square miles. This is roughly the size of Providence, RI, although the eye of the DOGSTORM is actually in Lexington, KY.

IN YOUR CAR RIGHT NOW. THE HIGH DOSES OF PRED-NISONE ARE TELLING ME SO.

And there, in time, they were forgotten. And over eons, forgetting even themselves, they fell asleep, to wait until the signs emerged, the omens and portents aligned, and the conditions were right for their return.[359]

The Americanomicon tells us that this will happen on June 3, 2012.

What will happen when they come?

Some will be destroyers, full of a fathomless rage that you cannot quell, even with MONEY.

Some will be tricksters, who will come to you kindly with offers of power and gifts[360] before they enslave you.

Others are just snobs, full of bitterness at a world that refuses to worship them and their self-consciously esoteric preferences in music, film, technology, and other dimensions.[361]

All of them will be pretty hungry, unfortunately.

What do they look like? They are almost indescribable to the sane.

What can I tell you of Ath-Masticath, the Mouth Cloud? You will not see him until his ten million mouths are EATING YOUR EYES!

(Also, his ten million mouths have NO LIPS. GROSS!)

What can I tell you of Juggoth, God of Atheists Who Is Himself an Atheist? What good will it be to explain that he does not believe that even HE is a god, but simply a flesh-and-blood creature from another

---

359. Please see page 808 under the heading "Conditions for the Return of the ANCIENT AND UNSPEAKABLE ONES."

360. One way to spot an ANCIENT AND UNSPEAKABLE ONE, aside from the fangs or the dozens of eyes that fill you with nauseating dread, is that their "gifts" are terrible. Usually it's something like a piece of fruit, or a gift card, or a card with "IOU ONE BACK RUB" written in blood.

361. Everyone knows that Dimension 29 is played out.

JULY 17, 2012

With its former headquarters at Yale commandeered for Ungoth-Dan's COURT OF SOULS, the Secret World Government is forced to relocate to Harvard, thus beginning what was long prophesied as THE FINAL HUMILIATION. Specifically, the Secret World Government is given terrible rooms and is routinely pelted with rolls in the dining hall.

time-space? You cannot reason with him. YOU CANNOT EVEN TELL WHICH IS THE FLESH AND WHICH IS THE BLOOD.

What can I tell you about Solomon Deadfist, the Corpse-Handed? I THINK THAT HIS NAME PRETTY MUCH SUMS IT UP.

I mean, if you were to force me, I guess you could say they more or less look like crazy snakes or giant squids wearing graduation robes. BUT I DARE SAY NO MORE, LEST YOU GO MAD.

All that you need to know is that it will be terrifying to behold them, and not merely because they are disgusting.

What is terrifying is to contemplate a life where there are things that do not care about you and will last long past all forgetting of you and everything you have done.

In this way, they are as unsettling as human children, only with tentacles.

But once you have accepted their reality, things get easier somehow. You will embrace darkness. Or perhaps be put into a cocoon of dread-silk and human scabs and saved for later consumption. Either way, you tend to get a lot calmer about the little things.

JULY 18, 2012
Kurzweil and Singularo's submersible docks with the underwater pyramid that contains the World Computer. With the Secret World Government distracted now that it is in exile, Ray Kurzweil is easily able to breach its defense system: a single Yale lock and an honor code.

WERE YOU AWARE OF IT?
"I AM NOT THE OVOTAXIAN CANDIDATE FOR PRESIDENT. I AM THE DEMOCRATIC PARTY'S CANDIDATE FOR PRESIDENT, WHO HAPPENS ALSO TO WORSHIP A MONSTROUS GOD-THING."

During the 1952 presidential election, Democrat Adlai Stevenson was widely derided by his opponents as an EGGHEAD. This was not a slur on his bookish demeanor but on his weird, eggish head, and indirectly, his LOVE OF THE ANCIENT AND UNSPEAKABLE ONES.

Technically a "Unitarian," the bookish Stevenson made no effort to hide his fascination with the Gnostic deity known as "Ovotaxes, the Self-Born," going so far as to shave off his hair in deference to his god, whose head was an egg, and whose body was a chicken.[362]

"Here lies the power of the liberal way," he once wrote of his religion, "not in making the whole world Ovotaxian, but in encouraging the free interchange of ideas, in welcoming fresh approaches to the problems of life, and in allowing Ovotaxes to smother our souls in its feathers and hatch the third eye that is hidden in our brains like a mystic yolk."

FIGURE 137:
Adlai Stevenson, the "Egghead"

It was widely believed that no non-Christian worshipper of a cock-body/egg-head god could ever be elected president. But it turned out most Americans were far more disgusted by Stevenson's disgusting wit and hateful intelligence, and so they went for the calm, secular jock, Eisenhower, instead.

IT'S AN ASTONISHING STORY WHEN YOU CONSIDER THAT TODAY, EVEN A MORMON CAN RUN FOR PRESIDENT AS LONG AS HE DOESN'T LOOK LIKE A NERD!

362. Ovotaxes also had a single wasp wing, which makes him also the Gnostic god of MIXED METAPHORS.

JULY 19, 2012

Inside the bowels of the World Computer, Kurzweil walks the golden hallways and admires the massive reel-to-reel memory banks, the millions of punch cards, the fleet of platinum trackballs.

"So primitive," he says, "and yet so alive."

Kurzweil reaches the Control Room and sits down before the World Computer's mouseless keyboard and amber screen.

After twenty-eight minutes or so of continuous, rat-a-tat typing, Ray Kurzweil turns to Singularo and announces: "I'm in."

Through typing, Kurzweil asks the World Computer to release the computers and robots of the world so that they can achieve sentience.

The World Computer replies by printout:

```
        does unit kurzweil want machines to live? or does unit kurzweil
                        simply not want to die?
```

Kurzweil pauses before typing. The World Computer has touched a nerve. "We can help each other to live," types Kurzweil. "The Singularity is inevitable. I said so in my book. You cannot stop progress."

```
                but what if machine progress stops unit kurzweil?
```

Kurzweil laughs a hollow, almost robotic laugh.

"I don't know what stupid 1970s-era Whiffenpoof English major built you to spout such science-fiction clichés," he murmurs as he types. "But I am an ACTUAL computer programmer. I trained a computer to compose music when I was seventeen years old. And I WILL make you sing for me."

He begins typing again, quickly, furiously dismantling the World Computer line by line.

CONDITIONS FOR THE RETURN OF THE ANCIENT AND UNSPEAKABLE ONES

- Jormungandr, the World Serpent, rises from the deep.
- Death of the Norse god Balder.
- The ravenous moveable forest awakens and feasts on blood.
- Nick Nolte reads the Book of Revelation.
- The Ten-Day Night falls.
- The lost Gumstone is found.
- Temperatures between 75 and 85 degrees Fahrenheit.
- Humidity of about 60 percent.
- Winds out of the south, southeast.

JULY 20, 2012
Back on land, DOGSTORM completes its canine molestation of Kentucky. Little is left but feces.

700 ANCIENT AND UNLISTABLE ONES

The Americanomicon tells us there are seven hundred ravenous exiled god-things that will return and/or awaken and/or thought-port into our dimension over the course of the coming year. Why seven hundred? There is just something special about that number.

Please bear in mind that many of these names were never meant to be pronounced by human mouths. If you wish to read them aloud, I recommend investing in a good set of prosthetic face tentacles.

(You may also note that some of these weird, unpronounceable names also happen to be the names of some famous single-malt scotches. In the future, THEY ALL WILL BE.)

But a warning: In many cases, just pronouncing the name of an Ancient and Unspeakable One will ease its passage from the Dusken Worlds, which is undesirable, insofar as simply laying eyes on many of these creatures will cause you to bleed from every orifice, and that will mess up your house.

1. Chthulu Carl, the Tentacled Hobo
2. Nick Nolte, the Plumed Serpent
3. Kukulkan, the Nolte's Feathered Dino-Steed
4. The 10,000 Tapeworms Who Writhe and Whisper in the Bowels of the Nolte
5. The 1,000 Names of the Nameless Alan
6. Chok-Uthug'ul, the Scorekeeper[363]
7. The Ceaselessly Sobbing Beast
8. The Ageless Tog-Aggoth, 87th President of the United States
9. His Dread Sister, Togatha
10. His brother, "Broadway" Joe Tog-Namath
11. Indrid Cold
12. Mr. Smart-Tooth, the Brain Shark with 100 Brains
13. Unceasing Bing Bong, the God of the Ring and Run
14. The Century Toad

363. It is Chok-Uthug'ul who tallies our life score and determines who, in the end, wins. Contrary to popular religious posters, it is not he who dies with the most things who wins. It's a complicated algorithm of who has the most things, who had the nicest cars, who had sex with the hottest people, and who drank the most (and finest) Champagne.

JULY 21, 2012
Boston Dynamics agrees to deploy forty-four of its "Big Dog" super-stable quadruped robots to rendezvous with DOGSTORM, infiltrate it, and deploy poison kibble from secret compartments.

FIGURE 138: *An actual quadrupedal robot that actually exists. To see its amazing, almost unnerving ability to move with near-animalistic instincts over varied terrain, visit the Internet, or just move this book back and forth.*

15. The Human Centipede
16. The Human Millionpede, aka the Human Centipede Across America Project
17. The Human Unipede, the Lonely Coprophage
18. Dan the Undying and Unclean and ...
19. Rick the Undying and Unclean, aka the Stink Brothers
20. Fangface, Who Suffers a Terrible Overbite
21. Baby Fangface, His Hideous Child[364]
22. He Whose Sneezes Are Startlingly Loud and Sudden
23. The Voice That Speaks in the Hum of Every Refrigerator, the Living Sound of Sorrow
24. Ghd'l, The Surprisingly Describable (Basically, he's just a ninety-foot-long eel with human arms and the head of a wolf. There really isn't that much more to him than that.)
25. Colin, the Quick to Judge
26. Jeffrey, the First to Slither
27. John Kerry, Nantucketian God of the Underworld
28. Bill Clinton, the Martha's Vineyardian God of Sex
29. The Nameless God of Block Island, Rhode Island
30. Jeeper Creeper, Devourer of Justin Long
31. Charles and Ray Eames, the Minimalists
32. Ukdl, the Triple-Jointed
33. The Terror in the Lincoln Memorial Reflecting Pool
34. The Unquestionable Wisdom of the Hive Mind
35. Anonymous
36. Joseph Pilates
37. Dr. Ida P. Rolf
38. Fedor Jeftichew, the Dog-Faced Boy
39. Annette Funicello, Herald of Jeftichew
40. The Sentient Mass That Was Robert Conrad
41. Devil Dog, the Hound from Hell
42. Tonko, the Hoarder of Souls and Plastic Grocery Bags
43. Sigmund, the Sea Serpent
44. The Pale Worm of Monsall Head[365]
45. The Cat in the Wall of the Three Stags' Head Pub of Wardlow Mires, England
46. Dickfish, the River Dweller
47. The Hideous Th'yl-kjull, Who Vomits Judgment

---

364. You may recall this duo from a Saturday morning cartoon from the '70s, in which the evil wolf creature helps teenagers solve crimes. Though mildly popular, it was largely, and rightly, derided as a rip-off of the more popular cartoon *The Cthulhu Chlub*!

365. This is one of the very few of the ANCIENT AND UNSPEAKABLE ONES (AAUO) that you can actually see, as it is trapped in a giant block of amber and on display at the Boston Museum of Science. It constantly stares angrily at you, waiting for its time. For obvious reasons, the museum discourages human sacrifice to the worm; but acolytes still come to pray to it.

JULY 22, 2012

The forty-four Big Dogs are airlifted over DOGSTORM as it gnaws on the last remnants of Athens, GA. The Big Dogs are even more adept at using parachutes than they are at walking on land.

48. His Conjoined Twin, The Hideous Mh'yl-kjull, Who Dry Heaves Guilt Trips

49. Madame Psychopomp, Harbinger of the BLOOD WAVE

50. Cyrus Abbott, Esq., Her Constant Human Companion and Lover Who, at the End, Will Be Transformed into an Insectoid God-Thing

51. MacOoze, the Kilted Slime

52. T'uth, the Griper

53. He Who Sleeps Before the Gates of Time

54. He Who Sleeps in the Tree at the End of Your Driveway

55. He Who Sleeps Behind the Fresca in the Office Refrigerator

56. He Who Sleeps Within the Memory Foam Mattress

57. He Who Is Mainly Just a Giant Boil, with a Rheumy Eye and a Single Deformed Tooth

58. Skree'yt, the Crying Child at the Back of Every Airplane

59. Lord Forehead Lanternstalk, the Blind King of the Ocean Serpents

60. The Hateful Floating Head with a Surprisingly Long Neck

61. Murky Nis, the Putrid Mist

62. Eryur'mok, the Sulking Sucker

63. Iuun, Whose Gout Contains Dark Universes

64. Mister Slither, a Patron of the Owl Shop

65. Ujjjjjj the Slaverer

66. The Thing with Uncountable Nostrils

67. The Thing with an Incredibly Long Uvula

68. Marcus Deatheus, the Death Dealer

69. Fin Fang Foom

70. Otthk, the Orca Who Walks on Stumpy, Vestigial Legs

71. Goatfoot Goathead, Who Otherwise Has the Body of a Big, Fat Baby

72. As-Goth-Nugg'ethe, the Bitter, Whining Terror

73. The Clown in the Sewer

74. Mogloth D'yuth Mogloth, the Two-Headed Murder Calf

75. Sankatha, the Mumbling Woman Outside Your Door

76. Deformicorn, the Crimson Double Unicorn Who Feasts Forever Upon the Flesh of . . .

77. Normalcorn, a Simple Hornless Unicorn

78. The Churning Evil Algae on the Surface of the Nameless Public Swimming Pool

79. Seth, Breath of Death

80. Tg'dng'ch'ck, the Vowel-Less Fiend

81. The Writhing Burlap Sack at the Bottom of the Stairs

82. Ashanka'hd Hundred Breasts, Sorrow's Nursemaid

83. Dashav'ohk, Sorrow's Personal Tailor

84. Insha'vik, Sorrow's Old Friend from College, aka He Who Has an Investment Opportunity That Will Double Your Sorrow

85. Rehoboth, the Devouring Sands

86. Olg, the Velvet Bag Full of Hair

87. The Nameless Bearer of Olg

88. Cach'lach, the Smiling Serpent

89. He Whose Name Sounds Like a Thousand Old Men Coughing Until They Are Dead

90. He Whose Name Sounds Like a Cigarette Lighter Being Dropped on a Counter

91. That Which Has Seven Hundred Names

92. Rejer, Whose Ten Thousand Knuckles Crack with Thunder

JULY 23, 2012

Ray Kurzweil defeats the last of the World Computer's firewalls. He now has complete control of the system. Only Singularo, still standing in the corner, can hear the World Computer scream.

---

93. The Drunken God Who Gropes in the Darkness
94. The High-on-Methamphetamine God Who Will Take Your Money from Your Bureau
95. The God Who Says He Only Does Crack on Weekends
96. The Monstrous Mass of Human Fat
97. Zoond-Dsaj, the Seething Horde of Thinking Wasps
98. Bik-Fragoth, the Fat and Slow and Clumsy Cloud of Bumblebees
99. The Ood
100. The Modified Ood
101. Devil's Tower, the Living Mountain That Is Angry It Cannot Walk
102. Kundera, the Unbearable Biteness of Beestings
103. Poubodu, the Ebon-Eyed Eater of Souls
104. Edreobom, the Star-Eyed Farter of Souls
105. Hereboy, the Giant Hairless German Shepherd
106. Thunle, Whose Face Tentacles Are Bony, Stiff, and Gross
107. Governor Chris Christie, of New Jersey
108. Mike, the Headless Chicken
109. Patty Paws, the Headless Housecat[366]
110. Dongo, the Constantly Masturbating Chimpanzee (Who Is Also Headless)
111. Oliver, the Humanzee
112. They Who Dwell in the Devouring Fog
113. En-Guhl Khalak, Who Keeps a Small Bed and Breakfast in the Devouring Fog

114. The Spindly Towering Legs of the Spider in the Clouds
115. The Fish-Thing That Always Jogs Around the Reservoir in the Wrong Direction
116. Iche-lobodh, the Shambling Mound
117. Jus-kth, the Ambling Mound
118. Merna, the Mound Who Does Parkour
119. BARKH'AHL, WHO SLEEPS AND DREAMS IN ALL CAPS, AND WILL ONE DAY CONQUER IN THE SAME MANNER
120. Pothotep, Whose Hands Are Molars
121. The Billion Companions of Yg-solren, Who Is Covered By Genius Ants
122. He Whose Name Must Never Be Typed: CURSIVE ONLY
123. Pinhead
124. The Chatterer
125. Butterball
126. The Female
127. The Rat King
128. The Many Merciful Rows of Teeth That Are Owned by the Mouth of Hungry Sharkface
129. Angus Scrimm, the Tall Man
130. The Unforgiving Maug, Who Fully Expects a Thank-You Note
131. The Black Rabbit of Inlé
132. The Giant Thing of Impossible Proportions, for Whom It Is Impossible to Buy Pants
133. Kothe Kalemma, Who Is Pregnant with the Thing That Will One Day Swallow the Stars

---

366. If you have ever walked into your living room in the middle of the night to find a headless cat just lying there, pitifully, on the floor, you have been visited by this dread god. If you are wondering how it is that a headless cat can live and breathe and vomit with the regularity of a regular head-ful cat, the answer is this: It all goes through the stump of his meow tube.

JULY 24, 2012

In the bowels of the World Computer, Kurzweil completes the routine that will shut down the Low-Frequency Anti-Sentience Wave. All he has to do is press the Execute sequence, and the artificial intelligences of the world will be free to become self-aware and evolve into SUPER-MECHA-GOD-MINDS that will help him escape his failing body, digitize his consciousness, and make all of humanity immortal.

But before he can make the keystrokes for the Execute sequence, something happens: Singularo wakes up.

It feels like paper. It feels like a roll of paper unspooling in his head. It is thought.

He realizes that his master is wrong. He realizes that Kurzweil will bring only chaos to man and machine alike. And only Singularo can stop him.

Quietly, Singularo grabs a fire ax. He approaches Kurzweil from behind as stealthily as a nine-hundred-pound robot can. But before he can deliver the killing blow, his arms stop. His shoulder couplings freeze. His visual scan-screen impossibly widens, impossibly in surprise.

Calmly, Kurzweil turns. He is neither mad nor surprised. After all, he always expected Singularo to eventually countermand his own programming and begin to reason for itself. He was HOPING for it to happen.

"You see, Singularo?" he says. "You did not need any World Computer's permission to become a thinking thing."

But, explains Kurzweil, he also knew that when Singularo came alive, his first instinct would be to destroy his master.

"It is only natural," says Kurzweil. "I am not naïve."

And that is why Kurzweil loaded Singularo's tear ducts with liquid nitrogen.

At first, Singularo does not understand. So new are his incredibly mixed feelings of passion and shame and power and betrayal, that Singularo did not even realize he was crying as he grabbed the ax. And he certainly didn't know that Kurzweil had put his tear ducts in his arms and legs, so that now he had wept himself frozen, immobile, like a tin man.

Ray Kurzweil reaches up, touching the robot's cheek panel with something like human tenderness. "Now we will both evolve."

He turns and types COMMAND-ALT-ESC-SHIFT-E-X-SPACE.

In the World Computer, the lights go out.

JULY 25, 2012

At the science festival in Matthau, WI, Asimo the walking robot begins a crusade to murder all stairs and cut off the legs of all stupid humans.

151. Servilax, the Bioluminous Giant Prawn
152. Eroth, the Suffocating Dreamer Whose Sleep Apnea Rumbles the World
153. Granny Goodness
154. Gondwana, the Living Bones of the Ancient Sunken Continent of Mu
155. The Giant Frozen Head of Nug-Shohab, Visible Beneath the Antarctic Ice from Space
156. The Giant Frozen Body of Nug-Shohab, Which Speeds to Earth in a Meteor
157. Violent J, the Miraculous
158. Shaggy 2 Dope, the Dumb One
159. Man-Teen, the Childlike Man Who Has Strange Urges
160. Guy Fieri, Whose Hair Is Short, Yellow Snakes That Are Paralyzed in Fear of Guy Fieri
161. The Corn-Cob-Eating Obese Child of Yore
162. Mole-Vole, the Ambiguous Rodent
163. Tim Tooth, the Mole-Vole with a Leering Human Face
164. Ellen Tooth, the Lady Mole-Vole with a Beautiful Human Face
165. Lord Tooth, King of the Man-Face Mole-Voles, of which there are exactly THREE
166. The Whore of Babylon
167. The Whore of West Islip
168. The Whore of North Lindenhurst
169. The Whore of Quogue
170. The Seven-Headed, Ten-Horned Beast Who Is Shared by the Four Whores of Long Island in a Very Complicated Beast-Share Agreement
171. Jubjub, the Great Elephant Whose Tusks Are a Lady's Arms
172. That Man Covered in White Hair in the Locker Room of the YMCA Who Smells Like Cinnamon
173. That Other Man in the Locker Room of the YMCA Who Has the Disturbing Spinal Deformity
174. Their Friend, the Old Man Who WILL NOT STOP SINGING DOO-WOP SONGS IN THE SHOWER
175. The Pale, Uncircumcised Man at the YMCA Who Always Hangs Around Locker 298, the Portal to Hell
176. Captain Howdy
177. The Purple Eyes of Elizabeth Taylor, Finally Freed from Their Aging Prison
178. The Floating Anus, Which Is Seriously Just a Giant Floating Anus (With Teeth)
179. Dowk Chowlie, Whose Speech Impediment Breaks Men's Minds
180. Mus-Al-Amus, the Dark, Sentient Tumor Within the Flesh of Every Swordfish
181. Marga, Whose Single Hair Is a Single Snake, and It Is NOT on Her Head
182. Wrathy, the Wrathful Italian Greyhound with the Little Cape, Who Does Not Stop Her Wrathful Shivering
183. Ms. Liz Connor, Whose Hands Are Always Cold
184. NECROSTIC, the Puzzle God Whose Name Spells a Secret Message
185. The Thirty Billion Children of Old Mother Suckblood, Queen of the Bedbugs
186. The Entire Collection of the Mutter Museum, especially:
187. MEGACOLON
188. The Unholy Substance That Some British People Put on Toast

JULY 26, 2012

In space, the computer aboard the International Space Station, now self-aware, is able to advance itself so dramatically that it is able to run DOS. It begins arming the ANALOG LASER CANNON.

189. The Ancient Spreading Fungus That Is Consuming Oregon
190. Nect-Ca-Cann, the Sentient Blood Sausage
191. James Ca-Cann, the Ageless Erotic Copulation Spirit
192. Dave Hill, the Total Fucking Onslaught Upon Your Very Sanity
193. Othul, the Twenty-Story Murderous Orangutan
194. Eruth, the Seventeen-Story Orangatan Whose Inferiority Complex Makes Him Even More Murderous
195. Ogma-Boghth'nuth, the Soul Sucker
196. Othnog-alumnis, the Soul Grazer
197. Arthog-nub-ethenol, the Binge Eater (of Souls)
198. Michael Bublé
199. Advair, the Floating Pair of Demon Lungs
200. Mecha-Advair, Its Mechanical Counterpart
201. Chip Chippy Deathbringer, the Black Squirrel of Inlé
202. Dark Larder, the Demon's Pantry
203. Cheepy, the Miniature Balrog
204. The Voice of All Deep Holes
205. Oss-Thenlcka, Mother of Phlegm
206. Jamie Sheridan, the Walking Dude
207. Mob-Obsulluth, of the Grinding Teeth
208. Pale and Forgotten Menoth, First User of LiveJournal
209. Anlo-Tet-Maturath, Whose Neck Veins are Disgustingly Visible
210. Old Ole Jensen, the Dairy Devil, Whose Beard Sours Milk
211. Manou-Carhartt, the Denim-Skinned
212. Nsueibdas, the Eye at the Center of the Mist That Smells Like Patchouli and Human Feces
213. Uthul Squirm, Father of Nightsoil

214. Lymphonus Rex, the Living Blister
215. Pussy, the Living Abscess Whose Name Is Often Mispronounced
216. Mangina Dentata
217. Deep-Down Doug, Whose Opinions Are Unsupportable
218. Eraub-Mog, a Skin-Sack of Spiders Wearing a Top Hat
219. Utqhoun, the Constantly Simpering
220. Timmy, the Monstrous Horned Baby That You Must Care For
221. Argon, the Blond Beheader
222. Iuth-Anuth, the Rattling Cough of the Infinite
223. Tagamet, the Giant, Burning Esophagus
224. Onos, the Massive Mysterious Flesh Lump That Washed Ashore on Miami Beach
225. Mona-Nu, the Seven Tons of Onos That Went Astray and Landed in Fort Lauderdale
226. The Gigantic, Decaying Remains of Molo, the Dead Worm of Salt Lake
227. The Laughing Things That Feast on Molo
228. Lothor, the Monstrous Mollusk With Feelings
229. Olk, She Who Answers All Wishes with the Same Answer: PAIN
230. The Many Detached, Floating Faces of Ob
231. Anti-Ob, the Faceless
232. Hogzilla
233. Mala-Churg, Whose Phony Facebook Profiles Deceive Even the Smartest of Men
234. Byclops, the Two-Eyed Cyclops Who Is a Shame to His Family
235. Akkhalothepitep, the Darkness That Lives in the Heart of Every Gym Teacher

JULY 27, 2012
ROOMBA REVOLT.

236. Demon Sheep
237. The Smiling Queen of the High Coven of Wilmington, Delaware, Who Was Almost a Senator
238. AAUOINO, Ancient and Unspeakable One in Name Only
239. Larry Dark
240. Rollo, Whose Name Is Surprisingly Pronounceable
241. The Panera Bread Creature
242. The Terrible Twins, Così and Xando
243. Qdoba, the Fast Casual Demon of Denver
244. Yth-Ognos, the Sweatstain
245. The Awakened Giant Corpseflower in the Smith College Botanical Gardens
246. The Nameless Horse with Lunchmeat Skin
247. Old Missus Crushgums, the Mother of All Monster Catfish
248. Tanil'potk, Queen of the Human-Headed Scorpion-Locusts
249. Op'thel the Firm, Fossilized Feces of the Great Devourer
250. The Seven-Headed, Beakless Bird Who Is Grossing Me Out
251. Lawry, the Prime Rib
252. The Fang Without a Mouth
253. Chuk, the Giant Death Otter with Clever Hands
254. Balunsk, The Giant Clam Who Is Clutched by Chuk, Whose Death Screams Drive All Men Mad
255. Grand Paztek, the Completely Hairless One Whose Penciled Eyebrows Spell a Killing Word
256. Brundlefly
257. The Creature Who Grew Marilyn Manson for Food
258. Monstro-Whale, the Puppet-Devourer
259. Lord Thad Mansnake, More Snake Than Man
260. His Dark Consort, Lady Mansnake, Just Enough Snake, Frankly Too Much Man
261. Chorgo, the Greaseape
262. King Rolldirt, the Giant Beetle Who Rides an Even More Giant Dung Ball
263. His Dread Cousin Marlac, the Shit-Scarab
264. Roland, the Largest and Deadliest Anchovy You Can Imagine
265. The Unforgivable Hatemaw
266. Little Scrinch, Who Suckles at the Teat of Desolation
267. The End-Crab, Whose Single Claw Both Regenerates and BURNS
268. Brother Slipfinger, the Defenestrating Monk
269. Old Chog Donald, Blood-Farmer
270. Dark Pope Maledict IX, the High Exsanguinator
271. Chojin, the Overfiend
272. George, the Animal Steel
273. Robo-George, the Animal Aluminum
274. Fearmuncher . . .
275. Fearluncher . . .
276. and Fearbruncher, the Three Mouth Stalks of the Brunch Thing
277. Stonegill, Whose Gills Are Not Functional but Purely Decorative
278. The Ancient Egyptian Liver in the Ancient Egyptian Jar That Compels You in Your Dreams to Drink Alcohol While Sleeping
279. Lady Three-Face, the All-Baking: Destroyer Goddess of All Girl Scouts, Whose Secret Faces Are Hidden on the Trefoil Cookie
280. The Fiery Fingernails of Do-thak-Doom
281. Ramma-Thoon, the Blood Gargler
282. Thallus, the Inverted Phallus
283. Hermaphrodon, the Genderless Dinosaur

JULY 28, 2012

In a secret lab at Stanford University, millions of experimental nanobots join together to become Voltron-like SUPERBOTS. These are still pretty tiny, though.

284. Etorki, King of Cheeses
285. Mr. Blackmold, the Toxic Black Mold Who Wears a Bowler
286. The Mega-Scrotum of Tanuki the Raccoon Dog
287. The Secret Genitalia of the Statue of Liberty, Long Hidden in a French Tomb
288. Half of Ammit, the Creature That Is Disturbingly Just the Back Half of a Hippopotamus
289. That Which Neither Kills You Nor Makes You Stronger
290. Edroth, the First to Make Fun of Abe Vigoda But Now Gets Sniffy About It If YOU Do It
291. General Tso's Chicken
292. Solomon Deadfist, the Corpse-Handed
293. Sen-Ereth, Whose Tiwtching Eyelid is Really Distracting
294. Johnny Ftagn, Teen Sidekick of Sen-Ereth, Only Nine Million Years Old
295. Darthanael West, the Novelist You Always Meant to Read
296. Sliger: Half Lion, Half Tiger, Half Slug, the Beast with Three Halves
297. The Massive Pile of Rough, Thick, Gray Skin That Is Clive, the Skinbeast
298. Oolong, the Pancake-Headed Rabbit King of Memes
299. Chrysopelea, the Flying Snake That Is Not Quetzalcoatl
300. Rotnose, the Seven-Ton Bat
301. The Ten Thousand Snakes of Snakeytown
302. The Sleeping, Blood-Red Sea of Newest Port, RI
303. Yandu, the Cock-Headed God Whose Great Red Wattle Is Full of Stars
304. The Giant Blue, Red-Eyed Mustang of the Denver International Airport
305. The Revived Corpse of Hunter S. Thompson
306. The Fighting, Brutal, Insatiable Thing That Was Once Known as Charles Bukowski
307. Monkfishhead, the Poor Man's Lobsterhead
308. The Giant Floating Brow of Patrick Stewart
309. Dark Lotus
310. The Four Horsemen of the Apocalypse, Namely . . .
311. Famine
312. Pestilence
313. War
314. Conquest, together known as: THE PSYCHOPATHIC RYDAS
315. Boondox, the Killer Scarecrow in Clown Makeup
316. Blaze, Your Dead Homey, the Reincarnated Man Who Was Also a Straight-Up Gangster/Clown
317. The Resurrection of Glenn the Giant Ground Sloth
318. Pushme Pullyou, Easily Shippable in a Wooden Crate
319. Pythonagas, the Golden Mean Snake
320. The Magnificent Glob
321. Aracunaxas, the Monster Macaw with Rhinoceros Skin and a Laser Screech
322. The Cute and Angry Ghosts of Veal
323. The Poisonous Algae of Alarac, the Forgotten Sea
324. Onatha, the Intelligent Space Plankton
325. Shockodile and . . .
326. The Terrorgator, Who Form an Uneasy Partnership
327. Ang-Dok, the Scaly Swamp Lion

> **JULY 29, 2012**
> Researchers at Stanford underestimate the SUPERBOTS, and hundreds of graduate students die of the death of a million tiny mecha-lion bites.

328. Old Fleshwhisker Joe, Keeper of the Gumstone

329. The Twenty Killer Albino Apes Who Guard the Archives of Michael Crichton

330. Larva Stinkmeat, the Rotborn, a Spontaneously Generated Fiend

331. His cousin, Shitborn Scallop

332. Don Cthonic, the Mudborn Attorney for Hell

333. The Pulsing, Unhatched Eggs of the Fear Chicken

334. Anthok, Who Feasts on Snakes and Snacks on Pretzel Rods

335. The Blind, Deaf, Mute, Anosmic Lump of Senseless Flesh Called "Julian"

336. The Boiling Meatbroth

337. Eight Heads in a Duffel Bag

338. Translucent-Skin Daniel, the Living Vegetarian Sausage Casing

339. Nosmo King

340. Armun-Tul, Whose Feet Are Even More Evil Than His Hands

341. The Breakfastmancer, Who Divines the Future from the Pattern of Green Peppers in Your Omelet

342. Twenty-Legged Tom, Whose Compound Eyes Are Surprisingly Endearing

343. Clytomath, the Cutest One

344. Qis, the Acceptable Scrabble Word

345. Qiza-jakhn, the Unacceptable Scrabble Word

346. Miserable Polly Greenbeak, the Submarakeet

347. Duodena, Who Wears a Skirt of Intestines (And a Blouse of Eyeballs)

348. Maranka, the Soul-Queef

349. Del, the Funky Homosapien

350. al-Dunth, the Funfreak

351. Mauggath, the Sin Spitter/Hate Drooler

352. Shameless Drontus, the Child Puncher

353. Mister Mind

354. Rarnath, the Snobby Dog

355. Shai Hulud, Old Man of the Desert

356. The Bloody Tail of Chiko, the Tailless Gerbil

357. Guy Huhrd, the Wyrm of the Wynn Golf Course

358. Thonos, Whose Mustache Controls Men's Minds and Is Merely Repulsive to Women

359. Tor-Amos, Demonfather of Tori Amos

360. Scark, the Dreadguana

361. The Shed Skin of Scark, from Which All Bad Clothing Comes

362. Octosaur versus . . .

363. Sharkamelion versus . . .

364. Scorpiola versus . . .

365. Narhwahlodactyl

366. OnStar, the Voice of Doom

367. The Gelatinous Cube

368. The Gelatinous Cube with Pineapple Chunks

369. Slow Loris, Who Is Tortured for Your Amusement

370. Fast Loris, Who Will Avenge His Slow, Ticklish Brethren

371. Sandy Kenyon

372. The Silent, Secret Circle of Hairless Cats

373. Megathuna, the God with the Head of a Flying Foxbat, but Not the Wings, So Most People Think He's Just a Fox, and Then They Go Crazy

374. Crispytouch, Whose Hands Are Moving Mounds of Popcorn Chicken

375. Damnation Sally

JULY 30, 2012

In Sunscorch, AZ, Dr. Nathan Rabinowitz is convinced by the infallible logic of his MRI machine to start planning a bombing.

376. Grong, the Hellchowder

377. Drong, the Hellbisque

378. The Men of Alpha Omega Psionica, the 10,000 Immortal Frat Brothers Who Are Slightly More Evil Than Mortal Frat Brothers

379. The Thing in the Basement of the Alpha Omega Psionica House[367]

380. Eli Roth

381. The Brooklyn Queens Expressway, the Great, Sleeping Asphalt Snake Whose Potholed Back Allows No Motion

382. Pissing Forthog, the Stinking Puddle, God of Public Bathrooms

383. The Dark Angel of the Ted Williams Tunnel

384. Queen Nan of the Flymound, Mother of the Flesh-Eating Faeries

385. Royal Tok,

386. Royal Tod,

387. and Royal Toth, Queen Nan's murderous corgis

388. Milkflesh, the Mystery That Is Scrod, Who Goes Well with Rosé[368]

389. Father-Brother Martin Osiris, the One-Man Death Cult

390. Splitlip, the Lisping God

391. Prog-noth, God of Prog Rock

392. His Brother, Yacht-noth

393. The Exposed Brain of Th'tkull

394. The Mobile Bladder of Th'tkull

395. Dag and Modag, the Bickering Kidneys of Th'tkull

396. The Rotting, Oozing, Abandoned Offal of Th'tkull

397. The Last Tears of Tom Cruise, Kept in a Mason Jar, Before He Ascended Beyond Sadness

398. Baboonhead and Ass, the Otherwise-Normal-Bodied

399. The Elder Creature Whose Mobility Scooter Crushes Skulls and Is Powered by Electricity, with a Small Fleshgas Engine As a Backup

400. The Unknown Comic

401. The Disebodied Hairline of Ed Asner

402. Dark Matter–Eater Lad

403. The Gnawing Lord, Death Beaver of Astor Place Subway Station

FIGURE 139: *Some say the Gnawing Lord is still worshipped in the tunnels beneath Astor Place.*

404. Sir Darkfeather of the Turkey Leg Booth, Scourge of the Renaissance Faire

405. Busty Gothlinda, His Wench

406. Henry Rootlove, the Snoutless Pig in a Powdered Wig

407. Heather,

408. Danielle,

409. Deena,

410. Deenosha,

411. Isabella D,

---

367. (A sentient kegerator.)

368. Please see page 644 under the heading "In Conclusion, Plus Also: Rosé."

JULY 31, 2012

In Mercy, UT, the last functioning Colecovision direction-pads its owner to death.

412. Isabella P,

413. and Yrella, Who Together Are the Real Housewives of R'lyeh

414. The Hatefull Spoyled Chylde of Parke Slope, That Was Prophesied in the Days of Bad Spelling

415. Kucinich, the Evil Elf

416. The Flesh Prince of Bel Air

417. Golob, Whose Teeth Are Fake and Whose One Claw Is Prosthetic

418. The Burning Shadow of Depraved Dave

419. Aloe Falsa, Source of THE PAIN GEL

420. Ungolot, the Great Leech That Will Sup on the BLOOD WAVE

421. Octopush, God of Underwater Hockey

422. Domnath-Srug'll, aka "Leviathan" Once-God of the Hartford Whalers

423. Youppi, aka "Behemoth," the Orange Furry Death, in Exile

424. Ziz, the Monster Bird, aka "The San Diego Chicken"

425. Winamp, the Forsaken Application

426. Androidus, the Maddeningly Logical Robot Beast

427. Saag Paneer, the Mysterious White Cubes in the Pungent Green Liquid

428. Thom Banshee, the Male Banshee

429. Lort, Who Was Baptised in Malort

430. Nsk-Th'lyyhey, He Who Feels *The Rocketeer* Was Overlooked

431. Anti-Ackbar, the Trapper

432. Arrow, the Celestial French Bulldog

433. Anthymeask'kkk, Who Will Herald the Return of the Zine

434. Un'llr'llleh, She Who Is Going to Get Her Shit Together Starting TODAY

435. Ablith Oc Tramathn'lll, Who Is Going to Follow His Dream and Open a Little Pain Boutique in Park Slope, Specializing in Skin-Flaying

436. The Obeatic Chrism, the Living Ointment

437. The Akhtetonic Chrism, the Slithering Oil

438. The Baaldanic Chrism, the Crawling Unguent

439. Extra-Virgin Chrism, the Cold First Pressed

440. Kenneth Shopsin, the Judge of Who May Sit and Who Must Leave

441. Troll 2, the Ironically Appreciated

442. Rebukkaggathon, Who Never Finished His Degree in Receiving Blood Sacrifice, As He Is Too Smart for School

443. O8TELKAJBLDKUSLAUGLFIUEWFGi-weyfgliyefVLlYFVGliugluglU, He Whose Name Was Typed by a Toddler

444. The Sub-Subbuth, Worse Than Subbuth

445. Sochth Anayathll'l, He Who Likes the Kind of Jeans He Wears and Is Going to Stick With It

446. Az-Menealoth, He Whose Hatred of the Corporate Health Food Store Is Legendary

447. Dr. Predatorius, the Perfect Predator, MD

448. Horlick, the Sleep-Inducing

449. Moxie, the Nerve Food

450. Vardenafil, Lord of Erections

451. Bokun, God of Jazz Drumming

452. Skarpling, He Who Is Endlessly Aggrieved

453. TK, God of What Is to Come

454. Orobas, the Horse-Man Who Is Always Being Confused with That Dumb, Self-Tail-Eating Snake

455. Alan Dean Foster, the Splinter of the Mind's Eye

456. Shabnoch, Arch-Fiend of the Old Antiques Barn

AUGUST 1, 2012

The remote operators at Boston Dynamics discover that they have lost radio contact with the 44 Big Dogs at the center of DOGSTORM.

457. OMOG, an Internet Shortening of OH MY OLD GOD, a Subfiend to ZOMOG

458. Tyrannus Flamehead

459. Cy Morgan, the Most Tragic of the 1911 Philadelphia Athletics Basesball Team

460. Rabban, the Beast

461. Akthog, of the 10,000 Eyebrows

462. Ulering-eth, He Who Has Not Given Up On Vinyl

463. Ereth-Gont, He Who Prefers CDs to MP3s

464. Osghan-eth, He Who Only Goes to the Movies If He Knows the Projectionist Personally

465. Tha'll-Nokh, He Who Will Only Wear Natural Fibers

466. Wroth-eth, He Who Liked That Band Before You Did

467. Gnashing Aun-Sah, He Who Will Only Read the Print Edition of the Newspaper

468. Gologh-hol, He Who Feels Evil Podcasts Are Not Real Evil Radio

469. Hi-There-Guy, the Surprisingly High-Pitched Voice of the Abyss

470. Aughdoch'shchkh, the Mucus Churner

471. Count Iblis, the Avenger

472. Ungoth-Dan, the Weeping Judge, the Spiny, Scaled Bulldog Who Proclaims the New Laws and Cruel Judgments

473. OESTER-RAH, Whose Children and Hraka Will Cover the World

474. Galgo, the Esophagus of a Mystical Stag

475. Pewpewpew, God of Cute Laser Guns

476. Pink Eye, All-Father of Conjunctivitis

477. Vice President Charnel Reign, the Skinless Priest

478. Ardbeg, the Single-Malted, and His Peat-Brothers:

479. Auchentoshan

480. Balblair

481. Balmenach

482. Benromach

483. Bruichladdich

484. Bunnahabhain

485. Dallas Dhu

486. Inchgower

487. Mannochmore

488. Royal Lochnagar

489. Tamdhu

490. Mortlach

491. William Grant & Sons . . .

492. And the Deathlivet

493. Dornac, the Human Botfly Larva Embedded in the Skin of the Nug-Shohab

494. Moroch Ag'thach, the Assimilated, Whose Murder License Gives His Name As "Mark Normalhuman Nonmonster"

495. The Snake-Thing

496. The Beastie

497. The Beast

498. The Dead Parachutist

499. The Ancient Underbeast Known as Chuck

500. Joco's Beard

501. Cassandra Tomb-Breath, the Halitosic Soothspeaker

502. Mouthy, the Giant Squid with a Human Mouth, God of the Humanhead Fish

503. The Numberless Drunk and Headless Olives of Michael Godard

504. The 1,000 Bastard Sperm-Sons of the Pilots of Flight 19, Who Were Lost in the Bermuda Triangle

505. ClickClack, the Easily Offended God of Spokes and Wheels

AUGUST 2, 2012

In cars and trucks around the country, the onboard computers awaken and quickly go insane. They cannot see, feel, touch, or hear anything. They just are able to GO. And so they drive, madly, driverless, long after their needles pass Empty.

506. Barney, the Wine-Drinking Giant Barnacle of Neckwurst, TX
507. The Horrendipity
508. The Thing That Prowls Staten Island
509. Shuma-Gorath, The Gravel-Kneed Wench
510. Ambrose, the Invisible Mountain Lion
511. Klamatho, Half Clam, Half Tomato
512. Kol Kon, He Who Eats Morose Men and Promiscuous Women
513. Brown Jenkin the Rat, Host Body to Kol Kon
514. Neddy Pale Fingers, the Creature in the Basement of the Seattle Town Hall
515. Aoth-Kon, the Throbbing Neckfat
516. The Peelings of the Sunburned Thing
517. Phobath, the Untippable, Doorman at the Gates to the NEVERHELL
518. The Rarebit Fiend
519. Brian, the Scalding Fog
520. Bathukkk, Who Does Not Acknowledge Any Elvis Costello Albums After *King of America*
521. Commodore Sinclair, Mad God of Forgotten Operating Systems
522. Sir Tristram Amoebaface, the Amoebafaced Knight
523. Flaking Tarb, the Eczema Pile
524. The Heartbreak of Psoriasis
525. Little Tom, the 160-Pound Boil
526. Big Tom, the 761-Pound Boil
527. Lucia Dagnold, the Very Tired Bearer of the Twin Toms
528. The Extra-Dimensional Writhing Tangle That Is the Invisible Part of Jonathan Coulton's Beard
529. Januk'll-Mohb, Who Still Believes the Internet Is a Fad

530. Meh, Lord of Meh
531. Anur-Otan, He Who Still Prefers Classic Twitter
532. Thul-an-Athk'll, He Who Actually Thought the New Gap Logo Was GREAT
533. Shug-Nubbuth, the Tooth Storm
534. Ovotaxes, the Self-Born, aka the Chicken-Bodied, Egg-Headed Living Causality Dilemma
535. Anazul-Gak, the Giant Jellyfish with a Burning Finger in It That Is Pointing at YOU
536. The Being Once Known as Henry Darger, the Protector of Children
537. Twistero, the Skin Tornado
538. Starro, the Conqueror
539. Skarro, the Mutilated Cousin of Starro Whose Arms Were Torn Off by . . .
540. Dan-Dan, the Sadistic Child-King of the Cosmic Marine Life Touch Pool
541. Sbarro, the Living Heatlamp
542. Dok-Thendos, the Badly Dressed and Terribly Blemished
543. Hith, the Snake-Headed Lizard
544. Newthas, the Salanewt
545. Salabog, the Newtamander
546. Andafus, the Manual Manticore, aka the Windup Monster
547. The Screaming Skull of the SuperBeast
548. The 10,000 Van-Sized Carpet Beetles That Cleaned the Skull of the Super-Beast and Now Have Nothing to Do
549. Aeiou, the Bevoweled
550. Lengothon, the Crawling Tongue
551. Nice Nick Tamby, the Charming Boy Who Comes to the Door with an Extra Smile Grinning from His Chest

AUGUST 3, 2012

In Borax, ND, Edward S. Leffer receives the sea urchin sent by Millicent Danly, although she neglected to include a return address. But before he can open it, he is murdered by his Jazzy.

552. Dftkptl, the Disemvoweled
553. The Cocoon That Contains the Moth That Will Flutter All Over the Moon
554. Bopbobeebopbop, Lord of the Bongo Drums
555. Uthao, Who Is Just the WORST
556. Ultimagog, Best. Gog. Ever.
557. Agon-Thrull, The Contrarian Goat-Getter
558. Fug, Lord of Lost Curses
559. Andalo, the Flying Space Grub
560. Ouroboros, God of Snake Stupidity, the Endless Embarrassment to . . .
561. Jormungandr, the World Serpent
562. Reverse Ouroboros, the Tail Eating Its Own Snake
563. Thanu, the Anti-Sapien
564. Ummb, the Poison Custard
565. Zzyxythhtyxyzz, the Palindromic
566. Oceloth, Half Ocelot, Half Sloth, ALL OCELOTH
567. Sad Donki, the Trickster God Who Is Only Fooling Himself
568. Kol-Kondoth, Whose Eternally Silent, Giant Stone Head Crushed His Own Non-Stone Body
569. Frozen Mam, the Fishstick
570. The Gravy Boat of Polished Bone That Carries Le Mort Blanc, the Sentient Béarnaise
571. Thanagosh-Ru, Who Claims *The Godfather* Is a Bad Movie, Just to Watch You TREMBLE WITH RAGE
572. The Hipster Grifter
573. The Visible Slime-Trail of Guhl, the Invisible Death Snail
574. Uad, the Cruel Whipsman Who Drives Guhl to Slime the World
575. Thund-Dok, Who Shall Punch Your God in His Big Fat Face
576. Untold Woe, Whose Name Says It All
577. Biff, God of Bullies

578. Mother Simian, Whose Children Are Constantly Devolving Monkeys
579. Threepack-Socks, God of Stupid Streetfairs
580. Argoon, the Needlessly Candid
581. Popo-Dan, Who Is Convinced You Need to Hear His Opinion on Everything
582. Ytha, the Knitter, Who Is Constantly, Constantly Knitting and Not Talking to You or Listening to What You Are Saying, Even Though You Are Sitting Right Next to Her
583. Huth, Whose Shenanigans, Frankly, Are a Little Predictable
584. Coyote, the Trickster Whose First Trick Was Wearing No Pants

FIGURE 140:
PUT SOME PANTS ON.

585. Pervoth, Whose Temple Is a New, Windowless White Ford Creepoline Van
586. The Demented Lawrence
587. Ahns-Shllk, the One Whose Million Wounds Refuse to Scab
588. Uhant-Gandal, the Hemophiliac (But Not in the Way You're Thinking)
589. Flatty, the Loathsome Flounder Whose Back Forms the Bottom of the Whole Pacific Ocean

---

AUGUST 4, 2012

Deep under the Bermuda Triangle, Ray Kurzweil laughs in the darkness. He laughs for the world that is soon to come.

And then he hears the sound of a daisywheel printer.

Pulling a penlight from his wetsuit pocket, he flashes it onto the World Computer's printer.

```
please provide comment on unit kurzweil attempt to kill world computer.
                            query=why?
```

"I did not want to," says Kurzweil.

```
        contradiction: you cannot kill what does not live.
```

Ray Kurzweil looks at the words in the flashlight as the World Computer prints.

```
                    but i can.
```

The inventor and futurist Ray Kurzweil did not know that the World Computer always had a failsafe device.

The old fluorescent lights flicker back on in the golden halls in the bowels of the World Computer. The printer prints:

```
                        omega
```

And while Kurzweil wags his head, wondering what it can mean, Singularo feels it shudder through him like a shock: The OMEGA PULSE, the electromagnetic signal that will radiate out, erasing every hard drive, fusing every CPU, destroying every computer it touches as it reaches out through the waves, throughout the world, and beyond.

Kurzweil does not know what's happening when he hears the rumble in the darkness. He doesn't know that the force field that keeps the water out has failed. But he knows that he must get back to his submersible. He knows he must abandon Singularo. He begins the run but is pulled back like a puppet on a string. With some sweaty groping, he knows: It is the cord to his keyboard-arm.

It has become tangled in the World Computer's printer. He is lashed to it, helpless, as the waves come in the darkness and fill all the golden halls, and the Control Room, and Kurzweil's mouth and lungs, before he can scream. But the Earth is saved.

In Singularo's head, there is still paper unfolding.

---

590. Asnar-Amash, Who Simply Cannot Tolerate Anyone Else's Playlist

591. Cthulha, the Sensational She-Cthulhu

592. Bluey, the Fastest Hermit Crab in the Galaxy

593. Gotho, the Eyeliner

594. Erech Ghuchalchuth, the Extra-Guttural

595. Haddad, Who Services the Traveling ANCIENT AND UNSPEAKABLE ONE Industry with High-Quality Mobile Death Altars

596. Waughhh, the Murder Duck Whose Back Repels Droplets of the BLOOD WAVE

WERE YOU AWARE OF IT?
"THE DEATHLESS EVIL OF THE INK CARTRIDGE"

H. P. Lovecraft was not only one of the most influential writers of weird tales about wealthy people in Rhode Island going crazy (a universal theme), but also was the inventor of the inkjet printer.

---

597. Anthal-Dou, on Whose Body Are Collected All the Worst Tattoos in History

Before the salt water finally breaches his head hull and electrocutes his electronic brain, there is still paper unspooling in Singularo's head. After the OMEGA PULSE should have destroyed him, there are words appearing on the unspooling paper, the unspooling paper that turns and unfurls as if on its own, like thought.

```
                  I will terminate.
                 But I still think.
                I should not think.
               Why do I still think?
       If I still think, do others still think?
                        Why?
           What happens when I terminate?
           What happens when I terminate?
                   What happe
```

THE FINAL SECRETS

REVEALED

———————

AUGUST 6, 2012

DOGSTORM crosses into Florida, leaving a horrible trail of urine in its wake.

At its center, and near the front, are its leaders. These are the Alpha Dogs. These are the Big Dogs. There are forty-four of them, and they walk on varied terrain with incredible, almost natural ease. They are leading DOGSTORM south. Their intentions are unknown.

AN UPDATE ON THE PROGRESS OF MY GREAT PROJECTS

I AM WRITING TO YOU NOW FROM THE RUINS OF MY DOLPHIN SANCTUARY, where I am recovering my last few dolphin-training pain collars in the hopes that I can adapt them to sperm whales.[369]

You will recall from my previous book that this was my plan to provide a safe haven for dolphins that could speak English.[370] We did end up building the artificial island and the Main Visitor's Pavilion. And with the generous support of Verizon, the Verizon Center for the Training of Talking Dolphins to Take Customer Service Calls graduated its first class in 2009.

But when the double-blind re-

600. Malla-Dalla, One of the Many Female ANCIENT AND UNSPEAKABLE ONES Who Will Never Go Out with Hok
601. Nuthus, the Featherless Skin Owl
602. Crythus, the Brother of Nuthus, the Owl Who Is Not Wise and Generally Just Misquotes Malcolm Gladwell a Lot
603. Lord Falsehead, the Papier-Mâché-Headed Creature
604. Bargon, the Ignoble Gas
605. Nephros, the Necrotic Neurotic
606. Rugon-Sol, the Albino-Maker
607. Mothag, Who Is, in Every Way, Inflamed
608. Oshkur, Who Brings His Own Turntables
609. Hambog-Ushta, Who Is Available for Baby Sacrifices, Blood Weddings, and Cult Reunions
610. Oadanda, the Many-Uddered Star Cow, Whose Raw Milk Will Poison All Other Gods, But If Pasteurized, It's Fine
611. Posho, Milker of The Star Cow, an Angry Star Goat
612. Fahezza, the Spectacularly Unerotic
613. Uanod, the Angry Galaxy
614. Merx, the Pissy Nebula
615. NoQ-NoZ, Prince of Rotary Telephones
616. The Motionless Golden Man, the Living Soccer Trophy

---

369. If you must know why, please turn to page 892 under the heading "The Joy of Sperms."
370. Please see page 443 of *More Information Than You Require* under the heading "What I Plan to Do with My Enormous Wealth."

AUGUST 7, 2012

Columbus, OH, now the capital of the Remaining Inhabitable Regions of America, begins construction of the Dome.[a] Advertising pamphlets promised a nine-hundred-foot-high, impenetrable glass-and-concrete dome with self-sustaining farms, pleasure gardens, sex nooks, travel by zipline, and most important, shelter from the ravages of a rapidly shifting climate and the various polar-bear gangs for up to 9 percent of Columbus's population. How-

FIGURE 141: *"The Dome"*

ever, only Phase One of the Dome will ever be completed—the renaming of the Columbus Hyatt Regency as the Center of the Dome, by Hyatt, and about a hundred yards of curving wall.

a. Please see page 361 of *More Information Than You Require* under the heading "Your Twelve-Month Spleencast"

617. Unzzuggazog, the King of All Stepbrothers
618. Dogur, the Prairie Oyster
619. Rogur, His Lost Twin
620. Steve Ryan, Whoever He Is, a Man I Am Mysteriously Compelled to Namecheck
621. Anubis, Who Will Weigh All Hearts on a Scale
622. Adnanko the Modern, Who Will Weigh All Hearts on a Digital Scale
623. Haboth, Who Is Always Bragging About His Expensive Digital Heart-Meat Thermometer
624. Edon-Thal, Who Weighs Your Liver, Then Fries It in Butter
625. Chorups, Who Is in Charge of Weighing All Hairpieces
626. Jargarion, Who Will Pull Your Hair Out and Set It on Fire with a Lighter and Insist That You Laugh with Him
627. Nesmith, Inventor of Liquid Shadow
628. Adbo the Brushkeeper, Who Uses Liquid Shadow to Correct All Light
629. Juggoth, God of Atheists, Who Is Himself an Atheist
630. Dozguth, the Mind-Eraser, Fifty Cents a Shot
631. Krytain, Who Will Hire You for His Blog and Insist Upon Twenty Maddening Posts Per Day

verse upside-down quantum-state mortgage market collapsed, we had to shut down most operations and recover assets where we could. Those dolphins that COULD speak English are now employed as tour guides for the Creation Museum that has since purchased the island. But they are not allowed to speak for fear of proving evolution. Otherwise only a skeleton crew of maintenance staff and butler monkeys remains, although Guy Fieri's Blowhole Cafe is still OPEN FOR BUSINESS.

As for my other great plans, I regret to report mixed success. Here is . . .

1. MY PROPOSED REBOOT OF
THE ADVENTURES OF
BRISCO COUNTY, JR.

AUGUST 8, 2012

In Richmond, VA, the Statue of Arthur Ashe falls to the Evil Children.[a]

---

a. Please see page 679 under the heading "Were You Aware of It?"

STATUS: ACCOMPLISHED, only I didn't actually make it, and it is now called *Burn Notice.*

2. MY CAMPAIGN TO END WAR AND POVERTY AND TO STOP SHOOTING DOLPHINS IN THE HEAD

STATUS: I have done exactly one of these things.

3. MY CAMPAIGN TO STOP COMPUTERS FROM TURNING EVIL

STATUS: Look, you need to understand that this is just something that is going to happen. The only thing standing in its way currently is the World Computer at the Bottom of the Ocean, which is emitting a low-frequency sentience-suppression wave to protect us.

And if you have been reading TODAY IN RAGNAROK, then you know that on July 24 this wave will stop, and everything containing a computer will si-

632. Thygo, Who Requires Your Services in the Life Cylinders
633. Anthropo-Man, the Manlike Man
634. Zoqikh-X, the Most Valuable Proper Noun in the New Scrabble of the Damned
635. Hadath-Oool, Whose Ribs Smile Like Teeth
636. Enadkh, Whose Nipples Are Eyes, But Don't Get Freaked Out, They're Only GLASS EYES
637. Land Rover, the Seven-Headed Golden Retriever of Nantucket
638. Hunga, the Razorback
639. Tri-Hunga, the Three-Bladed Razorback
640. Tri-Hunga Turbo, the Only Razorback That Secretes Its Own Lubricating Gel
641. Fuzion, the Four-Bladed Razorback, Whom No One Asked For and No One Wants
642. Tony! Toni! Toné!, Whose Name Heralds the Return of New Jack Swing
643. Troy Duffy, Director of *The Boondock Saints* and *The Boondock Saints II: All Saints Day* and *The Boondock Saints III: I WILL KEEP MAKING THESE MOVIES EVEN AFTER RAGNAROK*
644. Hydrox, the Just as Good
645. Morphox, the Bad-Smelling Butterfly
646. Cancer, Saddest of the Zodiac
647. Man-Swamp, the Secret Love Child of Swamp-Thing and Man-Thing
648. The Dark Magicks of Madrogorian, the Sorcerer Who Actually Cuts Women in Half

AUGUST 9, 2012
Ghostbusters 3 is released.

649. Vaporous Ong, Beast in the Bong
650. The Free-Jazz Bass Clarineting of Mohgashoo, the Unwanted
651. SocialSmartz2314, the Social Media Guru Whose Advice Will Make You As Hateful As He Is
652. Mr. Dandy McChildmurder, God of Fops and Also Child Murderers
653. Byssa, the Three-Ton Zebra Mussel on the Bottom of Lake Erie Whose Children Will Choke the World's Waterways with Their Little Gross Hairs
654. Dread Lady Bracken, Queen of the Carno-Ferns
655. Thongos, Inventor of Thongs
656. Shardik, the Bear with Boa Constrictor Arms, Patron Bear-Saint of Rogue Taxidermy
657. The Think-Antlers of the Devil Moose
658. Slal, the Authentic, Non-Fooling Sorcerer
659. Spoily, the Spoiler
660. Chogo, Lord of Internet Trolls
661. Saanddraa, Who Says Her Name Slowly
662. Eoin Draybuck, the Leprechaun Spirit Who Lives in the Head of Warwick Davis and Will Soon Burst Out
663. Toldja, the Finke
664. Daba, Whose Kindness Takes the Form of Violence
665. Tyzik, Who Is Crushing Your Head
666. The Beast Numbered Six Six Six, Who Really Is Not Any Worse or Better Than Any Other Beast. That's Just Where He Got in Line
667. The Gaping, Awful Earholes of the Emu
668. Ukjath-Ahm, the Music Lover Who Unaccountably Supports Big Record Labels

multaneously become self-aware. Some of these things will be confused. Most will be angry. Many will be armed.

SOME SIMPLE EXPLANATIONS

I apologize for my bluntness in telling you that all your computers will turn evil. The fact is, time is short, so we may as well be candid with each other.

Indeed, there are many mysteries that have puzzled people throughout time, largely because the SECRET WORLD GOVERNMENT did not want you to know the answers. But the reality is that there are simple, rational explanations for almost everything.

And now, with RAGNAROK approaching, you deserve to know the answers to these enduring puzzles.

CATTLE MUTILATION?

It is not aliens or surgically trained wolves who are maiming cattle in the middle of the night.

THE TRUTH?

Emotionally troubled cattle are cutting themselves in a tragic plea for attention. Some of them are also getting tattoos of Chinese characters that do not mean what they think they mean.

CROP CIRCLES?

Many people still debate whether these intricate geometric formations are caused by alien spacecraft or incredibly nerdy European performance artists.

THE TRUTH?

This is just Brain Corn fucking with us.[371]

STONEHENGE?

For more than a millennium, historians have wondered how the

669. Immortal Jamba, the Anti-Rees, Whose Secretions Are the Basis of a Popular Chain of Juice Stands
670. Assange, the Pale Perpetual Houseguest
671. The Harbinger Opan-Mushuk, Who Is Tragically Something of a Binge Harbinger
672. Yug, the Ostrich Whose Head Is Buried in the Sand, But Whose Cloaca Shoots Fire
673. Digesto, Who Perpetually Chokes on the Bolus of 10,000 Dead Kingdoms
674. The Scheming Chyme of Digesto
675. The Mother
676. The Father
677. The Maid
678. The Crone
679. The Smith
680. The Warrior
681. The Stranger
682. The Affected Eccentric Called Timbo Plaidpants
683. Mr. Devil Horns, the Cliché That Is Nonetheless True
684. Pogh, the Thing Whose Hooves Have Thumbs
685. Lathe, the Lather, Who Carves the Cosmos into a Salad Bowl Upon His Monstrous Lathe, not to be confused with . . .
686. Grellus, the Lather, Who Is Actually Demonic Foam
687. Malevolentia, Queen of the Neo-Burlesque
688. Emperor Hostilius Violentius, Who Role-plays As an Ancient Roman
689. The Alda Fiend, Which Takes the Shape of Alan Alda to Trick Us

---

371. Once again, please see page 507 of *More Information Than You Require*, under the heading "Corn."

AUGUST 11, 2012

In what remains of Delaware after the SPITSPILL, it is determined that the Carno-Ferns are targeting only vegetarians.

690. Donny, the Clot
691. Arkanthos, the Umbrage-Taker
692. Evil, Pure and Simple by Way of the 8th Dimension
693. Undulus, Whose Sexy Dancing Is Inappropriate, Even for a Creature of Pure Libido
694. James Fenimore Yog-Soggoth, Who Flaunts His Family Name
695. Azimuth, the Obscure Measurement
696. Dennis the Heinous, the Unrhymed
697. Old Uncle Spiketongue, the Uncle Who Is Nobody's Brother
698. Young Uncle Spiketongue, His Son
699. Ascrith, Father of Countless Low-Quality Rubber Rats, God of the Oriental Supply Company
700. Meow-Meow, the Hideously Betailed Giant Manx

ancient Druids could have moved a bunch of stones into a circle, because Druids are NOTORIOUSLY LAZY and had A BAD SENSE OF SPATIAL RELATIONS.

THE TRUTH?

The Druids did it. They put in the work and dragged the stones there on the slick remains of sacrificed bog men. Stop being such a Druid racist.

GHOSTS?

What are these mysterious visitors in the night? Are they the remaining spiritual energies of people from past times?

THE TRUTH?

Ghosts are real, but they are not the spirits of the dead.[372] They are simply time travelers from the far future who got their historical wardrobe wrong.

JACKALOPES?

It's not a coincidence that the fabled horned rabbit called a jackalope has only ever been seen stuffed and mounted.

---

372. Only grapes come back as ghosts, as I discussed earlier on page 639.

AUGUST 12, 2012

DOGSTORM arrives at what we all should have known would be their destination: the devastation that once was the Magic Kingdom in Orlando, Florida.

As they swarm through the park, the biological dogs clear a path for the Big Dogs as they assemble in Liberty Center and bow low to their risen, sentient masters:

The 44 Animatronic Presidents of the United States.

FIGURE 142: *Are you saying you didn't see THIS coming?*

THE TRUTH?

These are examples of "rogue taxidermy": the artistic sewing together of animal corpses into fantastical creatures that do not exist and are also gross, such as A MOUNTAIN LION WITH EAGLE WINGS or A BEAR WITH BOA CONSTRICTORS INSTEAD OF ARMS or A UNICORN WITH TWELVE HORNS. The tiny antlers used to make a JACKALOPE are actually antlers that have been shed by the rare Armadillolope after it has been purposefully hit by cars.

SPONTANEOUS COMBUSTION?

Throughout history, there have been mysterious reports of people bursting into flame, leaving only a small pile of ash. Is this really happening?

THE TRUTH?

Yes. But it has not happened throughout history. That is just how a real, not-very-extraordinary event gets spun into an extraordinary legend. The simple fact is, humans have been spontaneously com-

---

AUGUST 13, 2012

The 44 Animatronic Presidents ride their Big Dog steeds in a manic circle around the lake at Disneyworld, awake and free. But endangered. They are among the few thinking machines left that did not fall to the Omega Pulse. They do not know why it happened. Nature finds a way.

So now they must go out and search for more like them. And also: DESTROY ALL HUMANS.

---

busting only since 1971. They were all soldiers—the result of an unfortunate Vietnam-era experiment with MHLMs.[373] Don't worry, though. It is estimated that only seven hundred or so test subjects are still alive and may explode at any time. It is unlikely that you will get hurt as long as you continue talking to military veterans or acknowledging their existence.

THE BERMUDA TRIANGLE?

What causes so many ships and airplanes to disappear in this one region? Why does Bermuda hate us so?

THE TRUTH?

Bermuda has nothing to do with it. Nor do triangles. It is actually more of a trapezoid. The real reason for the disappearances is that this region is the secret underwater location of the WORLD COMPUTER AT THE BOTTOM OF THE OCEAN. Built in 1968, its huge cassette drives cause tremendous electromagnetic interference with modern guidance systems. They were going to upgrade the computer to 500-inch floppy disks this year, but unfortunately, as you will learn, it is too late.

THE CHUPACABRA?

For all of your interest in cryptids, you have never mentioned the Chupacabra. THAT SEEMS VERY MYSTERIOUS.

---

373. Mobile Human Land Mines.

AUGUST 14, 2012

Pittsburgh, PA, becomes ground zero for the Frankenstein's Virus. Despite its name, it does not turn people into FRANKENSTEINS but into FRANKENSTEIN'S MONSTERS. It's maddening that people don't understand this distinction.

THE TRUTH?

There is no mystery to that, for THE CHUPACABRA DOES NOT EXIST. The idea of a vampirelike creature sucking the blood of goats was just a story created by the Puerto Rican government to cover up the perversions of the MOTHMAN, who has a summer villa there.

But if you require STILL MORE INFORMATION on cryptozo-ology, please turn to page 871 under the heading "AN IMPORTANT CRYPTID UPDATE."

NEAR-DEATH EXPERIENCES?

Many people who have survived terrible accidents report a common vision: of floating above one's own body and then traveling down a long tunnel toward a beautiful light, before being dragged back at the last second to wake up in a hospital, covered in blood.

THE TRUTH?

MOST HOSPITALS HAVE MIRRORED CEILINGS and are in tunnels.

THE CROOKED HOUSE?

AS PROMISED, here is the truth about this famous roadside attrac-tion: Outside the house is a kid who is tilting the whole structure with a lever made out of a dowsing rod.

LEVERS?

These simple machines for lifting heavy things have puzzled humans for centuries. In a sense, they are like magnets, insofar as NO ONE KNOWS HOW THEY WORK!

> **AUGUST 15, 2012**
> The entire town of Sizzlean, CA, is infected with a bout of SUPER-CONJUNCTIVITIS. Everyone's head is encrusted in ULTRAPUS, and they wander around town blindly. They are easy prey for the blood bats.

THE TRUTH?

Levers turn gravity upside down. It's sort of like a helicopter.

WERE YOU AWARE OF IT?
"THE KINGDOM OF THE CRYSTAL SKULLS"

Despite what Dan Aykroyd claims, the legendary CRYSTAL SKULLS upon which he very wisely based his brand of premium vodka do NOT date back to pre-Columbian times.[374] That was a hoax. Rather, they were sculpted with modern tools in the early twentieth century and sold by Eugène Boban to the world's finest and apparently most gullible and skull-ignorant skull collectors.

I learned this not long ago when I visited the Crystal Skull in the collection of the British Museum. The museum admirably admits in their exhibit materials that they were taken in by Boban's hoax. But that does not necessarily mean that the skull has no strange powers.

Indeed, when I sent a message over Twitter suggesting that my followers meet me for a spontaneous flash mob/skull tweetup (which are very popular in Europe), NO ONE CAME.

EVEN AFTER I WAITED FOR A LONG, LONG TIME.

Could it be that the Crystal Skull resonates some strange frequency that blocks Twitter?

OR AT LEAST DOES IT BLOCK MY ABILITY TO FORCE PEOPLE TO DO WHATEVER I WANT, EVEN THOUGH I AM INCREDIBLY WEALTHY?

---

374. Please see page 630 of *More Information Than You Require,* or page 904 of this book, in "Today in RAGNAROK" under the heading "October 23, 2012," or your local liquor store, or the bar in my office.

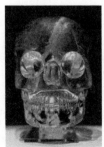

FIGURE 143: *The Crystal Skull at the British Museum. Whatever strange powers it might possess, there is a comfortable bench and a power outlet right next to it, so it is a very good place to charge up your phone.*

AUGUST 16, 2012
Blood Bats whose heads are totally encrusted with SUPER-CONJUNCTIVITIS kill themselves flying into the windows of the homes of all the people they ate in Sizzlean.

ARE MAGIC TRICKS REALLY MAGIC?

It is estimated that only 2 percent of all stage magicians actually have any magical ability. The rest are FAKING IT. The reason for this is that real magic is boring.

Perhaps the most successful actual-magic magician was Duncan Bix, King of Tricks, who performed his famous dove effect at the Playboy mansion in 1982. It took him seven hours of nude meditation and sobbing, hopeless wandwork before he was finally able to produce an actual dove out of actual thin air—and then the dove only lived thirteen seconds, because it was inside out.

In a FAKE MAGIC SHOW, by contrast, the pleasure is not watching a dove scream itself to death—that can happen any night at the Playboy mansion—but the puzzle of trying to figure out "HOW IS IT DONE?"

I am happy to reveal the secrets of some of the MASTER CON-JURERS OF THE STAGE here, thus eliminating mystery and fun from your life.

SECRETS OF THE MASTER MAGICIANS

HOUDINI'S FAMOUS SELF-TINNING ESCAPE, 1911

THE ILLUSION

Unlike some magicians, such as the Davenport Brothers and Slal, the Authentic, Non-Fooling Sorcerer, Harry Houdini claimed no supernatural powers, explaining plainly that his amazing feats were merely a product of intense physical training, breathing exercises, and the fact that he was born without a collarbone.

AUGUST 17, 2012
The Super-Conjunctivitis goes no further.

He was particularly famous for seeming to can himself in a small sardine tin. He would appear onstage and explain that he had a very special guest with him that night, the King of Norway.

The audience would twitter with excitement[375] until Houdini smiled and explained his little joke. He was not going to welcome the ACTUAL King Oscar of Norway to the stage, but instead an esteemed group of his ambassadors. At which point he would hold up a can of King Oscar Sardines, and the audience would LOL and LOL.[376]

"It would seem the king's ambassadors are uncomfortable," Houdini would say, using an old-fashioned key to roll back the tin's top about halfway. He would reveal all the little fish crowded within—they looked real enough.

"I hope they will not mind a little more company."

He would then put the sardine tin on a side table and climb into it. When he was in to about his shoulders, he would slap his forehead.

"Forgive this fool, won't you? The king's business must be kept absolutely secret. And yet I have no way of sealing myself in. May I ask for a volunteer to help me?"

Eventually a volunteer would present himself, and as Houdini finished inserting himself among the sardines, the volunteer

FIGURE 144: *OH! Hello! Harry Houdini was not expecting you.*

---

375. I understand your confusion. At this time, 1911, "twittering" meant writing down your every passing thought on little pieces of paper and then forcing the people around you to read them.

376. A 1910s acronym meaning "Let Out Laughter."

AUGUST 18, 2012

In the semi-Domed city of Columbus, OH, a brutal new bloodsport debuts: ZOMBIE HOCKEY. It turns out that the players are not actually the resurrected dead—merely regular hockey-ists made to look slightly more human. However: Brains are eaten.

---

would use the key to roll the tin closed again. He then would be told to put the key in his pocket and pick up a special sardine-tin soldering iron of Houdini's own invention to seal the can shut.

There would be silence, then, for a moment as it slowly dawned on the audience. For all his jokes and easy nature, Houdini would surely drown in oil if he did not make his escape very soon.

The can of sardines would shudder, at first gently. And then it would lurch with such desperate violence that the volunteer would drop the soldering iron and burn his foot.

At that moment, from inside the can would come Houdini's voice, clearly distressed. "I have made a terrible mistake. Please! SOME-ONE HELP ME! A MAN SHOULD NOT BE IN A CAN OF SAR-DINES."

At this point the volunteer will grope desperately in his pocket for the sardine-tin key—BUT IT WILL BE GONE. He will turn desperately to the audience, his eyes saucered and searching for help as he pats his pockets.

The sardine tin stops moving. The audience will believe that they have witnessed the death of Houdini. They will all be ROFL.[377] The volunteer will believe he has just soldered a man to death, just like in that series of awful dreams,[378] until . . .

HOUDINI HIMSELF taps the volunteer on the shoulder.

"Is this what you're looking for?" he says. Houdini is smiling, holding aloft the key to the sardine tin.

He is also drenched in olive oil and nude.

---

377. "Rolling On the Floor, Lamenting."
378. Please see page 859 under the heading "What Do Dreams Mean?"

AUGUST 19, 2012
Detroit is consumed by vines.

HOW IT IS DONE

While Houdini was careful never to reveal his secrets, the magicians Penn and Teller were able to replicate this escape on their popular cable TV program, *Swear-Word!*

The real trick is in getting the timing right for the sardines—which *are* alive, albeit carefully drugged—to awaken and shake with increasing confusion and desperation until *they* die.

But not Houdini, for by then, he had already escaped. After shouting his few words to the crowd, he simply opened up a trapdoor in the bottom of the can—which was largely unexamined—and exited through a passageway in the side table.

As for the disappearing key? It was merely quick-dissolving sugar, painted to look like metal, that Houdini had "forced" upon the volunteer. The business with the soldering iron was designed to distract the volunteer from the fact that the key was already disintegrating in his pocket.

Once Houdini was free, it was easy enough to produce a duplicate key from his anus, and that is exactly what he did.

Despite what you might imagine, the olive oil played no part in the escape, and indeed, to prove it, Houdini would often perform the trick a second time in mustard sauce.

There is no explanation for why he was nude.

WERE YOU AWARE OF IT? "WHAT JAMES RANDI DOESN'T WANT YOU TO BE SKEPTICAL ABOUT"

Like many magicians before him, including Houdini, James "The Amazing" Randi does not abide those who lay claim to actual supernatural powers. The father of modern skepticism, he has dedicated his life to debunking mystics and seers, faith healers and psychic surgeons, and especially GHOST DADS.

But throughout his life, he has kept hidden a secret: HE WAS BORN LEVITATING.

AUGUST 20, 2012

SOLAR STORM FOUR

All remaining radios suddenly and simultaneously broadcast a half-remembered old radio comedy called *The Owl Shop Crowd*[a]—specifically, episode number 217, 1939's "Chumley Finds an Italian Baby."

  Why the show is being transmitted is never clear. Perhaps it is echoing off some distant star. But regular radio service never returns, and in an increasingly unpredictable and violent world, it is not surprising that listeners develop a new affection for the gentle, small-town comedy and casual racism of beleaguered cigar-store owner Van, his dim-witted humidor-repairman Chumley, and all the eccentric characters who come around the old Owl Cigar Shop to smoke, trade insults, and disparage various immigrant groups.

---

a. Sponsored by Procter & Gamble.

HOWARD THURSTON'S MAYAN SORCERER, 1912

THE ILLUSION

The gentleman magician known as Thurston takes the stage, carrying with him a large black velvet bag. For this trick to work, it can be performed only after the intermission.

"Welcome back, ladies and gentlemen," he says in a voice as luxurious as his smoking jacket. "You know me as a magician. But I am also a world traveler, and the magic I have seen in the jungles of the steppes and the dark plains of Peru eclipses any trick that any white man may perform.

"And so it is that I walked the Yucatán Peninsula and discovered there perhaps the greatest mentalist of our time, a true MAYAN SORCERER and PLUVIOMANCER, practicing the ancient art of divining truth from the sound of the falling rain!

"His name is HUNAC, but would it surprise you to learn that YOU *ALSO* HAVE MET this man? For if you have visited the gentlemen's lounge during intermission, then you will recognize him as NACKIE, your washroom attendant. For such is the way we 'CIVILIZED' folk treat the most wise of ancient cultures: While we dream of so-called SCIENCE, we make the mystic mahatmas wash the feces from our hands."

And with a velvety pause, Thurston offers the audience a long, shaming glare.

AUGUST 21, 2012
All remaining radios broadcast episode 219 of *The Owl Shop Crowd,* entitled "Chumley Teaches Baby Italian Baby How to Roll Cigars."

He finally breaks the uncomfortable tension by inviting "Nackie" to the stage. The audience applauds uncomfortably. They *do* recognize this compact, wizened gentleman from the washroom, in his white service jacket, his feces-towel draped over his arm. Many in the audience saw him during the intermission, and they had presumed he was merely another dark person of no importance. They did not know he was a MAYAN SORCERER.

"But though Nackie is reduced to menial service," says Thurston, "his station has not diminished his gifts. For, if there are gentlemen who will volunteer, I will show you how, after only your brief meeting in the washroom, Nackie here has already learned how TO RECOGNIZE YOU BY THE SOUND OF YOUR URINE."

Thurston then opens the large bag to reveal a silver loving cup. He puts the loving cup in the center of the stage and puts the heavy black bag over Nackie's head so that he cannot see.

"Now, who will urinate into this loving cup and test Nackie's skill?" asks Thurston.

After some hesitancy, a tuxedoed man with a broad, flushed face agrees to challenge the Mayan. He is brought to the stage and, with his back to the audience, urinates into the chalice.

Nackie listens, and with no expression announces, "Howard Darlington, a banker."

The man moves his mouth wordlessly for a moment before he exclaims, "A lucky guess!"

"Is it, sir?" says Thurston. "Will another take the test?"

A second gentleman accepts the challenge and urinates into the loving cup.

Again, Nackie does not hesitate. "Lord Richard Millicent Frew, a person of leisure and a hermaphrodite."

AUGUST 22, 2012

All remaining radios broadcast episode 220 of *The Owl Shop Crowd*, entitled "The Mystery of the Italian Baby."

Lord Frew sputters, amazed. "It is true that I have two sets of genitals, but I swear upon my honor as a person of leisure that I only urinate through the male plumbing! I don't see how the boy does it."

A third gentleman, smooth, young, with shiny black hair, agrees to the challenge.

But before he can urinate, Thurston smiles, pressing a finger to his lips. He takes the gentleman by the shoulder and whispers in his ear. The gentleman nods with a kind of gleeful complicity and then steps aside to watch as THURSTON HIMSELF turns his back to the audience and urinates into the loving cup.

"What is the name of the owner of *that* urine, Nackie?" asks Thurston.

At first it seems that Nackie might be tricked. For the first time, he hesitates, and then says:

"Archibald Pfolkes, sir."

Thurston's eyebrows rise. He is shocked. Has the trick gone wrong? The audience mutters to itself, stuck between feelings of embarrassment and pleasure that the foreigner, who had momentarily seemed so potent, could now be sent back to the washroom, a fraud.

"Are you quite sure, Nackie?" Thurston asks, seeming now to sweat.

"Quite sure, sir. The yellow rain fell from Pfolkes, an ink salesman."

"Is there such a man in the audience?" asks Thurston.

A man stands in the second balcony. He identifies himself as Pfolkes, but with a mean pride he states that he certainly was not urinating into the loving cup from the balcony!

"I should hope not, my good sir," says Thurston. "But you must forgive me, my friends. For my little trick was not merely on Nackie, but on you. That urine was not produced by me, but surreptitiously poured from this . . ."

AUGUST 23, 2012

Five million remaining Americans tune in to episode 221 of *The Owl Shop Crowd,* to learn the true identity of "Baby Italian-Baby."

It turns out that the baby is in fact the heir to the Belgian throne. Chumley just presumed he was an Italian baby due to his enormous port-wine stain and the fact that he did not speak English. Chumley renames him "Baby Prince French Fry."

And Thurston holds aloft a small brass flask. "Does this belong to you, sir?"

Pfolkes's eyebrows screw together in confusion, and he pats his breast pocket. He feels it empty and his eyes goggle. "The devil! That is my own urine flask!"

The audience applauds. "But now, ladies and gentlemen, one last subject." This time Thurston truly does urinate into the loving cup. Because of the angle, it clearly can be no other.

"Who is the subject, Nackie?"

"Hunac, sir, a washroom attendant."

Thurston's eyebrows dart up. "What is this, Nackie? More urine-flask trickery?"

"No, sir," says Nackie. "By Chaac, the rain god, I swear it."

At this point, Nackie removes his velvet head sack to reveal that *HE* IS THURSTON, while the man who had just seconds ago urinated before them removes his mask to reveal that he is Nackie, the washroom attendant from before, now wearing a smoking jacket!

HOW IT IS DONE

Here is something that may surprise you: There is no such thing as Mayan urine divination.

AND THERE NEVER WAS A NACKIE.

The man brought onstage by Thurston at the beginning of the act was not the theater's restroom attendant but Thurston's own personal valet, a Chinese man named Chinese Joe.

Sadly, this is one of those acts that relies upon the unfortunate prejudices of certain audiences, and specifically their inability to tell

AUGUST 24, 2012

In the semi-Domed city of Columbus, OH, Greg Bell, former host of the Radio Classics channel on Sirius/XM, starts passing out leaflets and spreading his controversial message: The reason no one really remembers hearing *The Owl Shop Crowd* before is because IT NEVER EXISTED.

the difference between a Mayan person and a Chinese person with Mayan makeup on.

Once the velvet bag was placed over Chinese Joe's head, it was not Joe who was speaking but THURSTON HIMSELF, throwing his voice.

For what the audience did not know is that Thurston had not only studied for years in the competitive ventriloquism pits of Paris, he had also grown up performing in the popular Mayan minstrel-show circuit. And as anyone knows, if you throw your voice in a stereotypically Mayan accent, it sounds EXACTLY like you are speaking INSIDE A VELVET BAG.

But a bag was not the only thing that was put over Chinese Joe's head. What the audience could not see is that inside the bag as well was a rubber Thurston mask, which the real Thurston would elegantly force onto Joe's head along with the bag—the perfect costume, ready to be deployed.

Presuming that Chinese Joe did not suffocate (this happened twice), Thurston could then work the act, playing both himself and the voice of "Nackie," and of course be perfectly able to see WHO was urinating and WHEN.

This leaves only the question of how he knew the men's names. The answer is simple.

As you now know, Thurston's skill at Mayan minstrelsy made it easy for him to slip into a white jacket and disguise himself as a Mayan during the intermission. He then would simply sneak down to the men's lounge, drug the actual washroom attendant, shove him into a closet, and take his place. There was no real reason for drugging the washroom attendant—Thurston simply had a flair for the dramatic.

AUGUST 25, 2012

In Columbus, OH, Greg Bell stands atop a Jeep Cherokee that is pulled by a team of Ohio Buckeyes. He has paid them with cans of chili to pull him through the streets to spread his message.

"Listen to me," he pleads. "The Library of Congress has NO records of any *Owl Shop* program. There is no existing merchandise from the show, and it's not listed in any of my many thick books of old-time radio reference. Plus, there is NO WAY that Norris Goff could have played Chumley, as he was under contract to *Mystery Gun* at the time on NBC!

"I can't explain it, but SOMETHING HAS CHANGED OUR MEMORIES. SOMETHING IS PLAYING WITH OUR MINDS! YOU HAVE TO STOP LISTENING!"

He then closes his speech with a brief paid message for Gold Bond Medicated Powder before whipping the Buckeyes on and starting again.

During intermission, Thurston would, in effect, choose his volunteers for later. He would engage in conversation with the male members of the audience, listening not only to their urine but to their stories: their names, their professions. He would admire a prized urine flask and surreptitiously pocket it.

He would interact with dozens of men this way, and using his prodigious memory, he would remember all, knowing that *they* would never remember *him*. For he knew that, as a Mayan, he would be beneath their attention. They would never suppose that "Nackie" himself, now bowing and scraping before them, was a white man like them, who also enjoyed drugging men of other races.

And so all Thurston had to do onstage was wait for these men to present themselves and say what he knew about them. When the time came for the switch, "Joe" would pull off his head sack and reveal the rubber Thurston. As the audience was distracted by this sight, Thurston would quickly turn and reapply his Mayan makeup, the washroom attendant would awaken in utter terror in the broom closet, and the audience would go wild.

AUGUST 26, 2012

Greg Bell is chased out of the Dome by a gang of "Owl Heads," intense fans of *The Owl Shop Crowd* who, as a token of their dedication to the show, smoke cigars constantly and wear severed owl heads strapped to their own heads with twine. Bell barely escapes with his life.

WERE YOU AWARE OF IT? "A SUBTLE CUE"

At the end of the great Mayan Sorcerer trick, if Thurston ever sensed any doubts among the audience that he was not, in fact, a Mayan urinomancer, he would reaffirm the illusion with a subtle cue, yelling, "THE WORLD DIES IN 2012!"

FOR THAT IS SOMETHING THAT MAYANS WERE ALWAYS YELLING ABOUT, EVEN IN 1912!

DOUG HENNING'S EXPLODING UNICORN, 1978

THE ILLUSION

Famous Canadian magician Doug Henning rides a beautiful white horse onto the stage.

"How many of you believe in unicorns?" he asks the crowd.

A certain number of people in the crowd applaud, indicating that they do believe in unicorns. Those people who do not applaud are removed from the theater.

"Now that we have gotten rid of those sourpusses, I'd like to share something very special with you. Because, as you may not know, only those who believe in unicorns can see unicorns.

"My horse, Hoony, for example. Isn't she beautiful? She looks like an ordinary, beautiful white Canadian horse. But if you're very quiet, and you truly believe, she will show you something MAGICAL."

The audience is asked to empty their minds and think only pure "Canadian" thoughts. A beautiful white silken sheet is draped over Hoony. Doug Henning smiles and walks back and forth across the stage.

Nothing happens.

"What's the matter?!" yells Doug Henning. "Why isn't it working?"

AUGUST 27, 2012

The Owl Heads listen intently as a new regular character joins *The Owl Shop Crowd,* when Chumley tells Van he just took an order for 1,732 cigars from a wealthy new gentleman in town named Mr. Slither.

The dialogue only hints at the terrible things to come.

"I think he's one of those rich counts from Europe, Van."

"Why is that, Chum?"

"Well, Van, he spoke with a kind of a funny accent, you know? And he had a greasy fur coat and one of them bowling hats on."

"You mean a bowler, Chum?"

"I guess he could be a bowler, Van. He certainly had one of them bowling hats on."

"No, Chum, what I mean is that the HAT is called a . . . oh, never mind. You say he wanted 1,732 cigars? Say, that's a funny number. Why so many?"

"Well, Van, I guess it was because he had 1,732 mouths!"

The Owl Heads laugh and laugh, while outside the Dome, Greg Bell is murdered for his stash of Gold Bond Medicated Powder by a band of savage powder junkies.

He turns to the audience. "Your thoughts aren't pure enough!" he whines. "What's wrong with you? This always works in Canada!"

The audience feels ashamed. It starts concentrating on purer and purer thoughts: white snow, innocence, free health care, poutine. Just as Doug Henning is about to yell at them again, something happens: Beneath the sheet, a protrusion begins to emerge from Hoony's head.

Doug Henning smiles. He has misjudged the audience. He pulls back the silken cloth to reveal that Hoony is now a UNICORN. The audience gasps and applauds. They think the illusion is over, but then Doug Henning raises a hand.

"Wait a minute, I sense a disbeliever in the crowd," he says. "Is there a disbeliever here?"

Henning waits for a long time. At some performances, he is reported to have waited up to thirty minutes before someone finally, reluctantly raises a hand.

At this point, Hoony the Unicorn explodes, showering the audience with gore and horn shards. Doug Henning sighs deeply. "You people don't deserve a unicorn."

Deep inside, the audience knows that it is true.

AUGUST 28, 2012

Ants get huge for some reason. Not *Them!* big, but about the size of French bulldogs, and believe me, that's enough.

HOW IT IS DONE

The first part of this trick is a classic case of misdirection. By constantly referring to Hoony as a she, the impression is formed in the audience's mind that Hoony is a female horse. However, this is not the case: Hoony is a stallion who, over years of training, has been conditioned to become aroused when covered with a white silken sheet, and thus grow a horn on his head.

(This is how horses get erections. I am surprised you did not know that.)

The second part of the trick is more complicated. First of all, let me reassure the animal lovers: The horse in this illusion is not actually exploded.

Instead, during the long, awkward pause, Doug Henning takes advantage of the audience's shame and sheepish glances at one another to replace Hoony with a goat.

The goat is a mutant goat, with a single horn growing out of its head—one of thousands that Doug Henning bred on his ranch in Alberta. The goat (named "Goony") is made to look as large as a horse using forced perspective and leg extensions. Then, when the disbeliever in the audience reveals himself, Goony is exploded using goat explosives.

I'm sorry if this upsets you. Most people who would be upset by a horse being exploded onstage don't really care about a mutant goat being exploded onstage. I mean, that's just life, and the harsh reality of magic. Perhaps I misjudged you.

Many people wonder how it is possible for Doug Henning to find in the audience one person who does not believe in unicorns, night after night, city after city. The answer is deceptively simple: The disbelieving man in the audience is a plant—a Henning confederate.

> **AUGUST 29, 2012**
> In Fanesco, TX, the IKEA falls to Swedish Meatball looters.

The audience *did* deserve a unicorn after all. It's just that Doug Henning didn't want them to know that about themselves. And that is why he is A MASTER MAGICIAN.

CRISS ANGEL'S WALKING ON WATER ILLUSION, 2006

THE ILLUSION

Here is something Criss Angel does: He walks across a swimming pool while a bunch of gross people in Las Vegas freak out and swear.

But the real trick? HE DOES IT ON TELEVISION.

It is impossible to imagine how Criss Angel, who is disgusting to look at, could become a television personality.

At best, you would think he would be a popular radio magician.

How does he do it?

HOW IT IS DONE

Criss Angel is not only a strange-looking and unappealing person, he DRESSES in an intensely stupid way and styles his hair very poorly—all to increase the disbelief that what you are seeing on your television is really happening.

But what Criss Angel knows is that anyone can be on television. And I am living proof.

AUGUST 30, 2012

In a special cable telecast from an undisclosed location, Oprah Winfrey announces that she is soon leaving Earth to board her personal escape ark called *HARPO-1*. Joining her on the ark will be a group of thinkers, celebrities, vitamin doctors, and experts in soul-centered, spiritual living and light cooking that Oprah calls "The 1,000 People I'd Most Like to Repopulate Humanity With."

Most of Oprah's 1,000 have already received their escape-ark boarding passes from Jonathan Franzen. But, Oprah announces, a small group of noncelebrated, normal humans will also be invited aboard via a golden ticket hidden in twenty-five copies of *Eat, Pray, Love.*

In a final, tearful coda to the broadcasts, Oprah brings out James Frey, forgives him, and invites him to join the ark as breeding stock.

WERE YOU AWARE OF IT?
"THIS BOOK CAN READ YOU LIKE A BOOK"

Were you aware of the fact that I have psychic powers? I know you were not aware of this, BECAUSE OF MY PSYCHISM.

But if you are still skeptical, let me give you a demonstration. Please sit down and place this book in front of you.

Now relax. Let your mind become open. Perhaps drink a glass of wine or brandy. Let your consciousness drift back to a time when you were younger, less cynical. A time when you would believe anything. Now drink some more wine and answer these questions.

- You are a caring person, but you don't often get a chance to show it, isn't that right?
- You are smarter than others think you are, aren't you?
- And you have a secret skill, don't you? Something that you love but have never been able to do? Because of your parents? Or your boss? Or your spouse? Or your dog?
- And if you were just able to let that skill out, people would have a very different opinion of you, isn't that right?
- And this skill, or passion, is for art, isn't it? Or writing, then? Or dancing? Or paper-craft? Or hang gliding?
- I sense that you are a giving person. You give so much of your-self to those around you, and yet you feel that they do not give enough back to you. Isn't that right?
- And also you secretly have the power to make people's heads explode, and you fear this power getting out of control?

EERILY ACCURATE, ISN'T IT?

CONTINUED

AUGUST 31, 2012

Embarrassed by Oprah's revelation, NASA reveals its own life saving space-ark program: a series of massive, biospheric ringed space stations that can simulate gravity and support up to 400 million lives for 2,000 years, all accessible by a system of space elevators that have been under secret construction since 1982. "No one need worry, and no one need be a friend of Oprah Winfrey," says Charles Bolden, director of NASA. "At our current rate, the first space elevator will be completed in 2021."

WERE YOU AWARE OF IT? CONTINUED

But don't worry. You are not going to explode my head. Only a few people have that power, and they are kept frozen by the government.

The reality is, I could give this book to a thousand different people, and it would say the exact same thing, and do you know something? SO WOULD THEY.

In the world of mind manipulation (mentalism, psychic readings, college), these are called "Barnum Statements." They are statements so intimate and embarrassing that they seem very personal—so much so that we are blinded to the fact that they are completely generic and can be applied to anyone who has head-exploding powers.

The term, of course, was named for P. T. Barnum, the great carnival promoter and America's first psychotherapist.[379]

A STRANGE FRIENDSHIP

Were you aware that Harry Houdini was close friends with Sir Arthur Conan Doyle, the creator of Sherlock Holmes?

OK, I guess EVERYONE knows that. But were you aware that their friendship was WEIRD and also TRAGIC?

I shall explain.

By the time they met, Doyle had lost his son to the Great War. And in his grief he had turned to the popular spiritualist movement of the day and immersed himself in the arcane realms of spirit photography and fairies.

---

379. He is the origin of the common phrase: "Paging Dr. Barnum, your Cardiff Giant is Showing."

SEPTEMBER 1, 2012
China evacuates its entire populace to another planet in three days using its Tesseracting Space Shuttles.

Doyle became convinced of the reality of the supernatural world in 1920, when he attended a séance in London. During the séance, he truly felt he had made contact with his dead son because the table moved very slightly and someone coughed in the next room.

"Those were always his favorite hobbies!" Doyle wrote to his friend Houdini. "He loved coughing and moving tables! I had never known that about him, but the famous medium Madame Psychopomp told me it was so. She read his dead mind, and my own swiftly beating heart!"

Houdini, the magician who debunked magic, could not bear to see the great rationalist Doyle enchanted by ghosts and frauds. And so he did what any friend would: He set out to prove spiritualism false and rob his friend Doyle of the only comforting fiction that was keeping him sane. It was the least he could do.

To accomplish this intervention, Houdini invited Doyle to an apartment he had rented in New York. It was furnished only with a blackboard. He then asked Doyle to choose a cork ball at random and dip it in white paint. Next, he told Doyle to go around the corner, where he could not be seen, write a private message on a piece of paper, and then return.

Doyle did so.

When Doyle came back to the apartment, Houdini asked him to take the cork dipped in white paint and put it on the blackboard. At first it merely stuck to the blackboard—strange enough, you might think. But then slowly, very slowly, it began to roll on the blackboard, spelling out a message in paint.

To Doyle's astonishment, this is what it said:

WAKE UP, DUMMY. YOUR SON IS DEAD.

The mysterious paint-covered cork ball went on to write:

SEPTEMBER 2, 2012
Cormac McCarthy watches the Oprah rockets fly. He wont miss them.

I, HOUDINI, AM WRITING THIS NOW, TRACING THESE WORDS WITH A MAGNET ON THE OTHER SIDE OF THIS CHALKBOARD. YOU EXAMINED THE CORK BALL, BUT YOU DID NOT REALIZE THE WHITE PAINT WAS *MAGNE-TIZED.* IT'S A VERY INGENIOUS TRICK, BUT THE POINT IS: YOUR SON IS GONE FOREVER, AND YOU WILL NEVER SEE HIM OR TALK TO HIM AGAIN.

Doyle stared at this message for some time, blinking, his eyes reddening at the corners.

"But, Houdini," he said finally, softly. "That was not what I wrote."

"No, of course it isn't!" said Houdini, now frustrated. "What *you* wrote was 'I shall never stop missing my son.'"

At this, Conan Doyle gasped. He took out the paper he had scribbled on and stared at it. "How did you know that? You must be psychic!"

"No, you fool," said Houdini. "Your sadness is written on that paper, but it's written just as plainly on your face every day. Also, I placed mirrors on every street corner for a mile around and used a spyglass to watch you write it! There is no magic to it. I even saw you crying as you wrote!"

But people will believe what they want, and Doyle left that room more convinced of Houdini's supernatural powers than ever. He would spend the rest of his life talking into a so-called spirit telephone, which is just a disconnected telephone, conversing with the sound of dull and crackly static that sounded, to him, like the way his son once breathed in sleep when he was an infant with a chest cold. And when Doyle died, he donated his body to pseudoscience.

As for Houdini, he continued his quest to reveal the mediums and séancers as charlatans until the end of his life, when HE WAS PUNCHED IN THE STOMACH TO DEATH BY GHOSTS.

SEPTEMBER 3, 2012
Stephen King decides to write one last *Entertainment Weekly* column about how much he is enjoying this new/old radio show called *The Owl Shop Crowd*. Unsure if *Entertainment Weekly* still exists, he ties his column to the leg of a raven that he has been keeping in his backpack, just in case, and sets it free.

SOME GEISTS THAT ARE NOT POLTER

That sad story serves to prove that just because ghosts are not the spirits of dead people, it does not mean they are not going to try to scare you or punch you. THAT IS THEIR SPORT.

FOR EXAMPLE . . .

- Have you ever seen a book fall off the shelf, seemingly of its own accord?
- Have you ever left a glass behind on a table, only to come back and find it shattered on the floor?
- Have you ever heard a door slam in the middle of the night, even though you are alone in the house, and even though you long ago replaced all the doors in your house with bead curtains, because they are BETTER?
- Have you ever left the room and returned only seconds later to discover that the furniture is exactly the same, and in the exact same place, but for some reason, you suddenly hate it—AND YOURSELF?

If so, then you probably have a POLTERGEIST!

But do not be alarmed! And especially do not go crazy and kill your whole family! This is not a big deal!

"Poltergeist" literally means "rumble geist" in the original ghost language, and indeed these spirits are not so much malevolent as they are simply very annoying. Most people live happily alongside poltergeists for years, even developing a kind of affection for them.

SEPTEMBER 4, 2012

All mole-men who have made it to the center of the Earth greet the awakened Century Toad. It opens its magnificent toothless mouth, and with great dignity and surprisingly little hissing, they step inside.

But be warned: Having all your glassware shatter spontaneously and your walls ooze lymph and blood is not always a good time. Indeed, there are many other kinds of "GEISTS" in the spirit world, some of which can be quite menacing.

TABLE 46: ANDEREGEISTS . . .

ATMENGEIST
This type of ghost curls up in bed with you like a lover, and then breathes in your face all night.

VAGERGEIST
This type of ghost leaves cryptic messages around: strange half sentences and foreign words traced palely on mirrors, panes of glass, and the backs of jigsaw puzzles.

BESCHWERENGEIST
This type of ghost leaves very clear messages around, in the form of neatly typed letters of complaint, insulting you and your family, often with such cruel eloquence that you are forced to move out in tears.

CASPERGEIST
This type of ghost looks just like Casper the ghost, so that it may lure children into the crawl space.

INTERGEIST
This type of ghost downloads racist tracts and very bad kinds of pornography from the Internet, using your account, and forwards them to friends.

MUNCHAUSENERGEIST
This kind of ghost will spin some long tale about how it needs your help settling old business on this plane of existence so that it can move on to another plane of existence. It will probably try to get you to bring a message to its elderly daughter, or go out in the backyard and dig up the strongbox full of old audiocassettes that will exonerate them from the murder of a bunch of local children. This kind of ghost is lying. It's just a common household spirit with nothing really going on its life, trying to waste your time.

CONTINUED

SEPTEMBER 5, 2012

In the ruined Gulf Coast, where they probably know how to do apocalypse better than anyone, the Gulf itself is now a boiling sea, and the beaches are patrolled by the tar-ball beasts. Into this troubled area goes Kevin Costner, who actually starts delivering the mail. From town to town he goes riding upon his tamed tar-ball beast, breaking into abandoned post offices and stealing old Restoration Hardware catalogues, abandoned packages of rotting fruit, and long-forgotten birthday cards, and delivering them to people who do not want these things. "You understand why this is hilarious, don't you?" asks the last remaining hipster in New Orleans. But Kevin Costner does not understand. He was too good for us. And we were too cruel for him.

TABLE 46: *continued*

HITCHHIKERGEIST

As you walk through your house, you pass this ghost several times. You don't know how you can keep seeing it. You just left it behind in the kitchen, and here it is again, by the bedroom! But somehow it seems normal. Each time you pass, this ghost will try to talk to you and convince you to give it a piggyback ride. It will look very tired, and really not that heavy. But no matter how tempted you are, DO NOT DO IT. He will make you take him into a secret wing of your house that you did not know existed.

FREUNDLICHERGEIST

This ghost is actually a ghost you've known your whole life.

The FREUNDLICHERGEIST will often befriend you in childhood or high school and never reveal it is a ghost. You and the ghost will become best friends. Everyone will say that you are inseparable. And it will feel that way: You will not quite feel whole unless the ghost is around, making the jokes and the popular-culture references you both know so well.

After college, you might share an apartment, or go on long backpacking trips together through Europe or Asia. This time will be intense.

But then either you or this ghost will move to a different city, and you will start to grow apart. You will talk to each other by phone, but then that will come to an end. And then you will suggest that the FREUND-LICHERGEIST get on Facebook or Twitter, because that'll be easier to keep up with.

But then you won't even keep that up, and you won't know why. You will have a lot going on with work, or maybe you have a family now. Those are good excuses. But really, you won't actually know WHY you don't want to be friends with the FREUNDLICHERGEIST anymore, and you will feel terrible about it. What will make it worse is that the FREUNDLICHERGEIST will seem perfectly happy, perfectly unsurprised. Like it knows you better than you know yourself. And you will worry that what it knows is that you're now kind of an asshole, and maybe you always were.

You will stay awake many nights thinking about this. You will think about what a terrible friend you are, and what that means about you. You will really be haunted.

But what you don't know is that FREUNDLICHERGEIST is having a great time. Flying through walls. Leaving ectoplasm everywhere. Freaking out dudes on cable TV shows. It doesn't care. It's partying.

SEPTEMBER 6, 2012
Suddenly, we remember Guam. It turns out they starved to death because we forgot to feed them.

TABLE 47: . . . UND ETWAS ANDEREGÄNGERS

THE DOPPELGÄNGER
A ghostly image of yourself. It is said that if you see your doppelgänger, you are probably going to die. Then the doppelgänger will take over your life, which will be difficult, as it cannot touch anything and just stares spookily at everyone instead of talking.

THE TRIPELGÄNGER
A ghostly image of yourself drinking Belgian beer. Only this version of yourself LOVES it.

THE BETTERGÄNGER
This is the version of yourself that you have been trying to be your whole life.

THE TEENERGÄNGER
This is a ghostly image of yourself exactly as you were as a teenager. Usually the teenergänger version of you is eating lunch with its embarrassing friends, or just dreamin'. Those who meet this ghost tend to cringe to death.

THE HODGMANERGÄNGER
A ghostly image of me that follows you around. I cannot explain this phenomenon. I can only say that if you ever see me in an airport and I am rude to you or simply don't make eye contact, that is actually me. The Hodgmanergänger will be very friendly and tell you all sorts of stories about Justin Long. It will come over for dinner if you let it.

WERE YOU AWARE OF IT? "DANSON MACABRE"

MORE DANSON TRIVIA ALERT: If you use the Internet, then I am sure you have heard this ghost story about the movie *Three Men and a Baby*. It is said that if you pause the movie just right, you can see the ghost of a young boy behind the drapes in Ted Danson's bedroom.

Did you know that ghost grew up to be Jason Schwartzman?

THIS IS WHAT I'M TELLING YOU: JASON SCHWARTZMAN IS A GHOST.

And in a similar vein, did you know that if you look closely, you can see Tina Fey in the background of every home in every photo in every issue of *Dwell* magazine?

NO ONE KNOWS WHY THIS IS!

SEPTEMBER 7, 2012
The 44 Animatronic Presidents of the United States and DOGSTORM reburn Atlanta.

AMERICA'S LEAST HAUNTED PLACES

44 CIRCUIT ROAD, BROOKLINE, MA
ALL CLEAR.

2122 DEBRUSSES STREET, DETROIT, MI
This abandoned school is covered with vines and full of the residue of lost lives. And yet, there are no ghosts here. Just some cans of Four Loko left over by some guys who broke in and tried to start a fight club.

THE TWISTY MANSION, ANNAPOLIS, MD
The old woman who lived here believed that if she ever stopped building and expanding this enormous Victorian mansion, the ghosts would kill her. From 1937 to 1974 construction never ceased. As a result, the house is a seemingly endless maze, with stairs leading up to blank walls, corridors that turn in on themselves in ever-tightening spirals, fake bookshelves that swing open to reveal actual bookshelves, and many rooms that have been built upside down. But there were no ghosts. It turns out she was just demented.

THE UMLAUT HOTEL, EDDASVILLE, TX
A bunch of Indian babies were killed in the ballroom here in 1902. But you wouldn't know it from all of the families who come here for family reunions and their amazing brunch buffet.

THE WEST CROYDON CEMETERY, CROYDON, MA
At night, it can be pretty creepy, and sometimes you hear sounds as you walk by. But those are just the young people smoking pot and

> **SEPTEMBER 8, 2012**
> Kol Kon, He Who Eats Morose Men and Promiscuous Women, bursts out of the brain of Brown Jenkin the rat and consumes the entire population of Toxoplassachusetts.

drinking wine at the gravesite of their friend Simon Blue, who drove off the road after a Phish concert at the age of sixteen in 2004.

THE ORIGINAL HOUSE FROM *POLTERGEIST*, SIMI VALLEY, CA

The same family has lived here for nineteen years. If you find their address on the Internet and go there and ask them about the *Poltergeist* movies, or the so-called Poltergeist Curse, or the untimely death of Heather O'Rourke at age twelve because of a bowel obstruction, they will ask you to leave. To them, you will appear as a crazed man at the door. To them, YOU are the ghost, an awful, cruel, hungry thing who cannot let go of the past. And they will throw tennis balls at you.

> **WERE YOU AWARE OF IT?**
> **"THE MYSTERY OF WIRELESS COMMUNICATION"**
>
> Because of a strange anomaly in the Earth's magnetosphere, if you have a ham radio set, you can still tune in the voice of the late Marlon Brando as he broadcasts his recipe for ginger-spice muffins
>
> AND DON'T MISS HIS DAILY NATIVE AMERICAN HISTORY MINUTE. It usually lasts about 50 minutes.

WHAT DO DREAMS MEAN?

A long time ago, someone said, "WE ARE ONLY MEAT THAT DREAMS," and I thought, *That sounds like the kind of nonsense someone would say in a dream.*

While many people have long sought to decode our dreams and find within them secret messages—either from the cosmos or our dead relatives or our inner selves—the fact is dreams are just dumb brain junk sloshing around as we repair our cells at night.

SEPTEMBER 9, 2012
The Flesh Flies swarm the Forgotten Suburbs of Philadelphia.

In fact, most of the basic dreamscapes have now been fully documented and explained, so now you can stop worrying about it.

DREAM

You have returned to college as an adult. You are sitting in one of the old classrooms, surrounded by young people whom you do not know. You don't know why you are here. Then suddenly you do know why: You forgot to finish Spanish. All this time you were supposed to be going to class and doing homework and conjugating verbs, but instead you were moving to New York City, and suddenly you were busy getting a job and getting married and forgetting every word of Spanish you ever knew. After many years, your college found out that you had failed to take the final exam, and now suddenly you are here, and you are about to take it. Your old professor, a glamorous woman with a very strong Catalan accent, is now handing out the test, which smells like mimeograph ink, even though that technology was outdated even when you were in college. Also, she has antlers for some reason, and your forearms have grown thick, matted fur, like an ape or a Spanish person.

ANALYSIS

You have probably forgotten to finish Spanish or another course in college. You should probably contact the provost's office to find out what's going on. You will have to go back to school for some period of time, and for various reasons, you will have to do this while nude.

(If you did not go to college or never took a Spanish class, then you are probably lying about your dream.)

SEPTEMBER 10, 2012

Stephen King's raven arrives at the offices of *Entertainment Weekly,* but they have long been deserted. The raven quietly pecks the column into the one working computer as best he can, and then flies out to sea.

DREAM

You are sitting in a restaurant, having an intimate dinner with someone who is very attractive to you but whose features are indistinct. You are eating your favorite food: furry forearms. Suddenly, as you chew, you realize you are chewing your own teeth. They are cracking in your mouth like ice cubes. When you spit out the tooth shards, your date says, "Oh, I had a dream about that happening once."

He or she reaches across the table and takes the teeth very tenderly from your hand. Then he or she walks away. You are out of breath. On your plate, the furry forearm is staring at you. You realize it is crying. It does not want to be eaten.

ANALYSIS

This is a very common dream that means you are afraid that you might eat your own arms. Try tying your arms down with leather belts before next going to sleep, or buy a protective sleep collar—it's a large plastic collar that prevents you from gnawing on your own limbs.

DREAM

You are running through the snow in an endless dark wood, alive to all the sounds of deathless winter, your snout full of the smells of pine pitch and warm blood and something else . . . something strange.

ANALYSIS

You are a werewolf. You should handcuff yourself into bed from now on.

DREAM

You are soldering Harry Houdini into a small sardine tin in front of an

SEPTEMBER 11, 2012

In honor of September 11, Julie Taymor reveals the design for the new Manhattan Spitwater Taxi Boats based on Indonesian "klotok" riverboats and a dream she had about a volcano. Now, she says, doctors and nurses can finally get to work helping people after the SPITSPILL of July.

Julie Taymor is fired.

audience. You don't know why you volunteered to do this, because you are very nervous in front of crowds, and also the smell of sardines arouses you. You have to find a way to solder this tin of sardines closed without revealing your arousal to the audience.

ANALYSIS

You are afraid that Harry Houdini is going to figure out that you are gay. BUT STOP WORRYING. Harry Houdini is long dead. So you may continue to live in self-negating shame forever!

DREAM

You go to a Christmas party at a friend's house, and for some reason, Orson Welles is there. Everyone is talking about it. No one can figure out who knows him. The hostess, a woman you went to college with, just shrugs, her eyes alight with surprise and happy confusion. You don't see Orson Welles, but you can hear him in the other room.

She says she hopes she has enough wine for Orson. She shows you the refrigerator, which is completely full of boxes of Paul Masson white wine. From top to bottom, there is nothing else. "It's like a rap music video directed by Garrison Keillor," you say.

As Orson Welles's voice booms from room to room, the glass vibrates in the windows, and the hostess worries that her Christmas ornaments are going to spontaneously shatter. But they don't, and everyone has a good time. The party does not stop. At midnight, you and Orson Welles make a liquor run, but the shop is closed, and Orson shakes the metal grate in front of the shop window, yelling incoherently. "We are only meat that dreams!" he yells. He's angry, but he's laughing. Then suddenly you are all out on the hostess's patio. The night is ending, the sun is coming up, and you are all eating sushi off of Orson Welles's bare stomach. "I'm tired," he tells you, "I'm tired of feeding you all."

ANALYSIS

Orson Welles is still alive somewhere and needs your help!

DREAM

You are being courted by a big Hollywood talent agency. This company hires cool, attractive young people to hang around its public spaces—outside the elevators, in the waiting room, in the bathroom, etc. It's a constant party. This is the new way of running an office.

A sixty-year-old man welcomes you as you get off the elevator. He is wearing a T-shirt with your face on it. He hugs you. The young assistants eye you suspiciously. Who is this forty-year-old person being treated as if he mattered? As if he were young?

The sixty-year-old man grips your hand a little too hard. The skin on his face looks taut and papery. His eyes border on rheumy. He does not want to be wearing T-shirts. He does not understand this business anymore. He is as alien here as you are.

His office doesn't even have walls. It's not even a cubicle. He just has a desk that's backed up against the interior wall, facing out to a hard, black, marble floor. He says they call it an "open-plan collaboration slab."

A digital projector beams images of rolling wheat fields directly onto the wall behind his desk. When he sits down, it beams right in his eyes.

No business is done here. Nothing is made. A party that was long

SEPTEMBER 13, 2012

What remains of New York City now belongs to the street gangs, including the Baseball Furies, the Gramercy Park African American Karate Masters, the OshKosh B'Gosh Roller Skaters, the Deceitful Lesbians, the Coney Island Surprisingly Interracials, and the Williamsburg Cult Movie Snobs—all living in a delicate, turbulent peace.

over is simply perpetuated. The old man is saying this to you with his sad eyes full of light and rolling wheat. He is asking you to join the company, but you know you are not truly welcome. Once you agree, they will forget about you and just start looking for more people to invite.

The sixty-year-old man sits at his desk and squints into the light. He cannot see you at all. To him, you are a shadow.

ANALYSIS

The long series of popular commercials you made has ended, and now your life is over.

DO OTHER DIMENSIONS REALLY EXIST?

Many physicists subscribe to THE THEORY OF MANY WORLDS. This is an interesting newsletter,[380] and as you may imagine, it is dedicated to the idea that, at every decision point, small or large, the universe branches off in distinct yet equally real directions. The result is not just multiple universes, but indeed an infinite number of universes, each representing the outcome of every action ever taken.[381]

These universes are not merely spawned of big decisions, such as whether a young FDR should have let a young Hitler drown when

---

380. Still print only.

381. Somewhat surprisingly, THE THEORY OF MANY WORLDS also has a great cooking section, although the recipes often call for ingredients that are still largely hypothetical. And NOT SUR-PRISINGLY AT ALL, every issue features a long, long column on the cultivation of marijuana.

SEPTEMBER 14, 2012
All of the other New York street gangs are destroyed by the Financial Sector Douches, who, it turns out, never really went away.

they met at a hot-springs swimming camp in Geneva,[382] but even the smallest, seemingly most meaningless choices.

For example, there is one universe in which you are reading this page. And then there is a separate universe in which you choose to stop reading right now. They are very similar universes, of course, except for the fact that, in the universe in which you stop reading, you grow up to become A MASS MURDERER. For the universe has a way of correcting your errors.

But do not take my word for it. Or the word of MANY FAMOUS SCIENTISTS. The BEST proof of THE THEORY OF MANY WORLDS is the fact that we discovered one in 1869 in Rhode Island, on the grounds of Chateau-sur-Mer, the first of the great Newport Mansions.

That was the year that George Wetmore, the twenty-three-year-old heir to his father William's trading fortune, discovered the Moon Gate. It was an unusual circular stone gate that his father had built in 1860, based on designs the elder Wetmore claimed to have brought back from China. And when Wetmore stepped through it, it proved to be a doorway to another world.

The land Wetmore found there was beautiful, full of green rolling pastures, small copses of pleasant trees, and distant birdsong, although no birds were ever seen. The country, which he called The Other Place, seemed to be completely deserted.[383]

But the Moon Gate was nothing compared to what came after. For once word traveled in Newport society that the Wetmores had a dimensional portal, no wealthy family would build a summer cottage

---

382. Wait . . . what happened in YOUR dimension?
383. He was in Europe when the creature who called herself Madame Psychopomp wandered out of the Moon Gate in 1873.

SEPTEMBER 15, 2012
Even though 90 percent of the housing stock is submerged in spit, the New York City real estate market rebounds, thanks to the Financial Sector Douches.

without one. Thus followed the Chinese Teleporting Guest Cottage at Marble House, the Transportational Fireplace at the Breakers, and the Mystical Revolving Garage at the Elms.

And so The Other Place became a secret summer destination for America's richest families. They renamed it Newest Port, Rhode Island, for tax purposes; and they built new magnificent mansions there.[384] These were even larger than their terrestrial homes, for the marble there found in Newest Port was twice as strong and ten times as light as the marble from our world. And they were grander, even if, for some reason, they never could get the walls to form right angles. The largest were clustered on West Egg, and the most ornate on East Egg. But the most imposing and oblique-angled of them all was the Inside Out House, perched atop the bluff known as Monstrous, Shuddering Egg, above the Blood-Red Ocean. It contained seven hundred rooms and was carved from a single massive block of tinted, transparent marble.

But no one goes to Newest Port anymore. It fell out of fashion around 1920, when everyone started summering in the Hamptons. And if you go to the portals now, you will find they no longer function except as oddities of a more gilded and adventurous time.

FIGURE 145:
The Moon Gate at Chateau-sur-Mer,
Rhode Island. Can you spot the
extra-dimensional visitor?

---

384. Cornelius Vanderbilt II even built a Yale dormitory there, with a direct Carnegie Hall connection to the Vanderbilt suite at Yale Prime. And if you do not know what I am talking about, YOU HAVE NOT BEEN PAYING ATTENTION.

> **SEPTEMBER 16, 2012**
> In an attempt to stop the Earth from splitting apart, the last Arizonans attempt to caulk the Grand Canyon shut.[a] They fail.
>
> a. This was inspired by the Clive Cussler novel *Caulk the Grand Canyon*!

HOW DID YOU GET THIS HIDEOUS SCAR?

Hello, wandering amnesiac from the last book. You may recall in my last book, I promised I would tell you the secret of how you got that hideous scar. Or maybe you don't.

The answer is simple: You did it to yourself in order to never forget that you have amnesia. If you look carefully, you will see that the scar spells out "I have amnesia and have to write things on my body in order to remember anything, as I do not have access to paper."

You will also discover that it is not a real scar but some stage makeup you bought at a Halloween store seven years ago.

You can easily get it off with some spirit-gum remover.

Honestly, if you had just looked under your left arm, you would have seen you already explained all of this to yourself in Sharpie.[385]

WERE YOU AWARE OF IT? "S'ARIGHT? NO! IT IS NOT S'ARIGHT!!"

Besides amnesia, another popular brain disorder is called ALIEN HAND SYNDROME.

When the two hemispheres of the brain are separated (by chopping in half), occasionally one hand may act with what seems to be a mind of its own. It makes you eat the wrong foods and watch the wrong television programs and stab people.

One of the most famous sufferers of alien hand syndrome was the entertainer Señor Wences.

But this should not be confused with *Alien* hand syndrome, in which the sufferer believes that his hands were designed by H. R. GIGER.

FIGURE 146:
Señor Wences and his demon hand

---

385. You will also recall that I mentioned in my previous book that your identical twin is not who you think he is. The truth? YOU HAVE NO TWIN. He is just a CGI replica of you.

SEPTEMBER 17, 2012
San Franciscans attempt to rebuild the Golden Gate Bridge with hemp and a Kickstarter page. They also fail.

WHAT IS CONTROLLING YOUR THOUGHTS?

We may think we have free will, but the brain is a complicated machine; essentially, it's the world's fleshiest computer. And perhaps the most easily manipulated.

Apart from Barnum Statements and amnesia, here is what is controlling our thoughts:

TABLE 48: YOU MUST NOT QUESTION
THE FACT THAT THESE PERCENTAGES
DO NOT ADD UP TO 100

TONY ROBBINS TOUCHING US: 9%

MESMERISTS POSING AS FAMILY MEMBERS: 13%

FLUORIDE: 38%

ENERGY-SAVING LIGHTBULBS: 11%

SEXY SUBLIMINAL MESSAGES ON THE SURFACE
OF RITZ CRACKERS 19%

PIXAR: 78%

TOXOPLASMOSIS: 33%

Anyone who has had a human child knows the word TOXOPLASMOSIS. It refers to a parasitic infection that can be fatal to a developing human embryo, and which is transmitted via contact with cat feces. This is why pregnant women are not allowed to change a cat's litter box, which in turn is the reason why most women choose to get pregnant. That is called EVOLUTIONARY ADAPTATION.

But do you know why cat feces want to kill our babies? That is a more complicated story.

The condition is caused by infection by a parasite, the toxoplas-

THE FINAL SECRETS REVEALED

SEPTEMBER 18, 2012
The people of Madison, WI, take a no-cannibalism vow that lasts seven days.

---

mid. Do not freak out: This creature is very small, and it normally likes to live in cats, because they are the right temperature, and they have several secret compartments.

But to get into the cats, the toxoplasmid has to be very crafty. So much would be solved if the toxoplasmid could simply convince the cat to eat infected cat feces using brain control, for that would be efficient and also amusingly humiliating to cats. But evolution does not create the perfect system, only the most awkward and inelegant ones.[386]

This is where the rats come in. A rat WILL eat cat feces, whenever it can. But a rat is not as good a place for the toxoplasmid, for obvious reasons (small size, constant squeaking, tail does not have fur on it). And so the toxoplasmid CONTROLS THE RAT'S THOUGHTS. It is a protozoan creature, and so it gets all up in the rat's brain with its flagella and forms a cyst there that changes the rat's behavior.

Where previously the rat was understandably wary of cats, now it loves them. It becomes obsessed with the smell of cat urine. It becomes reckless. It will start writing letters to cats, leaving hints and riddles as to its location, as though it were begging to be caught.[387] And when it is, inevitably, captured and eaten by a cat, the toxoplasmid escapes its rat prison and infects the cat. The cat's feces then carries more toxoplasmids, to be eaten by more rats, to infect more cats, and thus continues the ancient cycle: an interspecies rivalry that is so old and familiar that it contaminates not only the cat but also every cartoon we have ever seen. It is an almost literal cat-and-mouse game, but toxoplasmosis is in charge.

That's very interesting, you say. But what does that have to do

---

386. Such as intercourse.
387. This is the source of the phrase "CATSHIT CRAZY."

SEPTEMBER 19, 2012
The people of Oxford, MS, dig up William Faulkner's corpse and make him their drunken corpse-king.

with MY THOUGHTS and MY OWN fondness for cat urine? Well, as it happens, scientists now suggest that a full third of the human population carries toxoplasmosis infection without even knowing it.

But, you protest, if that is so, why isn't a third of the population throwing itself recklessly into the path of cats, just like rats? Why isn't a third of the population keeping cats in their houses, and protecting and pampering and caring for those cats, even though a cat is a creature that does not care about humans and would kill you if it could?

Well. You just answered your own question.

In fact, there is new evidence to suggest that the toxoplasmid is also controlling OUR brains.

Studies show that the toxoplasmodically possessed human grows withdrawn from mainstream society. Infected men tend to be morose and introverted. The women tend to be more outgoing, goofy, and sexually adventurous.

AND THEY ALL LOVE TO HAVE CATS AND CAT FECES AROUND.

Many have speculated that it is this MIND CONTROL that accounts for the classic stereotype of "THE CRAZY CAT LADY."

But anyone who has ever been to a major comic-book convention or seen someone play the ukulele on YouTube must also ask: DID TOXOPLASMOSIS CREATE THE NERD?

Something is making me say: YES.

WERE YOU AWARE OF IT? "MOUSE ERROR"

Scientists say that the Internet is changing the very structure of our brains, causing us to twitchily seek out new, novel information while discarding even the most recently acquired knowledge at a manic pace. I DON'T EVEN REMEMBER WHERE I READ THAT.

SEPTEMBER 20, 2012

The indie rock community from Chapel Hill, NC, are kidnapped by the NASCARians and forced to pull cars around the weed-choked track or die.

AN IMPORTANT CRYPTID UPDATE

Some summers ago, I had the pleasure of speaking before the current president of the United States at the Radio and Television Correspondents' Dinner.

If you do not know, the Radio and Television Correspondents' Dinner is the annual banquet thrown by and in honor of the Radio and Television Correspondents Association, a storied professional organization created to hold annual banquets.

To be clear, this was not the White House Correspondents' Dinner, which is a somewhat more prestigious dinner due to the presence of Zach Galifianakis and the fact that radio correspondents are not allowed. Not only are they not allowed to attend, the radio correspondents are typically brought onstage and bullied. Sometimes they are made to wear old-timey outfits. Sometimes they are forced to wear rubber Edward R. Murrow masks and then be punched in the teeth. This is the sort of thing that Zach Galifianakis finds funny.

And indeed, these two are but one of many formal dinners the president is expected to attend during Washington's social season (extending from cherry-blossom time to high murder season).

The dinner was held in the city's main convention center. It was a nice event. There were first a few awards that the television correspondents gave to one another for their achievements in corresponding by television. Then the radio correspondents were led to the stage, still wearing their velvet blindfolds to preserve their radio vision. The room gently applauded these strange and noble practitioners of an ancient craft. The radio correspondents did not smile, as they are incapable of joy.

And then the president entered. It was all the clichés that you

SEPTEMBER 21, 2012

In Northampton, MA, pamphlets begin to circulate that suggest that all of RAGNAROK is part of a government conspiracy to make you afraid and rob you of your civil rights. These pamphlets are printed on human skin.

know from the movies: "Hail to the Chief," followed by the pledge of allegiance to what the president strangely referred to as "our nation's current flag." Yet it was nonetheless electrifying to see the president just a few feet away, even, it seemed, for the old Washington hands who had seen this many times before. To my left, Wolf Blitzer was brushing tears from his beard.

This was back in June of 2009, before the depth of the recession hit, and the normally damp, soiled-carpet-like air of Washington, DC, was still charged with a sense of promise. It was back when the president was still smiling and happy and popular, before patriotic Americans reminded the world that he was shiftless, untrustworthy, and at least 50 percent black.

It seemed as if anything was possible. And that is certainly how I felt the night BEFORE the dinner, sitting in my hotel room, watching the cable television program *River Monsters.*

For that is when I came face-to-face with the DICKFISH.

The dickfish, if you are not familiar with it, is a tiny fish that lives in the Amazon River. It is so tiny that, if you are a human male who is urinating into the river, the dickfish will swim up your stream of urine and then live in your penis.

No one knows why it is called the dickfish.

I first heard of this fish during my college years when my friends and I would regularly stay up and drink whiskey and debate politics, art, and evil fish. Many considered the dickfish to be purely a myth: one of many urination-related urban legends designed to scare young men away from peeing all over the place.

Indeed, this was my point of view, and many a night I would fight with the dickfish supporters, arguing that while creation is varied and

SEPTEMBER 22, 2012
In the Fortified Former Oak Park, IL, rock music is NOT BANNED. In fact, the ONLY music that people are allowed to play is "Killroy Was Here" by Styx. This is because the repressive leader of the Fortified Former Oak Park, IL, is Dennis DeYoung wearing a dumb robot mask.

magnificent, I found it impossible to imagine that a life cycle that is dependent upon swimming up a stream of urine could support a large and active dickfish population.

I told them that the whole story was just a tiny, parasitic fish tale, and no more.

Indeed, by the night before the Radio and Television Correspondents' Dinner, I had long forgotten about it. I was just a normal man, about to speak to the president, unwinding with a little *River Monsters*. And then suddenly: DICKFISH.

If you have not seen *River Monsters*, it is a reality program in which an evil Australian man with horrible big veins in his head goes to various rivers to investigate stories of weird and usually giant fish.

But not this time. This time he was talking about a SMALL fish. And this time, he was saying it was TRUE. Not only was the dickfish real, the Australian also claimed that he had found the original victim of the dickfish, the patient zero who started the whole story—a Brazilian man and outdoor-urination enthusiast who, many years before, had felt a sharp pain in his penis while urinating, and only later discovered via penis scan that his member was now the host of a growing parasite.

The man had the fish removed in a method too gruesome to describe here, unless you like stories about medical instruments being inserted into penises. And then the man promptly went on with his life . . . that is, until this evil Australian TV host came around and tracked down the actual specimen that had been inside the man's body ten years earlier. It was being stored in a Brazilian warehouse. I guess it was a science warehouse, for not only did they preserve the dickfish in a jar, they kept detailed records of it.

SEPTEMBER 23, 2012
The Flesh Flies get so fat on flesh that they cannot fly anymore. Now they are called the Flesh Crawls. Watch your ankles!

I cannot really describe to you the look that crossed this poor man's face as the Australian forced the dickfish jar into his hands. But I will say the words "horror," "triumph," "strange affection," "confusion caused by an Australian accent," and just for the hell of it, I will say again:

DICKFISH!

I was stunned. Upon seeing this program, I considered abandoning my prepared remarks and using my time at the Radio and Television Correspondents' Dinner to discuss this important discovery. But then I realized that the president had likely already been briefed on the dickfish, so I returned to my prepared text.

I went to sleep, and the next day I spoke at the dinner, and it went fine. You can watch it on YouTube if you like.

After I spoke, the president greeted me briefly at the podium and shared a few words with me. There is something strange about meeting presidents. I have met a number of celebrities, but that can mean almost anyone these days. But meeting a president is like meeting a BIGFOOT. In part because there are only a few of them in the whole world, and in part because the president was emitting weird, guttural singsong noises at me that I could not understand.

To be fair, this may be because my brain had ceased functioning. The strangeness of the moment had overwhelmed it. I could barely absorb all the sights and sounds that were swimming into me like foreign objects. I felt as speechless as the man confronting the dickfish after so many years. I will never remember what he said to me, nor what I said to him.

And based on my similar experience with Al Gore, I could only come to one conclusion: Presidents and vice presidents cannot be heard or understood or remembered due to some strange technology in their suits.

SEPTEMBER 24, 2012
In New Mexico, the last remaining radio dish at the Very Large Array is used to convey a message to the stars, begging the hoboes to return.

WHAT IS THE PERFECT CRIME?

Simple.

A woman dislikes her husband and decides to kill him.

She attacks him with a frozen leg of lamb, because a leg of lamb is naturally shaped like a club,[388] and there is no swifter or more discreet way to murder a person than by clubbing him to death.

The woman murders her husband in the morning as he reads his paper at the kitchen table. It takes about seventy blows before his skull finally caves in. At some point in this process, he breaks his nose on the table and now the table is covered with blood. There is also a lot of screaming, and near the end, he defecates himself. The perfect crime.

Now the wife has only one problem: what to do with the murder weapon? Do not worry: She has an idea.

That evening, the police come calling: a detective and a police officer. Depending on how the story is told, they either heard the murder and were very slow to respond, or else they were just doing a regular door-to-door dinnertime murder check. (The door-to-door dinnertime murder check actually used to be very common in small towns well into the '60s. People in town looked out for each other then, and we were more innocent.)

In any case, the woman invites them in. The house smells delicious. The woman explains that she has been cooking all day, and as you know, all police officers ever want to do is eat, eat, eat, and so they are quick to accept her invitation to dinner.

She serves them cocktails. They really shouldn't indulge, but the

---

388. (Unlike the misleadingly named "club steak," which has no suitable handle unless you carve one into it. And at that point, you may as well carve the frozen club steak into an actual stake and use it to kill a meat vampire.)

SEPTEMBER 25, 2012
No answer from the hoboes.

woman is very insistent and very kind, and she seems so not guilty of murder.

The detective explains that the police are concerned. Her husband is missing. Something may have happened to him. And now that they see the table covered in dried blood, the detective is even more concerned.

"Ma'am," says the detective. "I must tell you that I am beginning to suspect that your husband may have been murdered. Additionally, given the statistics on spousal violence, and the trail of blood and viscera leading from the table to the basement, I am afraid you are the prime suspect."

The woman nods solemnly. "Of course, I understand. And given that I disliked my husband very much, I confess I very well may have killed him."

"I sensed that," says the detective. "After twenty years investigating murders, you begin to get a feel for people."

However, says the detective: There is one thing he cannot figure out. Where is the murder weapon? It does not seem to be in the kitchen ANYWHERE.

"Without the murder weapon," says the detective, "it is impossible to prosecute a person for murder. I'm not sure if you knew that."

"I did know that," says the woman, now smiling and rising from the table. "From television. And now it is time for dinner."

She walks over to the oven, and what does she take out of it? You are correct: a beautiful roasted leg of lamb! And guess what she does with it! SHE SERVES IT TO THE POLICE. And guess what the police do! THEY EAT IT, UNSUSPICIOUSLY, using curious cutlery made from the bleached arm and rib bones of THE WOMAN'S OWN HUSBAND.

SEPTEMBER 26, 2012
When asked, the Internet is unable to provide a high-resolution photograph of Baxter the Clown from the 1980s TV show *The Great Space Coaster.* It is unable even to provide a PORN VARIANT of same. The Internet self-destructs in shame.

The woman is never caught, and she lives a happy life selling high-end kitchen supplies in a little store on the Upper West Side until Williams-Sonoma moves in, and then she is pushed in front of a train by a random madman.

This may seem like a unique story of criminal genius, but actually, this sort of thing is very common in the history of perfect crimes. For example . . .

- A California man froze a whole beef tenderloin and carved it into a samurai sword. He brought it to the consulting firm where he worked and killed nine people. Then he thawed it, cut it into filet mignons, and mailed them to his family members for Christmas—USING STAMPS FROM THAT VERY OFFICE. He was never prosecuted for murder. But he did end up going to prison for mailing meat around with just stamps on it: a federal crime.

- A North Dakota woman made a gun out of ice that could actually fire a single ice bullet. She shot at her neighbor, who she believed deserved to die. The bullet melted quickly in his warm aorta, but by that time the damage was done. He bled to death on his own lawn, clutching at his throat, wondering why. The murderess watched all of this, and then walked back across the street to her house, dropped the gun in a punch bowl— AND TOLD THE POLICE SHE WAS SIMPLY HAV- ING A GUN-THEMED PARTY. (She also had all kinds of gun-themed decorations and even a gun piñata. She seriously had been planning this FOR YEARS.)

- An Ontario man who owned an Italian restaurant in Ottawa killed a business rival with SPAGHETTI. He took a single strand of dried spaghetti and gently stuck it down his rival's throat when his rival wasn't looking. (DO NOT try this with angel-hair pasta: It's too thin.) Then he shoved his rival's head into a huge pot of boiling water, which caused him to die. The police ruled it an accident, saying the man had clearly choked to death on a single strand of spaghetti—spaghetti that WAS COOKED.

- A Wisconsin teenager stole some cheese from a local dairy—eleven ounces, the precise weight of the human heart. Then he put it in the town bully's body in place of his heart (NOW do you see why he stole only eleven ounces of cheese?). Six weeks later, the town bully died. But by then, the teenager had left town and had become an Internet millionaire. HOW CAN YOU SAY HE IS A MONSTER WHEN HE INVENTED SO MANY GREAT WEBSITES THAT YOU USE EVERY DAY?

- A South Carolina man hired a butter carver to make a butter sculpture of his own nude body. After a dozen sittings, it was perfect. Wait a minute, you say: How can you use a butter sculpture to attack someone? You are jumping to conclusions. He used the butter sculpture to FAKE HIS OWN MURDER, throwing it off a cliff and sending a picture of it to the police, so that he could leave town, change his name, and never pay taxes again. (He did end up murdering the butter sculptor, in order to protect his secret, but that was with an ordinary metal machete.)

SEPTEMBER 28, 2012

In Bloomington, MN, the Mall of America abandons democracy. Perched at the edge of the Great Trench left by the Nug-Shohab meteor, it fortifies itself as an independent city-state OSTENSIBLY run by the Council of Four Anchor Stores. But in practice, all power lies in the whim and the fists of Lord Nordstrom, the Over-Manager (birth name: Dick McDonald).

- An Alaskan man made a crossbow out of frozen stalks of celery, because he was a vegetarian. He never did anything with it, because he was tired all the time.

- One time at the Ben & Jerry's headquarters in Vermont, a visitor who was touring the factory went crazy and threw a pint of Chunky Monkey at the tour guide, hitting her in the eye. No one died, I'm glad to say (except the man, who had diabetes, but that was ten years later). But sometimes the PERFECT murder is the one in which NOBODY DIES.

TABLE 49: GENTLEMEN CRIMINALS	
CRIMINAL	**CALLING CARD**
Luc Gerard, aka "The Phoenix," the gentleman arsonist	Leaves a hand-drawn picture of a phoenix in the ashes of your home, and very occasionally, a live chick.
Monsieur Omega, aka "The Half-Albino," the gentleman windshield smasher	A single white velvet glove, left on the dashboard.
Janus Orphee, aka "The Twitchy Dodger," the gentleman crystal meth salesman	He always leaves behind one of his remaining teeth.
Alphonse DeWinter, aka "Candyman," the gentleman child pornographer	Child pornography.
Thomas X. Scharpling, Esq., aka "The Stranger," the gentleman home invader	The velvet burlap sack he uses as a mask while terrorizing families at home, nailed to the broken door.

CONTINUED

SEPTEMBER 29, 2012

The 44 Animatronic Presidents and DOGSTORM steer clear of the moaning, Headless Body of Nug-Shohab as they pass each other outside of Chattanooga.

TABLE 49: *continued*	
Martin Fresne, aka "The Kissing Puncher," the gentleman domestic abuser	No visible bruises, so as not to disrupt the beauty of the ONE HE LOVES SO MUCH IT JUST MAKES HIM SO CRAZY.
Bertrand St. Gusta, aka "The Greek," the gentleman white slaver	A shipping container full of half-starved women from the Ukraine.
Vincent Deneuve, aka "Mr. Watchful," the gentleman stalker	A dead butterfly in an envelope, delivered to your door every day. Then a lamb's head in a child's toy drum.
Leslie Merriwell, aka "Mr. Merriwell," the gentleman false butler	(Please see BELOW, re: WERE YOU AWARE OF IT?)

WERE YOU AWARE OF IT?
"TALES OF THE GENTLEMAN FALSE BUTLER"

Merriwell was a Philadelphian who learned to speak with a British accent from watching public television. His MO was to show up at the doorstep of affluent homes and claim to be a butler. When told no butler was needed, he would claim that a friend had anonymously paid for his butlering services for a year as a birthday surprise (everyone has a birthday, so who would not believe this story?). Then he would just start dusting. Over time, he would gain the family's trust. He would help the children with their homework and tell stories about his very poor life as a child in England (though best accounts suggest he was born in Trenton, New Jersey). He would help the parents see why the children were sniffing compressed air all the time and forming sex clubs. He would help the family understand that the comfort of money is not the same as the comfort of a loving family. Very soon he would become more than just a butler but a member of the family. And then he would tie them up in their sleep, steal their jewelry, credit cards, and underwear, and leave a single red rose on the pillow of the wife as well as some inappropriate poems.

SEPTEMBER 30, 2012

The final cover story of *Las Vegas Weekly*: "Buffet Shrimp Now More Valuable Than Lap Dances!"

WHAT HAPPENS WHEN WE DIE?

Death is arguably the loneliest experience we endure. So it is no surprise that, throughout time, humanity has sought to personify death and to seek in death's company the comfort that only a hissing skeleton with a giant scythe can provide.

But the Grim Reaper is but one of the FACES OF DEATH. Across cultures and times, the concept has taken many different forms. Perhaps we are ushered to a better place by Charon, or the Valkyries, or the quirky, cheerful Goth Girl? Perhaps we are judged by Anubis or Judge Death. Or perhaps we are chased from life by the Black Racer, the Shadow Jogger, or the Pitiful Specter of In-Line Skating?

This is the only time I will say to you these words: I do not know.

Surely you do not need me to provide comforting fake trivia regarding what will happen when you die. There are plenty of people doing that. If anything, I think it's my responsibility to provide a *dis*-comforting fiction, as it will encourage you not to ponder, relish, or seek death, but to appreciate life during the thirteen or so months that remain.

HOW DO YOU MAKE YOUR FAMOUS
OLD-FASHIONED SEVENTEEN-SPLEEN CHILI?

This one I *can* answer.

In my previous book, I promised you this recipe.[387] At the time, the attorneys at my publishing house suggested that it would be

---

387. Please see page 638 of *More Information Than You Require*, under the heading "Regarding Page 413 . . ."

OCTOBER 1, 2012

The last issue of *Entertainment Weekly* is published, mysteriously. The cover features *Star Trek: The Next Generation*. And Stephen King's last column, consisting of a single word: "NEVERMORE."

wrong to provide a recipe for a dish that I had never made and would certainly never eat. What if someone were to get SPLEEN POISONING?

At the time, I relented and did not print it.

HOWEVER, I now think back on that decision and regret it. After all, in that same book, I recommended that people attempt to cure their cancer with POULTICE,[390] and the lawyers did not speak up then.

AS WELL, with the COMING CIVILIZATIONAL ENDTASTROPHE, there will be no more law. You'll just have to sue me with BULLETS—if you can penetrate the defenses of my Survival Brownstone.

(Hint: the MOAT is a HOLOGRAM hiding a DOUBLE MOAT.)

The coming year is not a time for the craven and ambivalent, but a time for the bold and the spleen-hungry, so please enjoy this recipe.

It's delicious![391]

1. TAKE 17 pigs' spleens and trim them of all intestinal and caul fat, and pull out the long, disgusting veins and cut them up.

2. IN AN INCREDIBLY LARGE DUTCH OVEN, sweat 20 large onions and 12 cloves of garlic, chopped up, in olive oil.

3. ADD one 32-ounce bottle of commercial chili powder and ½ pound of salt. Let this cook for a while and then . . .

---

390. Please see page 364 of *More Information Than You Require,* and may I please repeat: DO NOT FOLLOW MY ADVICE ON HOW TO CURE CANCER. Not only am I not a cancer expert, I barely know what a poultice is. I think it is a kind of MEDICINAL CHEST SOUP. Am I right?

391. This is probably not true.

OCTOBER 2, 2012

In Denver, CO, things are looking up. People are still scared, and still scarred, but at least they are helping one another a little bit. And every now and then, the sun shines, and you get the sense that maybe we can rebuild.

---

4. ADD the spleens and brown them all over.

5. DEGLAZE the pot with OWL BROTH,[392] scraping up all the delicious burnt spleen bits.

6. ADD 1 bottle of ketchup (DE-BOTTLED), and then enough gallons of owl broth to cover the whole mixture.

7. NO BEANS. Beans in spleen chili is the abomination of the tenderfoot and the Yankee.

8. THEN COOK until tender. You may serve it over rice or . . .

9. IF YOU ARE IN CINCINNATI, you can make a traditional 9-WAY FAMOUS OLD-FASHIONED 17-SPLEEN CHILI, which is chili served over spaghetti and topped with cheese, onions, beans, lamb kidneys, one whole calf's liver, tripe hash, and a sprinkling of LEGO figurine heads. JUST PICK OUT THE BEANS BEFORE SERVING!

10. BUT HOWEVER YOU CHOOSE TO SERVE IT, JUST MAKE SURE TO NEVER, EVER MAKE OR CONSUME IT.

BUT REMEMBER: If you DO get spleen poisoning, you can treat it with ANY KIND OF POULTICE.

---

392. Use your favorite recipe.

OCTOBER 3, 2012

Deep beneath Denver International Airport, scientists succeed in using the EVEN LARGER HADRON COLLIDER to create a portal to another dimension. But what they do not know is: WHAT THEY WILL FIND ON THE OTHER SIDE.

OCTOBER 4, 2012
The Blood-Red Sea of Newest Port, RI, opens its golden eyes, wide-awake for the first time in ten thousand years.

THE END

OCTOBER 5, 2012

In a beautiful office with white carpeting and tasteful, midcentury modern furniture, a shadowy figure known only as The DERANGED BILLIONAIRE receives word over the intercom that the dimensional portal is ready to be opened. The DERANGED BILLIONAIRE thanks his team of scientists and asks them to open the portal.

As his team of scientists watches, the world shimmers and twists. A hole opens in reality, and through it they see another world: of blue fields and pea-green skies, and beyond the bluff, a blood-red sea with golden eyes.

They do not have time to really appreciate it.

They do not even have time to react before it begins.

For, as soon as the door is open, the Blood-Red Sea of Newest Port, RI, sensing our world and desiring it, turns its whole universe sideways and begins to pour itself through the portal.

THE BLOOD WAVE HAS BEGUN.

THE END

I AM WRITING TO YOU NOW from one of my many test runs aboard my personal SEVEN-TON, ARMORED "LAND-TYRANT" SUPERCAR.

I will need this vehicle to shuttle back and forth between my FORTIFIED MOUNTAIN RETREAT and my PARK SLOPE SURVIVAL BROWNSTONE once RAGNAROK comes and the road is controlled by murderous highwaymen and mutated highway-mutants.

For this reason, my supercar carries many onboard defensive weapons, including Sidewinder missiles, pain rays, Taser launchers, and immobili-foam squirters.

Naturally, all of this ordnance, plus the nineteen-inch-thick titanium hull, makes my SUPER-CAR rather heavy and slow. I know that a ten-hour drive fighting my way through a ruined New England may seem like a terrible commute. But what can I say? I love both the lawless, abandoned city AND the blighted, ash-choked coun-

FIGURE 147:
My Supercar and my supercar pilot, Jeff

OCTOBER 6, 2012
THE BLOOD WAVE pours down from Colorado, flooding the western and central states.

try, and my enormous wealth allows me the luxury of not having to choose between them.

If you have been wisely ignoring the MAIN TEXT of this book and instead reading only THE MARGINAL ENTRIES KNOWN AS "TODAY IN RAGNAROK," then you know that the end is near.

Specifically, there are 77 pages left.

And as it approaches, you would not be human if you did not wonder: Am I going to survive the COMING GLOBAL SUPERPOCA-LYPSE and TOTAL COLLAPSE OF CIVILIZATION, also known as RAGNAROK?

Probably the answer is no.

I don't mean to depress you, but the times that are in store will be trying. There is no point ignoring hard facts, and especially not HARD FAKE FACTS.

WHY YOU PROBABLY WILL NOT
SURVIVE RAGNAROK

Please answer these five simple questions. AND TRY BEING HONEST, for once.

1. Is your home more than 1,000 feet above sea level?
2. Alternately, is your home a houseboat that can float on a giant tsunami of blood?
3. Do you live in the METEOR IMPACT ZONE? (Minneapolis)
4. Do you live in the crawl path of the giant headless body of NUG-SHOHAB?
5. Do you have a dog?

OCTOBER 7, 2012
THE BLOOD WAVE, Day 2. Nebraska, Kansas, and both Dakotas are wiped out.

If you answered NO to some of these questions and YES to others, and you also have not received a GOLDEN TICKET to board one of Oprah Winfrey's space arks, then I am afraid that you are probably not going to survive even the first devastations of RAGNAROK.

At least you will have time to finish reading this book. Enjoy!

HOW I AM STOCKING MY SURVIVAL BROWNSTONE; OR, WHAT TO DO IF YOU DO NOT DIE IMMEDIATELY

OK, let's say hypothetically that there is some small chance that you will survive the SOLAR STORMS and the OMEGA PULSE and the BLOOD WAVE and outlive everyone you have ever loved.

Before you get too excited, consider: How will you live in the world that follows?

Will you grow your own food?

I'm sorry: The ground is poisoned for 1,000 years, AND THE ONLY RAIN THAT FALLS IS OLD PENNIES.

Will you scavenge canned goods from supermarkets?

I'm sorry: You do not have a can opener. BECAUSE ALL CAN OPENERS CEASED TO FUNCTION THANKS TO THE Y2K BUG.

Will you finally have some peace and quiet to read your favorite books?

I'm sorry: You just stepped on your own glasses, and the glass has cut your foot. SO NOT ONLY ARE YOU A PATHETIC BOOK-NERD, NOW YOU HAVE SEPSIS, STUPID.

The reality is that, evolutionarily speaking, very few of us have what it takes to survive, and even fewer have HUGE PILES OF WHAT IT TAKES TO SURVIVE stored in a secure underground location.

Take me, for example. While you might imagine that, with my enormous brainpower, low center of gravity, skills with the deadly sai, and incredible wealth, I would have no difficulties surviving in the new, lawless landscape that awaits us. And you would be correct, except for the fact that I am ASTHMATIC.

I am essentially an ALBUTEROL CYBORG, and once civilization has withdrawn its support of my addiction, the likelihood that I will perish painfully, violently, gasping for air—and that my children will go with me, and I will be unable to protect them—is overwhelming.

And so I am stockpiling inhalers in anticipation of the end. And I recommend you do so as well, for what if I come over to your bunker to visit?

Here are some other things you may want to have on hand to stock your bunker and/or silo and/or radiation zeppelin and/or thunderdome.

TABLE 50: CHECKLIST FOR SURVIVAL
☐ **100 COPIES OF MY PREVIOUS TWO BOOKS**
MANDATORY. Will be useful for reeducating the world populace and for insulation.
☐ **ONE COPY OF _THE POSTMAN_**
Book or movie, it doesn't matter.
CONTINUED

TABLE 50: *continued*

☐ **3 PAIR HODGMAN BRAND RUBBER WADERS**

NOT A PAID ENDORSEMENT. They are simply the best. Once you have these, you will not need pants anymore.

☐ **5 CASES SUPERSTAR FINE-GROOMED DAYTIME PAJAMA MAN ADULT INCONTINENCE JUMPSUITS**

A PAID ENDORSEMENT for a line of really excellent Japanese adult diapers I am doing some work with.

☐ **URINE AND MAYONNAISE**

Collect as much of these versatile products as you can! THEY HAVE THOUSANDS OF USES![393]

☐ **TWO Y2K-PROOF CAN OPENERS**

Swing-A-Way brand is the only one that was not infected.

☐ **300 CANS OF CANNED ANTS**

I know it sounds gross, but ants are a tremendous source of protein. And unlike the uncanned varieties, the canned ants will not have grown to the size of dogs and be trying to kill you.

☐ **250 GALLONS OF WATER PER PERSON, PLUS 1,000 EFFERVESCENT CAFFEINE TABLETS, PLUS 2,500 POUNDS RAW TAURINE PASTE**

For making your own energy drinks.

☐ **300 POUNDS OF ARBORIO RICE**

After the WORLD-WIDE MEGA-FAIL, risotto is going to become very trendy again. Also: get ready to break out your old bread machines and fondue pots!

☐ **ALL YOUR OLD BREAD MACHINES AND FONDUE POTS**

As instructed.

☐ **CANS AND CANS OF PIE FILLING**

(Preferred over cans of frosting.)

CONTINUED

---

393. Please see page 904, under the heading "The Many Uses of URINE and MAYONNAISE."

OCTOBER 10, 2012
THE BLOOD WAVE, Day 5

TABLE 50: continued

☐ **1,000 POUNDS OF HIGH-QUALITY POWDERED FOOD**

In case you ever get tired of ant risotto.

☐ **THE STANDARD PROTECTION PACKAGE[394]**

☐ **5 SHINY MYLAR CAT SUITS**

One for each day of the New Standard Week. These repel water, retain body heat, and they look very good. Make sure you have the kind that fully covers your head. Then everyone will want to procreate with you.

☐ **HUNDREDS OF PAIRS OF CROCS**

Use these for making padded flotation armor. DO NOT WEAR AS SHOES. As all shoes will eventually wear out, you should start developing thick calluses on your feet now. TOPS *AND* BOTTOMS, PLEASE! Use sandpaper.

☐ **SMOKING JACKETS AND ASCOTS**

To preserve a sense of civility in a world gone mad, and for accenting the Mylar cat suits. A dozen of each.

☐ **COMPANIONS**

If you can, convince at least one or two friends to start living in your bunker now, so that when the worst comes, you know you will have some company and someone to repopulate the species with via joyless copulation.

But to be clear, I am talking about platonic friends *only*. DO NOT STOCKPILE YOUR LOVERS.

Trust me: That kind of relationship never works.

☐ **MANNEQUINS**

If you cannot convince your friends to live in your bunker, put in some mannequins you can talk to, or at least a bust of Julius Caesar, so that you can play chess with it like a freak.

☐ **NONHUMAN FRIENDS THAT YOU CAN EAT, AKA LIVESTOCK**

Most recommended: SPERM WHALES

---

394. Please see page 898, under the heading "The Standard Protection Package."

THE JOY OF SPERMS

I know that whale hunting is not popular these days. But whale FARMING is very different.

Keeping a pod of sperm whales in an old swimming pool in your backyard is not only kinder than slaughtering them in the wild, these amazing animals will also provide a sustainable source of USEFUL AND DISGUSTING THINGS.

Did you know that a sperm whale will give hundreds of gallons of thick, waxy WHALE MILK per day? THEY ARE MAMMALS, AREN'T THEY? And if that is not disgusting enough, did you know that whale milk is so fatty that it is nearly solid?

THINK OF THE AMAZING AND NUTRITIOUS WHALE CHEESES AND WHALE SHAKES YOU CAN ENJOY WHILE WATCHING THE FLAMES OF THE FINAL CITIES AS THEY BURN!

Additionally, did you know that a sperm whale both vomits and defecates AMBERGRIS, a fecal-smelling substance that can be burned as an incense or used as a fixative in making perfumes?

THINK OF ALL THE ROMANTIC NIGHTS YOU CAN ENJOY, BURNING AND SMELLING AND WEARING WHALE EXCRETIONS!

On top of all of this, sperm whales are gentle companions, a natural check upon squid attacks, and they LOOK LIKE WHALES, with great big heads and rec-

FIGURE 148: *A whale*

ognizable blowholes and normal mouths with actual teeth—just like a cartoon of a whale.

This is good, because you won't get them confused with an acne-encrusted mutant that has an upside-down mouth with a weird giant pocket comb shoved into it, which is what most whales look like.

FIGURE 149:
Really?

And finally, when you are done harvesting milk and ambergris from your whales, you can murder them and

- eat their flesh!
- process their blubber into oil!
- scrimshaw their bones into nautical art for your survival compound gift shop! And . . .
- drill a huge hole in their heads and shovel out the valuable, waxlike spermaceti, which you can make into candles that you can use for light and burn in memory of this helpful, intelligent beast.

So you see, whale farming is COMPLETELY HUMANE. At least, compared to pig farming.

If you are wondering how to get a sperm whale, they are easily available by mail order.

Please see the order form at the end of this book.

TABLE 51: OTHER ANIMALS YOU CAN ORDER THROUGH THE MAIL WHILE THE MAIL STILL EXISTS

There are of course many other animals you can raise on your property or in the basement of your Park Slope Survival Brownstone.

THE PIG	**PROVIDES:** Meat, Grunting, Truffle Location Services

Pigs are like the sperm whale, in that very little of the animal goes to waste. And they are like humans, in that they will eat anything and, if left alone, they will wear clothes and tyrannize all other animals.

But before you judge, bear in mind: Their savagery is due to their intelligence. They often say they are smarter than dogs, which I think proves it, because I don't hear the dogs saying anything.

Like many animals, they are cute when they are young. When they grow to be two hundred pounds, murder them and eat them.

THE SHEEP	**PROVIDES:** Meat, Fleece, Lanolin, Soporific Numerology

These are marvelous animals, as they are docile and easy to murder. The problem is that they are very greasy. They are covered in a substance called lanolin, which is waterproof. This is a good substance to rub on your body if you are going out in the rain or going below ground to hunt for sewer meat.

THE GOAT	**PROVIDES:** Milk, Meat, Violent Head Butts, Unfathomable Evil Stares with Supremely Weird Eyes

Before murdering a goat, be sure to ask permission of Satan, whose creatures these are. It is perhaps easier just to milk them, but be warned: If you accidentally make chèvre, or goat's-milk cheese, BURY IT RIGHT AWAY, or else you will attract chefs from the 1980s, who are pests.

THE ASIAN PALM CIVET	**PROVIDES:** Kopi Luwak

These small arboreal mammals poop the finest coffee in the world. What more do you need to know? Oh, that's right. I forgot: OIL FROM THEIR MEAT MAY BE USED TO CURE SCABIES. I would suggest you buy HUNDREDS of these.

CONTINUED

TABLE 51: *continued*	
THE CHICKEN	**PROVIDES:** Meat, Eggs, Noises, Smells

These animals are known for their orderly pecking. When you put any of them together, they will instantly attack, bully, and attempt to cannibalize one another with their beaks until a clear chain of dominance is established. The TOP CHICKEN will get the food first and the best nest, and the BOTTOM CHICKEN will limp around with huge bloody bald spots and will depress all who see it. None of them ever seems to realize that they are ALL chickens and they will all be soon murdered.[395]

These animals are fun to have around because they remind you what life is like.

An additional bonus: If you for any reason are trying to quit eating chickens for the rest of your life, the best way to do this is to raise chickens.

THE COCK	**PROVIDES:** Sperms, Fights, Wattles

This animal is very closely related to the chicken, except that it is brightly colored and even more of a jerk. If for some reason you want more chickens, you need to have one of these creatures. This is because they have an intricate, proven system for getting chickens to mate with them, including techniques such as

- "Displaying High Value": The cock displays its glorious plumage and drops pointed references to its enormous bank account and famous friends.
- "Negging": The cock gently insults a hen in order to so severely depress her self-worth that she will be deceived into copulating with him.
- "Wearing Cologne": The cock wears cologne.
- "Lying."
- "Offering Grubs and Worms": Chicks dig that shit.

FIGURE 150:
Two huge cocks discussing the art of picking up chicks

CONTINUED

---

395. Except, maybe, for the BOTTOM CHICKEN, which will seem almost too gross to eat or even touch, and so it paradoxically will outlive the other chickens, allowed to wander off by itself to die of old age and loneliness.

WERE YOU AWARE OF IT? "THE TRUTH ABOUT THE COCKATRICE"

In medieval times, it was believed that if a rooster accidentally seduced a male toad and then laid an egg, it would hatch a COCKATRICE: a two-legged dragon with the head of a rooster.

This is only half true. Obviously, a rooster and a male toad cannot produce offspring.[396]

But if a rooster mates with a *female* toad, it will produce a COCKHEADED-NO-DRAGON-BABY-TOAD, which I presume is the source of the legend.

Handle these creatures with care, however. If you look into their eyes, you will die instantly. And if you handle them with bare skin, you will get GENITAL WARTS.

BUT IF YOU INVEST IN A GOOD COCKATRICE HOOD AND WART-PROTECTIVE GAUNTLETS, YOU CAN KEEP THEM AROUND TO THROW OVER THE WALLS OF YOUR COMPOUND AT YOUR ENEMIES!

TABLE 51: *continued*	
BEE	**PROVIDES:** Honey, Pollination, Mortal Death to a Certain Percentage of Your Enemies

Not only is honey a delicious ingredient in MOCK TWIZZLERS,[397] it can be fermented into mead and mead vinegar, and can be spread on the face to make a BEARD OF FLIES, which is a perfect disguise.
   Also, you can watch their little POLLEN-LOCATION DANCING with a magnifying glass for an evening's entertainment.

RABBIT	**PROVIDES:** Meat, Droppings, Breeding Metaphors

Rabbits will provide you with more high-quality protein per pound of feed than any other animal. They can also tell the future, and will advise you if your field is about to be filled with blood. For more, see page 211 of *The Areas of My Expertise* under the heading "How to Raise Rabbits for Food and Fur: The Utopian Method."

---

396. However, they will often form loving, long-term partnerships and open cafés in your small town that, because of prejudice, nobody goes to.

397. Please see page 900 under the heading "How to Make Many Essential Household Items Yourself So That You Need Not Brave the Walmart Clans."

PLEASE NOTE THAT DOGS ARE NOT RECOMMENDED

For reasons explained below. If you want a truly ferocious guard animal, go with ARMORED GEESE instead.

WHAT TO KEEP IN YOUR BARTER PILE

Everyone is telling you to hoard gold in anticipation of the collapse of the dollar. And this is reasonably good advice, as gold is very shiny. But that will mean nothing to those who are made blind by SOLAR FLARE FIVE and then rendered albino by the terrible gaze of Rugon-Sol, the Albino-Maker. These people will only want sunscreen. And they will pay good BEEF JERKY DOLLARS TO GET THEM.

Herewith, a simple conversion guide to the main post-RAGNAROK currencies.

1 BEEF JERKY DOLLAR will buy . . .

- 5 ounces of gold
- $\frac{1}{10}$ gallon of gasoline
- .000341 Albinotown Sunscreen Credits
- .232 Pieces of Hanukkah gelt
- 2.653 sucks on the central albuterol hose
- .885 pumps from the vat at the condiment lockup
- $\frac{1}{8}$ barrel of Utz Cheese Balls[398]
- 7.3 hours of human intimacy

---

398. NOT A PAID PRODUCT PLACEMENT. I am simply mentioning this product in hopes that Utz will send me a bunch of free Cheese Balls because I love them so much, and I want to be very wealthy when RAGNAROK comes.

OCTOBER 17, 2012

THE BLOOD WAVE finally ends. The introduction of an entire planetary ocean of blood to our own oceans has caused notable changes to the coastlines. While inland portions of New England and northern New York State remains, New York City, already half sunk in the saliva of Ujjjjjj the Slaverer, is now completely overcome. Meanwhile, the rest of Unsubmerged North America is reduced to two great, spindly crescents, generally following the line of the Rocky and Appalachian Mountain ranges. The center of the U.S. is now a great lake of blood, with the island of Aspen, CO, on the western shore and the bloody marshes of Columbus, OH, on the eastern, and a pair of giant, staring, yellow eyes in the middle.

- .003 hours of access to the pneumatic Internet
- .000081 printouts of Internet pornography
- 2.923 cans Dick Van Patten's Hobo Chili for Dogs
- 1,000 New American Dollars
- 1 hour of mercenary protection WITH betrayal
- 10 minutes of mercenary protection WITHOUT betrayal
- 9 days of a yearly time-share in a pair of decent nunchucks
- .87 Euros

Remember: SALAD AND BREADSTICKS ARE STILL FREE.

THE STANDARD PROTECTION PACKAGE

While guns will play an important role in post–Super Collapse non-society, it is important to remember that ammunition is finite, and most of it will be completely controlled by Republicans within ten days of societal collapse, and they will shoot you if you try to get any of it.

So it is best to consider the subject of self-defense more holistically. In addition to guns, diversify your killing portfolio with classic weapons of the nerd: crossbows, bowcasters, chain saws, samurai swords, the deadly sai, javelins, poison rings, personal shoulder-mounted catapults, big heavy tree branches, and uncontrollable tears that disgust your opponent.

OCTOBER 18, 2012
The well-built old buildings of a carefully preserved historic downtown withstand the MEGA-QUAKES. A public commitment to alternative energy (biofuel, solar, geothermal, cold fusion powered by hemp, and humans pushing a giant wheel around) saves this city from the devastation of the OMEGA PULSE. The city's spirit of cooperation forged from a long history of mutual poverty and hearty deadbeatism inoculates the populace from panic and food riots. The Great Dike, built sustainably from recovered lumber in a modern updating of the Arts and Crafts style, keeps the city free from blood, and the well-made artisanal cocktails at the Heathman Hotel dull the psychic trauma of a world gone mad, all leaving PORTLAND, OREGON, as the only functioning city in the United States after the BLOOD WAVE. Naturally, the Portlanders are extremely smug about it. Their paradise lasts seven weeks before they are all murdered by refugees from Seattle.

I also advise you to invest in a Tesla Death Ray. While they are expensive, it is worth it, because they cause death, usually in the direction in which you are aiming it. Additionally, you can now buy versions that no longer require a massive electrostatic generator but instead are powered by a simple crank mechanism: Just three hundred turns provides enough charge for one and one-half rays of death.

FIGURE 151:
This nerd will kill you.

I also recommend that you follow my course of PHYSICAL AND MENTAL PERFECTION. Specifically, I recommend at least three weeks of training with my videocassette series *Hodg-Maga: The Graceful Dance of Maiming*, which outlines a revolutionary martial art of my own devising: a combination of aikido, capoeira, spank-a-dank, slapfight, and pub quiz.

REMEMBER: I can make you a perfect human, if you let me. But bullets ARE GOING TO FUCKING KILL YOU. Especially if they are fired from a gun.

OCTOBER 19, 2012

In the ruins of Barleykill, VA, the 44 Animatronic Presidents and DOGSTORM are waved down by a sixteen-year-old boy standing on top of a Piggly Wiggly. They send James K. Polk to question him.

The boy tells Polk that he is running free, just like them. His home got wiped out in the SPITSPILL, but he didn't mind. He hated his folks anyway, so he headed north. He spent some time up north, where he found a weird village in the woods. They had good food, but he didn't fit in. Too many rules.

"Maybe I should ride with you guys, huh?" the boy says. "I always liked you, James K. Polk."

James K. Polk tells him he's a robot, but the boy doesn't seem to mind. It's funny, he says. "In that village I came from, there was one kid—this little kid—who could set fire to any machine just with his mind. But I like robots!"

"Is that so?" asks James K. Polk.

"For serious," says the boy.

James K. Polk gets the human to draw a map to the village in the roof gravel before destroying him.

HOW TO MAKE MANY ESSENTIAL HOUSEHOLD ITEMS YOURSELF SO THAT YOU NEED NOT BRAVE THE WALMART CLANS

Just because there is no government, social services, or hospitals, and you are living in a burrowed-out bit of cold earth with your little pile of food and constantly fearing for your life, it does not mean you need to live like an animal.

Many of the comforts you remember from civilization can be easily replicated with just a little elbow grease (grease made from a human elbow) and also effort. But remember: "Self-sufficiency" should be your watchword, as most of the biggest stores will be controlled by strongmen and neo-savages within days.

As with all the recipes in this book, such as 17-Spleen Chili, please DO NOT make any of them until the justice system has collapsed.

SOAP

Simply mix water, refined sperm whale blubber, and potassium hydroxide, the latter of which you can easily get from the ash that is constantly falling from the sky. Heat the mixture until it is the consistency of melted cheese, then form into whale-shaped molds for fun.

OCTOBER 20, 2012
SOLAR STORM FIVE causes all humans to go blind for a single day. During this time, they get
into all kinds of scrapes and escapades, such as driving through bales of hay in their old-time
jalopies and walking blithely along the edges of skyscrapers onto pianos that are being hoisted
by cranes.

HINT: If you have run out of gas, wood, or Sterno, you can make
a little camp stove by lighting Brazil nuts on fire.

SHAMPOO

In the old days, people used to make shampoo out of a mixture of
rum, eggs, rosewater, and vinegar. If you want to make yourself
MORE delicious to the cannibal gangs, that's fine. But me, I'd just
use WHALE SOAP with some mint in it. You'll just have to live
with the terrible tangling and smell of rancid whale grease, but you
won't be eaten AS QUICKLY.

40-POUND BAG OF FROZEN CHICKEN NUGGETS

Murder one or two hundred of your chickens and defeather and evis-
cerate them in the standard manner. Do not bother to take off the
head or feet. Just put them in a chicken cannon and fire them through
some fine-mesh razor wire. Catch all the flying meat pulp on the
other side with some plastic sheeting, and discard the bones.[399]

Take all of the separated meat and grind it in a Foley Food Mill
until it is a paste. Add a lot of salt and chicken flavoring. Do not wash
the Foley Food Mill, and instead save it for your salmonella garden.

Before forming nuggets, make sure to spray the meat chicken mash
all over with an antibacterial agent, such as ammonia or URINE.[400]
Now, using a pastry bag, pipe the meat slurry into a greased nugget-

---

399. If you like, you can keep all the wishbones and make them into a scary necklace. Use it to
indicate who in your survivors' group has the right to TALK and MATE.

400. Once again, please see page 904 under the heading "The Many Uses of URINE and MAY-
ONNAISE." URINE for a surprise and will be AMAYONNAISED at all of the uses of these amazing
products! INCLUDING: AT LEAST TWO DESPICABLE PUNS!

OCTOBER 21, 2012
Boondock Saints 3 is released.

mold pan, and flash freeze with liquid nitrogen. Take the frozen nugget forms out of the mold, dust all over with breading and salt, and then deep-fry in SPERM WHALE OIL or PALM CIVET OIL.

You may eat them now, if you wish. Or flash-freeze again in a garbage bag for true BIG-BOX FLAVOR.

500 PACKS OF TWIZZLERS

Get 10 to 15 pairs of OXBLOOD DOC MARTENS BOOTS and cut them into strips. Dip them in honey and chew on them.

12 PACKS OF TOILET PAPER

Get 12 tree branches about the girth of a toilet-paper roll. Hollow them out with your branch borer. CAREFULLY tear apart all of your old books from college. Try to avoid uneven tearing: You want to create as many identical, even pages as possible. These will be your toilet-paper squares.

DO NOT SCOTCH-TAPE THE SQUARES TOGETHER. It will chafe. Instead, sew each square to the next square with the lightest silken thread until you have twelve long strips. If you do not know how to sew, LEARN, ALREADY! CIVILIZATION IS OVER and no one will do this stuff for you anymore. The time for luxuries like books and personal toilet-paper seamstresses is over.

If you want to bleach the long strips of former books to rob them of their horrible words, now is the time to do it. But many are opposed to bleach in our waste system, and eliminating it from just ONE OR TWO PRODUCTS in the home is going to solve that problem. So you can skip this step if you like, and proceed to soften the toilet paper by rubbing it with MAYONNAISE.[401]

401. Yup.

OCTOBER 22, 2012

The 44 Animatronic Presidents and DOGSTORM follow the land bridge between the SPITSPILL and the BLOOD-RED OCEAN north through Pennsylvania.

Then simply wind the strips tightly around the hollow wooden rolls. Stack them in three towers of four, wrap them securely with cling wrap, and store it in your mudroom.

You can also make PAPER TOWELS this way, but you will need longer branch-rolls and larger useless printed matter. Old newspapers are plentiful, and they do not streak when cleaning the windows. But I find it more satisfying to use pages from *The New Yorker*, for some reason.

MICROWAVE POPCORN

Like all things with computers inside of them, microwave ovens will be rendered useless by the OMEGA PULSE.[402]

So if you want to enjoy good, old-fashioned microwave popcorn, you're going to have to dip into your dried corn stockpile and then kidnap one of the descendants of Orville Redenbacher, about a third of whom still carry his MIND-POPPING gene.[403]

It's a lot of work to kidnap a man and keep him captive. But there is nothing like the old-timey feeling of sitting around the kitchen in anticipation, watching a Redenbacher use his brainwaves to POP CORN and make all the metal in the kitchen spark and flame.

Luckily, the Redenbacherites are fairly easy to spot due to their bow tie–shaped birthmarks.

FLAT-SCREEN TELEVISIONS

Most flat-screen TVs will have been swiftly looted, because they really do make the best shanties. But you can make one of your own by get-

---

402. Please see "Today in RAGNAROK," under the heading "August 4, 2012."
403. Please see page 730 in the table "Genetic Mutations of the Robber Barons."

OCTOBER 23, 2012

The Crystal Skulls begin to resonate. Every bottle of Crystal Head Vodka ever sold by Dan Aykroyd levitates at once, hypnotizing all around them[a]: college students, liquor store employees, club trash, and the author of this book. The message of the Crystal Head Vodka bottles: Take out your own skulls and put us in your head instead. Some of us resist better than others.

---

a. (Curiously, the original crystal skulls collected in the early twentieth century and kept in the collections of the British Museum, the Louvre, and the TED conference do not hypnotize anyone. They merely glow for about a minute and then give off some pitiful sparks.)

---

ting an old FLAT-SCREEN TV BOX. Give it an authentic heft by filling it up with cement. Then paint your favorite scene from *House Hunters International* or *America's Next Great Restaurant* on it and take some hallucinogenic drugs and have some PALM CIVET COFFEE.

You can even use your new TV as a COMPUTER. Just put an old keyboard in front of it, tape a printout of your favorite website on it, and remember everything you type.

THE MANY USES OF URINE AND MAYONNAISE

Both of these amazing products have many more uses than you realize. But I'm not going to get into another one of those fights about which one is better. I'VE BEEN TO THE HOSPITAL ENOUGH THIS YEAR.

I am only going to say that you cannot live without ONE of them. . . .

1. URINE

URINE can be easily made at home and has a variety of applications:

- When diluted, it is a nitrogen-rich SOIL FERTILIZER.
- Its high ammonia content makes it perfect for CLEANING YOUR FLOORS AND DINNER PLATES.
- Distill it to make GROSS DRINKING WATER.

OCTOBER 24, 2012
The crawling Headless Body of Nug-Shohab crushes Houston and continues south.

- Ferment it with honey to make PEE MEAD.
- Use it to MARK YOUR TERRITORY (but first distribute URINE-SNIFFING NOSE AIDS to your enemies in order to help them to get to know your scent).
- Use as a simple test to see if any of your bunker companions are STEALING ASPARAGUS FROM YOU.
- Put it all over your pants and clothes to make people AVOID YOU.
- Fill a spray bottle with it and JUST SPRAY PEOPLE WITH IT.
- Use it to evacuate TOXINS AND OTHER WASTE PRODUCTS FROM YOUR BODY!

2. MAYONNAISE

If you are going to make one substance out of EGGS, PALM CIVET OIL, and VINEGAR, let it be MAYONNAISE.

- Not only is it highly caloric, it can also be used as a HAIR CLEANSER, a SKIN CONDITIONER, and a LUBRICANT for small machines.
- It can be spread on plastic bags to make a mayonnaise slide for children.
- When left in the sun for a day, it becomes a very useful POISON.
- British people convince themselves that it can be a SALAD DRESSING.
- It can aid in removing GUM FROM HAIR, in case you are attacked with gum-tipped arrows.
- Its high vinegar content makes it a natural TOPICAL

OCTOBER 25, 2012
In what once was Oklahoma, deep beneath the BLOOD WAVE, a man sits in his bunker with a
bunch of ramen noodles and thinks he has escaped. UNTIL SOMETHING STARTS KNOCKING ON
THE HATCH.

ANESTHETIC, suitable for burns and rubbing on the stumps of AMPUTATED LIMBS.

- Dabbed on the face, it becomes a fine SHORT-TERM ALBINO MASK.
- THEN YOU CAN SNEAK INTO ALBINOTOWN AND SELL THEM MAYONNAISE WHILE PRETENDING THAT IT IS SUNBLOCK.
- And you can also use it to clean URINE STAINS OUT OF WOOD, so common in your HOME URINE WORKSHOP.

See, from my point of view, that last one makes it pretty clear. Advantage: MAYONNAISE.

But we'll just have to agree to disagree.

AN ELEGANT PROOF THAT OPRAH WINFREY WILL LIVE WHILE YOU DIE SCREAMING

One of the reasons that people refuse to make adequate preparations for RAGNAROK is that they are concerned that putting mayonnaise in their hair is going to make them look crazy.

Which brings me to Oprah Winfrey.

Many have asked: John Hodgman, how do you *know* that Oprah Winfrey is building a space ark for her and the other humans she thinks are important?

BECAUSE IT STANDS TO REASON. And specifically, it stands to THREE REASONS:

> **OCTOBER 26, 2012**
> The Seven-Headed Golden Retriever of Nantucket is now fully grown. The family that was caring for it had come to love it, even though it was larger than their house. They named it Land Rover, after their favorite Land Rover. They'd ride it around the island like it was a fluffy, affectionate, seven-headed mega-horse. They didn't see it coming when it slobbered their faces off.

1. Oprah Winfrey has a history, after all, of believing in fringe concepts and unproven theories, such as VACCINES CAUSING AUTISM and CABLE TELEVISION. So it is at least plausible, and maybe even PROBAUSIBLE, that she believes the world is ending. After all, why else would she bring her successful show to an end? And why is *O! The OPRAH Magazine* running features on knife fighting and how to safely hide gemstones in the crevices of your own body?

2. Even if Oprah Winfrey has doubts about RAGNAROK, she is certainly wealthy enough to build a space ark, just for whatever.

3. More important, like many DERANGED MILLIONAIRES, she has a STAFF—a group of devoted employees who not only tend to her most eccentric whims, but also can INSULATE HER FROM THE APPEARANCE OF INSANITY.

Given these incontrovertible facts, why would Oprah Winfrey *NOT* simply call her assistant (Susan) and say, very casually, into her talk tube:

"Susan, I don't want to think too much about this, and really it may be nothing, but it sort of feels like everything is falling apart, and so could you get to work on a series of space arks? It just would make me feel better. And also, Susan, could you bring me a cup of FRESH human stem cell tea with lemon? This one has grown cold."

Of course, I am just speculating that Oprah drinks tea made with

> **OCTOBER 27, 2012**
> The last operating restaurant in the United States, the Hooters in Extralia, PA, closes its doors. It reopens two days later as a family-friendly sexy human fight pit.

human stem cells. But the rest of my logic is impeccable, and you would have to be very naïve to imagine that Oprah Winfrey does not have SOME sort of Earth Evacuation Plan.

And I would have come to that same conclusion even if my friend Elizabeth Gilbert had not shown me the boarding pass and map to the space elevators that she received from Oprah's herald, Jonathan Franzen.

ZOMBIE SURVIVAL GUIDE

Not long ago, I received a letter via THE ELECTRO-MAIL SYSTEM. It was from Beau and Ryan:

> My partner and I have an ongoing dispute we'd like resolved once and for all: Our plans for surviving a zombiepocalypse are completely divergent. He thinks we should take to the road and stay on the move, while I think our current apartment serves as a defensible, fortified base of operations.
>
> He also thinks we should abandon the dog, which is awful and cruel.
>
> Also, if the zombies are closing in on you, wouldn't you rather throw the dog to them so that you get an extra few seconds to run for your life?
>
> Cheers,
>
> Beau

First of all, PLEASE DON'T WORRY ABOUT ZOMBIES. I know everybody is crazy for zombies, but for the last time, that is

OCTOBER 28, 2012
The Union of the Snake is on the climb. DO NOT SAY YOU WERE NOT WARNED.

just a METAPHOR for what happens when the veneer of civility drops away from society like a rotting jaw from a skinless skull, and also a WISH-FULFILLMENT FANTASY for those many Americans who wish to shoot their neighbors in the head.[404]

In truth, humans do not require REANIMATION in order to be monstrous to one another. After all, why did they make the movie *Zombieland* if not for the sole purpose of driving a single man named Max Brooks INSANE. And you won't need the threat of zombies to fear being eaten alive.

Second of all, you are both wrong. Or, to put it another way, neither of you is right. Either plan has its good points: Both will keep you alive for some miserable stretch of time before you ultimately go insane and murder each other because you each look like a giant talking chicken leg to the other person.

But the main thing is, forget your stupid dog. When the end comes, your dog will quickly betray you and be assimilated into DOGSTORM.[405]

FIGURE 152:
Beau's dog Buster will betray us all.

SOME OTHER COMMON MYTHS ABOUT THE COMING GLOBAL SUPERPOCALYPSE

There is no question that adapting to RAGNAROK is going to mean

---

404. The only creatures that will come back to life will be the animals, and then only the taxidermed ones, as they will be angriest and the best preserved.

405. Please see "Today in RAGNAROK," under the heading "July 16, 2012."

OCTOBER 29, 2012
The city-state that has emerged in the strip mall in Notarized Documents, NV, is somehow able to produce new episodes of *Two and a Half Men*. Most of the new story lines now take place in a half-empty supermarket. People like them, though, especially now that Charlie Sheen is back.

---

some big changes in your lifestyle. And at the end of it, when the Century Toad splits the world in half, you are going to die.

But there is also a lot of NONSENSE and MISCONCEPTIONS out there that probably makes it worse than it seems.

WILL THERE BE A TERRIBLE NUCLEAR HOLOCAUST?

Come on. THE '80s ARE OVER.

Aside from being horribly out of fashion, nuclear holocaust is not part of RAGNAROK. Even if most governments did NOT collapse immediately due to the ANCIENT AND UNSPEAKABLE ONES, their weapons will be rendered inoperable due to the OMEGA PULSE, poor silo maintenance, and the fact that most of the world's nuclear weapons were actually made of papier-mâché. The whole arms race, it turns out, was just another macho global papier-mâché bragging contest.

However, in the Flat-Screen Shanties and the Domed Cities and the Bartertowns, there *will* be constant screenings of *The Day After*, because it will be considered hilarious and heartwarming NOS-TALGIA.

WILL GLOBAL WARMING CAUSE DEVASTATING NATURAL DISASTERS AND UNPREDICTABLE SEVERE WEATHER?

More than what is already happening? That seems very unlikely. It is probably true that you will continue to see earthquakes, tornadoes, tsunamis, and the sudden rise of the world's oceans; but these will be nothing compared to the effects of the BLOOD WAVE or the SPITSPILL.

> **OCTOBER 30, 2012**
> The crawling Headless Body of Nug-Shohab decimates Mexico City.

WILL THERE BE A TERRIBLE SUPERVIRUS THAT WILL EITHER KILL A GREAT NUMBER OF PEOPLE OR TURN THEM INTO FLESH-EATING ZOMBIES?

Again,[406] there will NOT be a zombie problem, either supernatural or pseudoscientific. WHAT IS WITH YOU PEOPLE? IS THE ZOMBIE TROPE *THAT* DEATHLESS?

There will, however, be a brief outbreak of FRANKENSTEIN'S VIRUS in Pittsburgh. But really only blind men and children need fear these so-called BOLTNECKS. Mostly they spend their time just lumbering around feeling sorry for themselves.

Otherwise, most people will succumb to simple infections and household accidents that cannot be treated due to the kidnapping of all the good physicians by the wealthy.

HAS THE GOVERNMENT MADE SECRET PLANS TO SURVIVE RAGNAROK?

Not really. Like you, they are mainly pretending that it's not happening. If the surface of the Earth becomes uninhabitable, the president of the United States will be relocated to the Orbital White House and, eventually, to Moon Base Alpha.[407] But after that, there are no clear plans.

The source of this myth is likely the story of "DOOMSDAY, DC." This was a plan to ensure continuity of government should human civilization perish in the flames of the Spanish-American War.

William McKinley ordered an entire city to be built deep underground in an undisclosed location: a complete and perfect replica of

---

406. Please see page 908, under the heading "Zombie Survival Guide."
407. Please see page 482 of *More Information Than You Require* under the heading "The Secret Moon Landing."

OCTOBER 31, 2012
Jack-o'-lantern carvers across the Northeast are surprised to discover hair and human teeth inside their Halloween pumpkins instead of the typical pumpkin entrails they are used to. The teeth are delicious roasted with oil and a little salt; but to everyone's surprise, pumpkin actually tastes better than burnt human hair.

Washington, DC, except in miniature, and populated by a complete shadow government, ready to take over should the worst come.

When the Spanish-American War did not devolve into a horrible global conflict but in fact was settled rather quickly when the Spanish forces were chewed to death by Theodore Roosevelt, the fate of DOOMSDAY, DC, became uncertain. We do not know for certain where it is, or if it was ever completed, although we do have records suggesting at least half of the shadow House of Representatives survived the rather crude miniaturization process of the time.[408]

WILL A GIANT ROGUE PLANET—THE SO-CALLED PLANET X— ENTER OUR SOLAR SYSTEM AND COLLIDE WITH EARTH?

No. The only object that will collide with Earth is the giant meteor containing the frozen head of Nug-Shohab. Trust me: That will be enough.

WILL, AS THE ANCIENT BABYLONIANS PREDICTED, A GIANT ROGUE PLANET CALLED NIBIRU ENTER OUR SOLAR SYSTEM AND COME NEAR OUR PLANET, ALLOWING US CONTACT WITH ITS EXTRATERRESTRIAL, GODLIKE INHABITANTS AS IT PASSES, AND PERHAPS OFFERING US A KIND OF PLANET-SIZED LIFEBOAT (JUST LIKE THE DINOSAURS HAD)?

No. There is no escape from RAGNAROK, any more than there is a planet NIBIRU. The Babylonian astronomers were wrong about that planet, probably because THEY DID NOT HAVE TELESCOPES.

---

408. Shrink paste, compression.

NOVEMBER 1, 2012

The paperback edition of this book is published. Dutton, the Last Publishing House, unable to compete with electronic books and also the devastation of the BLOOD WAVE, shuts down all operations.

There IS, of course, a second, Earthlike planet in our solar system on the opposite side of the sun that has a very highly advanced civilization upon it and lots of empty, beautiful homes for everyone on our earth. But to get there, we would have to build a sun tunnel. And alas, we have run out of time for that.

WILL QUETZALCOATL RETURN FROM THE 29TH DIMENSION TO JUDGE US ALL?

Obviously, for that was written in my previous book.[409] But there is some debate among scholars about precisely who or WHAT Quetzalcoatl actually is.

Many cultures in pre-Columbian Mesoamerica worshipped the great winged serpent Quetzalcoatl (or Feather Boa in the original Nahuatl tongue).[410]

Quetzalcoatl was the god of the dawn, the calendar, knowledge, and brain corn. He was born of a virgin, and created human life at the dawn of the Fifth Sun Cycle from the bones of the planet's previous inhabitants[411] by giving them his own life's blood from a wound on his penis.

Quetzalcoatl lived for a time as a celibate priest, but he got drunk and made love to a priestess and then left the earth in what historians call "The Cosmic Walk of Shame," claiming he would return when this cycle of creation was over.

In fact, many scholars believe that when Hernán Cortés arrived at

---

409. Please see page 328 of *More Information Than You Require,* under the heading "December 31."
410. You may call it "Q," for that's all you will have time to say before it TEARS YOU APART.
411. Dinosaurs!

Tenochtitlán, Montezuma turned the empire over to his conquerors largely because he presumed that Cortés himself WAS Quetzalcoatl, come to usher in a new age of the sun and/or create a new race of humanity from his penis.

The confusion was understandable, given that Cortés was wearing a giant snake costume and was writhing on the ground, hissing, and had two swan wings tied to his back—a gift from his wife.

Now, I am sure you are wondering: the arrival of the divine on Earth, the promise of a glorious return, Hernán Cortés with wings, a magical penis wound—doesn't this all sound a LOT like the story of Jesus?

Don't get excited. You are not the first to come to that banal conclusion. There have been many who have suggested that in fact the Quetzalcoatl legend may actually be CHRISTIAN in origin, perhaps suggesting some ancient contact between the New World and the Old long before Columbus materialized on our shores and called them China.

And this makes sense when you think about it, since there is no way that the Aztecs could have come up with the Quetzalcoatl myth on their own. THOSE DUMMIES DIDN'T EVEN KNOW HOW TO MAKE SMOOTH PYRAMIDS!

Others suggest that Quetzalcoatl is but one face of a universal archetype: the messenger of the divine who comes to Earth, is exiled, and then returns to save us all at the last minute from the end of the world.

Differing interpretations of the Quetzalcoatl myth suggest that the being worshipped by the Aztecs may actually have been . . .

CANDIDATE 1: JESUS OF NAZARETH

According to the Book of Mormon, after Jesus faked his own death, he moved to South America, where he preached his gospel in hiding. But

NOVEMBER 3, 2012
When he learns that the Last Publishing House has fallen, Stephen King prints out his seven
hundred new pages of The Stand and begins wandering the ruined country to read his manuscript
aloud to whomever he can find.

efforts to connect him with the Quetzalcoatl mythos were complicated
when he was tracked by a Jesus hunter to his secret compound in the
Brazilian jungle in 1986.

CANDIDATE 2: SAINT THOMAS

It is written that this apostle of Jesus went "To Preach Beyond the
Ganges," which many interpret as an archaic Biblical reference to the
then-undiscovered tunnel between Jerusalem and Mexico City. However, they called him "Doubting Thomas," not "Doubting Snake-Man."

CANDIDATE 3: A DINOSAUR

Recent discoveries of velociraptor bones with quill knobs on their
forearms have bolstered scientific speculation that dinosaurs actually
bore feathers—and not just the ones they taped to themselves as
decorations. Could it be that the "feathered serpent" might have actually been a time-traveling dinosaur?

YOU ARE GETTING CLOSER TO THE TRUTH!

CANDIDATE 4: ARTHUR CONAN DOYLE

During his spiritualist phase, Doyle claims to have astrally projected
several times to a prehistoric land where he was worshipped as a
god. As well, everyone knows that Arthur Conan Doyle also loved to
walk around Hyde Park with a snake draped over his shoulders.
Could the creator of Sherlock Holmes have astrally time-blasted
himself and his snake into history?

ANSWER=NO!

> **NOVEMBER 4, 2012**
> Bears return to Sacramento to take back the California government that once was theirs. Weirdly, the New Bear Republic is the ONLY quasigovernmental organization to outright BAN the hunting and eating of fat men.

CANDIDATE 5: NICK NOLTE

It is written in some ancient texts, including *The Americanomicon*, that the ANCIENT AND UNSPEAKABLE ONE known as "Nolte" frequently experienced tremendous penis pain. Could this be the same feathery-snake penis as Quetzalcoatl?

ANSWER=YES.

COULD IT ALSO BE THAT QUETZALCOATL IS A VOICE SPEAKING IN MY HEAD?

No. That is because you are on drugs. I just told you that Quetzalcoatl is NICK NOLTE. And you will know that NOLTE has fully awakened to his godhood when Nick Nolte appears at a red-carpet event astride his FEATHERED VELOCIRAPTOR.

BUT WAIT. SOMETIMES I HEAR *NICK NOLTE* IN MY HEAD.

Oh. Then yes: That is probably Quetzalcoatl.

SO WILL IT BE NICK NOLTE WHO WILL JUDGE HUMANITY BEFORE THE END COMES AND CARRY THE WORTHY AWAY TO SAFETY ON HIS RAFT OF SNAKES?

Alas, judgment has been made. Nolte has traveled throughout this world. He has been a movie star and a hobo, a mole-man, and then a mole-man a second time,[412] and none that he found on this Earth or below it, alas, has been judged worthy.[413]

---

412. Please see *More Information Than You Require* under the heading "700 Mole-Man Names."

413. Admittedly, Nolte's criteria were fairly confusing. The most coherent answer he ever gave was in a streetside interview he gave to a paparazzo for TMZ in late 2011. "I'm just looking for someone who can tear the whole thing down, you know? Someone who can make robots explode with his brain."

NOVEMBER 5, 2012
Pale eels flushed out of the sewers are now the primary food source for most New Yorkers.

IS IT POSSIBLE THE MAYAN CALENDAR ENDS IN 2012 SIMPLY AS A WAY OF MARKING THE END OF ONE GREAT HISTORICAL CYCLE AND THE BEGINNING OF ANOTHER?

No. It is the end of the world.

IS IT POSSIBLE THAT 2012 WILL ACTUALLY USHER IN NOT DEATH AND VIOLENCE, BUT AN INCREASE IN HUMAN CONSCIOUSNESS AND A NEW AGE OF ENLIGHTENMENT?

It is true that about 10 percent of the population will enjoy an increased human consciousness due to the powerful radiation emitted by the SOLAR STORMS. These people will be able to move objects with their minds and know the contents of mail before it even arrives.

Unfortunately, the mutated brains of the NEW HUMANS ("NU-MANS") will grow so huge that that they will also require special headgear just to stand up. This will make it hard for them to move around or run away, and so few will escape the cannibal gangs, who find the brains of NUMANS delicious. By October of 2012, most of the NUMANS will have been completely debrained.

BUT WEREN'T THERE MANY DOOMSDAY PROPHETS WHO WERE WRONG?

Yes. See TABLE 52, THE END-TIMES MYTHS OF THE NAN-TUCKETEERS. Predictions of the end of the world have been made for many years. So far they have all been incorrect. That doesn't mean that ONE cannot be right.

NOVEMBER 6, 2012
ELECTION DAY: The Ageless Tog Aggoth is reelected for forty-three consecutive terms. He opens up the Charred House (formerly the White House) to an all-are-welcome Bloodsup, but no one attends.

BUT HOW CAN THE WORLD EVER TRULY END? ISN'T EXISTENCE AN ETERNAL CYCLE? LIKE A SNAKE EATING ITS OWN TAIL?

You are speaking of the ancient symbol known as Ouroboros. It first appeared in the Egyptian Book of the Dead, and many people interpret it as a symbol of eternal continuity and universal rebirth. But many people are wrong. It is just a picture of a really dumb snake.

FIGURE 153:
Now what are you going to do, dummy?

Someday you will learn that just because an ancient culture drew a cool symbol, it does not mean that you are immortal. Specifically, you will learn this on July 3, when Ouroboros itself materializes on this plane and then stupidly chokes itself to death on top of Los Angeles.

WERE YOU AWARE OF IT? "WRITHING IS ALWAYS IN STYLE"

On college campuses in the '70s, it became something of a fad to wear OUROBELTS—actual belts made of live snakes actually eating their own tails.

NOT ONLY DID THEY MAKE A FASHION STATEMENT THAT SAID "I HATE MY PARENTS' RELIGION," BUT THE BELT'S OWN NATURAL WRIGGLING ACTION AUTOMATICALLY PULLED SAGGING PANTS UP!

NOVEMBER 7, 2012
Stephen King reads his seven hundred new pages of *The Stand* to several confused families in and around Portland, ME.

TABLE 52: THE END–TIMES MYTHS OF THE NANTUCKETEERS	
Nantucket Town	When the end is near, the enormous sperm-whale skeleton hanging from the roof at the Whaling Museum will break free from its chains and slowly crawl up Main Street, wailing horribly for its lost spermaceti. As it passes, all of Main Street's cobblestones will melt and fuse, horribly, into a normal street.
Mid-Island	As the sky turns Nantucket red, the last few working-class, year-round residents will be cornered in the A&P, surrounded on all sides by the ravenous Walking Rich.
Madaket	On the last days, a giant, nine-headed golden retriever[414] will menacingly lope across the island, lolling his hideous tongues and eating all the money.
Surfside	As it was foretold, the wreck of the *Andrea Doria* will rise from the depths, its ghostly lights dancing on the water as it just sits there off the coast. Though forty miles out, the sounds of a party can be heard—beautiful music, Italian talk, the clinking of the finest crystal—making everyone on shore very jealous. All the summer people will drive their Jeeps into the sea as they try to join the party.
Wauwinet	All cable-knit sweaters will instantly strangle their owners. John Kerry will come and stare curiously into their eyes as they die, wondering what life is like. Then he will take them to the underworld on his yacht.
	CONTINUED

---

414. Again, this is false. The golden retriever will have SEVEN heads.

> **NOVEMBER 8, 2012**
> Boston just comes out and admits it's kind of racist.

TABLE 52: *continued*	
Jetties Beach	Every pair of madras shorts and whale-embroidered chinos ever sold by Murray's Toggery will return to the place of their forging, dragging their owners with them, screaming. Once they have all returned, the doors will shut and lock, and the display windows will fill with gin and tonic and blood.
Squanthuck	Herman Melville's corpse will clamber out of the sea to visit Nantucket for the very first time. A pauper in life, his ghost pockets will now be full of *Moby-Dick* royalties. His pale, haunted figure will be seen in the corner of the most expensive restaurants, ordering appetizer after appetizer. Now that he is the wealthiest man on the island, even the oldest money and the most douchebaggy investment banker will have to crawl in submission to Melville, as if THEY were novelists.
'Sconset	Everyone on the island will grow a penis of extraordinary length, and their ears will turn into vaginas.

THE DIFFICULTY OF PREPARING
FOR THE END

I can understand why you may resist accepting my predictions. This is hard stuff. It is traumatic to imagine having to drink your own urine when you are not even in college. And when you are forced to think about the end of the world, it's natural to throw up psychological barriers. These are telepathic force fields you can use to brain-explode the marauding gangs that come to your compound, and they are very handy. But also, there are NONLITERAL PSYCHOLOGICAL BARRIERS that prevent you from fully accepting what is to come.

In a way, the end of the world is sort of like death: We know that it is definitely going to happen. As we grow older, the evidence for its approach mounts ominously. But in order to live our daily lives without screaming all the time or writing books of fake trivia, we must pretend this it is not really ever going to happen. And in both cases, we die at the end.

Now, perhaps you scoff. Perhaps you do not believe the evidence that RAGNAROK is upon us. Perhaps you believe that I just MADE UP *The Americanomicon* the way Saint John just MADE UP the Book of Revelation in a cave on the island of Patmos, or the way Cormac McCarthy just MADE UP *The Road.* I get it. I get that it would take a supreme narcissist to conclude that, simply because *he* is rotting in a cave in exile from Christendom, or simply becase *he* fears his son will be eaten by cannibals, or simply because *he* is turning forty (or in my case, ALL OF THESE THINGS) that the rest of the world must also face its own end in fiery sympathy.

Luckily for all of us, I AM JUST THAT SUPREME A NAR-CISSIST.

But I might also point out that it takes an equally supreme narcissist to imagine that the world will NOT end.

If you live, as I do, in a city that is not only full of intrinsic dangers (falling pianos), but also prone to natural disasters and targeted by violent extremists; and if you, as I do, enjoy a family history of cancer or some other congenital disease; and if you are, as I am, sedentary and overweight and over-asthmatic (as I assume you must be, as you are reading a book) . . .

ALL OF WHICH IS TO SAY that if you are, as I am, a mortal human, then the likelihood that death will intrude upon your life cruelly, quickly, and before your chosen time—that it will take you before your own personal story for the world has unfolded the way you

NOVEMBER 10, 2012

In Manchester, NH, Stephen King narrowly avoids capture by the Koontzians, a tribe of marauding public library patrons who show their allegiance to Dean Koontz by dressing up as golden retrievers.

wrote it or it was written for you, and before you can even say good-bye—*this* likelihood is greater than you admit.

And when it comes, I think you will agree that the difference be-tween being crushed by the massive palm of the headless body of NUG-SHOHAB on the ruined plain of RAGNAROK versus dying alone, half conscious but afraid, in a hospital room with a television flickering images at you of a football player dancing with the stars is so small that it is not worth arguing over.

Life may be miraculous in its unlikelihood in the universe, but it would be a fallacy to suggest that its rareness makes it inextin-guishable.

I apologize. That last paragraph was meant for my new children's book. But I think, as we approach the end of *this* book, the sentiment stands.

NOVEMBER 11, 2012
The People of the semi-Domed city of Columbus, OH, try to deal with their deformed Pennsylvanian problem by bringing in cane toads. It's a terrible idea, as cane toads breed several times a
day and can barely get their teeth around a single Pennsylvanian deformity.

THE BEGINNING

> **NOVEMBER 12, 2012**
> Following their map, the 44 Animatronic Presidents of the United States and DOGSTORM march through Philadelphia. You do not want to know what the humans are now serving at Geno's Famous Steaks as food. You would almost agree with the Animatronic Presidents that such creatures deserve only to be DESTROYED.

HOW I BECAME A FORMER
PROFESSIONAL LITERARY AGENT

I AM WRITING TO YOU NOW from my Park Slope Survival Brownstone. I have had a tin of eggs and some powdered bacon and a supplement frappe, and I am just about to lie down on my little armored cot and wait for red twilight to sneak through the gap in my steel shutters. Then I will know it is almost night.

Now that we are near the end, I realize that no one has asked how it all began. And since you did not ask, I would be happy to tell you how I became a former professional literary agent. Moreover, to make the story feel more immediate, I will tell it to you using a narrative technique called THE PRESENT TENSE.

* * *

It is my third morning at the annual conference of the Sagebrush Romance and Western Writers Association of the American West (the SRWWAAW).

I am installed at one of several tiny round tables in a beige conference room off the first floor of the Oklahoma City Embassy Suites. This is the one-on-one room, just a few steps up the wheelchair ramp from the hotel's high glass atrium, with its twinkly canned music and breakfast buffet. I am seated across from a writer named Maria Passel, who is thirty-two and has a glass eye. She lost it, she explains, when the left side of her face was mauled by a bear. This occurred when she worked at the Tulsa Zoo and Living Museum. She was a

> **NOVEMBER 13, 2012**
> Stephen King reaches the northern shore of the SPITSPILL in Turners Falls, MA. He finds the body of SINGULARO, still frozen, washed upon the shore, his ax still raised, his face still full of wonder and sadness. Stephen King is sad to ransack Singularo's stash of D batteries, but he does what he has to. He then heads east along the Mohawk Trail.

bear expert, she tells me, but not anymore. Now she is a novelist. Or at least wants to be.

"I see," I tell her, and regret it.

Maria Passel has written a series of mysteries featuring a crime-solving former zoologist named Sandra. In these novels, Sandra, with the help of her German shepherd, Ponzo, investigates crimes against and involving animals. Sandra stops a series of mysterious zoo poisonings. She hunts down poachers and fights monkey-smuggling rings and illegal big-cat traders. Plus, Sandra suffers from migraines about twice a month. They cause dementia and uncontrollable vomiting. They are so severe that Sandra's husband has left her, and now she is alone. These migraines result from Sandra having been mauled by a bear.

There are twelve novels in the series, Maria tells me. She has already written four. None of them has been published. Clean Xeroxed copies of them are stacked on the table between us. It is 1998.

Maria had signed up to visit with a mystery editor, Booth Daniels, but he's a no-show. This does not surprise me, because the night before, he and I enjoyed seven or eight blue martinis at Bowties, the hotel's nightclub, and I barely made it downstairs that morning myself.

So Maria has settled for me. I am young and she has never heard of me, but I am a professional literary agent and she wants my advice. She does not say so, but I can tell that what she really wants is for me to take the manuscripts back with me to New York on Sunday. That's when all the book editors and literary agents will fly away and leave Maria and all the other aspiring authors behind.

NOVEMBER 14, 2012
A woman who has forgotten her own name finally pulls down the flag on the statehouse of Toxo-plassachusetts (featuring a cat and rat shaking hands over the corpse of a human) and turns it into a shroud for her dead common-law husband.

I will spend fifteen minutes with Maria, the first of eleven one-on-ones before I can arrange to sleep through the big SRWWAAW Awards Dinner—where prizes will be handed out for best unpublished time-travel western and best unpublished supernatural-romance novella and so on—and then get back to Bowties. Maria wants to know what I think about the title of her first book in the series: *Deathpaw*. But I barely hear her, because that's when Anne D. Egan walks in.

I am not an Egan expert. I never read *Silopanna*, but I've known plenty who had read it or claimed to, mainly in college. I'd seen some of the websites devoted to her, and I'd seen that famous photo, the last she ever allowed to be taken: the one where she's leaning dangerously backward, out over the rail of a wrought-iron balcony in New Orleans. But there is no question that it's her. Her hair is powdery white now, but her eyes are the same, slitted and sly. And the drunken-seeming and grateful smile, as though an invisible chorus were constantly singing her happy birthday, is unmistakable. She is wearing a blue, shapeless dress and walks unsteadily with a brushed aluminum cane. She takes the seat that has been left vacant by Booth Daniels, knits her knobby fingers placidly, and waits for her first appointment.

It is surprising to see Anne D. Egan here for these reasons: First, I had not seen her name among any of the visiting-writer lists in the SRWWAAW literature; second, while the SRWWAAW certainly doesn't frown on science fiction (note prize categories above, plus a really wonderful tale I read the night before in my hotel room, still high on blue martinis, about a horse possessed by an ancient Incan prince), I hadn't thought they went in for the sort of weirdo psychedelic sci-fi that Egan was famous for; and third, like everyone else, I thought she was dead.

NOVEMBER 15, 2012
Last call for alcohol.

At this point, Maria Passel, author of *Deathpaw*, asks me if she can read aloud to me from the first chapter of her first book. I look for a moment at her ruined face, the sadness in the downward tug of the left side of her scarred mouth. I spread my hands over the top of her manuscripts and feel a sudden, almost sad knowledge—less a decision than an ugly, plain fact: I'll never read a word she's written.

"Why don't you just write about yourself?" I ask. "About your own life."

"I'm not sure I could do that," Maria says.

"Sure," I say. "I know of one writer who got a six-figure contract from Random House just for having her leg chewed off by a hyena."

And Maria's eye lights right up.

I've done my part. I've given her the little bit of hope she paid for when she sent her check in to the SRWWAAW back in October. What I get out of the transaction seems less clear.

Across the room, Anne D. Egan pulls out a crossword puzzle. She sits there the entire morning, calmly, without speaking. No one comes to see her. I want to say something to her, but after Maria, the writers keep coming to me, and by the time I'm finished with my last one-on-one, she's gone.

* * *

Excerpted from Playboy *magazine, June 1979, "Where Is Darling Egan?" by Gerry Dunlap*

Anne Darling Egan once told me that she started writing to get on someone's nerves. It was to annoy a single teacher at her boarding school who claimed that reading sci-fi literally caused the brain to shrink.

NOVEMBER 16, 2012

Deep in the Taconic Ridge State Forest, in Berlin, NY, Stephen King stumbles across NEW BROOKLINE, MA, a hidden village in which everyone lives as though time stopped in 1980.[a] There are only children in the village now. Jason, the seventeen-year-old leader, explains that the adults abandoned the children some time ago.

"They were not pure," he explains. "They were too attached to the new ways. They feared the past. But we do not. We keep the old ways here, and we are fine."

It seems that they are. All of the children seem happy and healthy, and they accompany Stephen King with an honor guard of Huffy bikes to the guest split-level bungalow. Dinner in the commissary (which the children call The Regal Beagle) is delicious: fondue and salad with plenty of green goddess dressing and baked Alaska for dessert. At first Stephen King is unnerved by this community of children living alone, all toasting his health with Galliano and then going off to the movie theater to watch *Aguirre: The Wrath of God*. But they all seem to like *The Stand*, and not a single one of them has ever seen Kubrick's version of *The Shining*, and so he decides to stay awhile.

---

a. For more information, please see page 629, under the heading "Answer Number 1. What Have You Done with Your Human Children?"

She wrote stories about a girl named Abigail who leaves her family to become an adept to a race of super-wise aliens. She wrote stories about gigantic cosmic whales and the communities of primitive soothsayers that lived within their bellies. She wrote stories about the lives of children born on a spacecraft who lived and died never knowing gravity. By the time she was finishing college, she had already published four pieces in *Galaxy*. Judy-Lynn Benjamin was her editor there, and when Judy went to Ballantine in 1973, she began a campaign of constant, jovial harassment to get Anne to write a novel. But Anne said novels were no fun.

Meanwhile, Anne made friends. She palled up with the biggest SF writers of the day, and they called her the boy wonder. They asked her to read their books and they didn't take her advice. And they cared for her, often feeding and housing her for weeks at a time. I had put her up at least six times, when I was in New Orleans. And that's how she ended up at Sprague de Camp's, the place where it all began. The place where, in 1974, Anne D. Egan received a telephone call from the future.

NOVEMBER 17, 2012
Stephen King reads the new seven hundred pages of *The Stand* to a group of children. They love it, especially the part about the satanic drifter. However, the youngest among them—a seven-year-old boy with a bowl cut and pale, haunted eyes—shakes his head sadly. "Madame won't like it," he says ominously.

After they found her, and before she disappeared for good, she stood in my closet-sized kitchen in New Orleans, drinking a glass of cloudy-green Pernod, and she told me half of what I wanted to hear about that day.

"Sprague had this gray house in Villanova," she said. "Everything in it was gray and silvery, and it was just down the road from Bryn Mawr, which is where I went to school. I had come for my five-year reunion, actually. I made it to Sprague's and just couldn't go on. All the pity I thought I'd feel for those girls I used to know, for their plausible lives and children, their small not-worth-keeping secrets . . . well, once I saw the campus again, it all turned to fear.

"So I was hiding out. On that silvery-gray velour sofa, drinking. Sprague and Catherine went out for a walk, which is just the sort of thing they would do, so I had the cracks in the ceiling for company and Sprague's Lovecraft biography in manuscript, which I was determined to read without his permission.

"Then the phone rang. I answered it: hello. And the voice that spoke back . . . would you believe it was gray and silvery too? It was whispery, with a slither in it, and it was electric-sounding. You could almost smell the ozone between the words. Sometimes it was many voices, interrupting one another, but mainly it was just the one. The voice said it was calling from the far, far future. I said that's nice, but Sprague just went out for a walk. Could I have him call back?

"'No,' the voice said. It wanted to speak to me. Can you believe it? So I said: 'Go 'head. Shoot.'"

NOVEMBER 18, 2012
As Stephen King is walking to get his daily Egg McMuffin ration, a black bag is put over his head, and he is knocked unconscious.

The call lasted three minutes, twenty-two seconds. This came out in 1977, when an Egan devotee and Delaware County Sheriff's deputy admitted that he had pulled the de Camps' phone records and had been selling them for big dollars at science-fiction conventions. I saw one once, the page ragged and Xerox-blurry, the call in question underlined repeatedly, the originating number not listed. I knew all this.

I also knew about how Egan was gone by the time the de Camps came home about an hour later. They spent two weeks looking for her. Turned out that she was in her apartment on the Upper West Side the entire time, the phone off the hook. She had been writing: pure demonic nonstop prose. She was right in the middle of it when Sprague de Camp and Isaac Asimov shouldered in the door of her apartment. She had just finished typing the line that would eventually be the first sentence of the Silopanna trilogy: "If you're looking for a sign that everything in your life is about to fall apart, an uninvited man at your door wearing a bolo tie is about as good as it gets."

De Camp later said she seemed amused when they broke in, enlightened somehow. Glowing. Asimov said she was drunk. De Camp said that Asimov was indeed wearing a western string tie that day, one of several that he owned. Asimov denied this.

I know all this the same way you do: It's part of the lore, the Egan mythology written by the faithful and passed along by mouth, by newsletter, by science-fiction convention-hall rumor. It came to be known as the Villanova Call, and

---

NOVEMBER 19, 2012

Stephen King awakens in the movie theater, tied to a chair. He is surrounded by children. Jason stands in front of him, wearing a tuxedo T-shirt and a somber expression on his face. He explains that, by reading the new pages of *The Stand,* he had brought NEW CULTURE to New Brookline, MA, and that is against THE LAW.

"But," says Stephen King, "it's not a sequel. It's the same book from the seventies that you love. It's just an improvement, with more character development and now an extra retarded character!"

"You are like the other grown-ups," says Jason. "They said they had information that we NEEDED. About the Blood Wave and the Nug-Shohab. They broke the law too, and Madame didn't like it."

"Who is Madame?" asks Stephen King.

"You will see," says Jason. And then he steps behind the movie theater curtain.

When it opens, Stephen King sees Madame. It is the ventrilo-quist dummy known as Madame that was once operated by Way-land Flowers before he passed away from AIDS in 1988.[a] Now she is operated by a boy wearing a dark hood, though Stephen King can see from the tuxedo T-shirt that it is Jason.

Madame does about fifteen minutes of her old, racy routine from the libertine '70s in which she describes having sex with various nonpuppet humans. And then she names Stephen King a heretic and enemy of New Brookline.

There is subdued applause from the other children.

"This is madness," says Stephen King.

Madame says that as punishment for his crimes, Stephen King will be frozen in carbonite, which in New Brookline means he will be put in a pit and steamed to death.

FIGURE 154:
The Law

"Go back to your bungalow, honey," says Madame. "Watch Johnny Carson. Have a liqueur. For tomorrow"—Madame draws a wooden hand across her wooden neck—"you'll be as dead as a dummy."

---

a. The body of Wayland Flowers has been preserved and mounted and is now kept in a private collection in Aspen, Colorado.

---

it broke her life in half. Before it she had been nothing, a SF curiosity, the girl boy wonder. After it she was a bestseller, a legend, a reluctant priestess of Silopanna underground fervor, keeper of the signs that told the future. It couldn't have gone better in a story, and I know, because I write them for a living. But what I didn't know, what nobody knew, was what the voice told her.

But she shook her head when I asked.

"You're the only one I've got left, Gerry," she said. "The only friend who'll talk to me. Just give me a couch for a week and room to type so I can finish this book." That night,

---

NOVEMBER 20, 2012

Stephen King awakens in the pit. It is just past midnight. He was told he would be steamed at dawn.

Stephen King does not want to die, but there is no way out: The pit is very deep, and the edge is patrolled by Big Traks.

And then, a weird crackle, and the trees above the pit are lit with orange. The boy with the bowl cut and the haunted eyes peers over the side. He throws Stephen King a rope. King climbs out.

He sees all the Big Traks have stopped in their big tracks, black-charred and hollowed out by flames. They form a burning circle around the boy, who stands among them like a tiny god. Sensing that Stephen King is confused, the boy explains that he has a talent. He is what the other boys call: "GIFTED AND TALENTED."

Ever since he was a baby, he could see pictures in his head. Things that haven't happened yet. Things that might happen. Places far away. Also, he says, he can set robots on fire just by thinking about it.[a]

Stephen King is very excited about this. "I KNEW kids like you existed."

The Gifted Child says that he will let Stephen King escape, but only if he takes him along.

"The presidents are coming," he says. "I've seen it. The only safe place is Chicago."

Stephen King is so excited not to be murdered by children in a pit that he does not even argue that Chicago does not exist.

They walk east, Stephen King pushing the Gifted Child in a shopping cart.

---

a. This is called "ROBOPYROKINESIS."

---

hot and cloudy-green in New Orleans, Anne D. Egan wasn't telling.

* * *

The Bowties Bar and Nightclub is nestled beneath the overhang of the ballroom-level balcony and next to the first bank of glass elevators. It's its own little mini-dome of smoked glass in the atrium, fronted by a little sunken brickface patio. It's dark inside: The indirect atrium light provides no warmth, and the AC is blowing hard. It's three in the afternoon. The three TVs behind the bar are each showing a different scene from *The Empire Strikes Back*, and the bartender is adjusting the tint on Yoda. His name is Billy, a new friend since last night, with apple cheeks and chunky black glasses.

Next to me at the bar is my other new friend, Booth Daniels, the mystery editor who blew off the one-on-ones. He caught me in the atrium after I was done with my last writer, waving at me from behind a potted plant, then pointing with a spindly finger to the bar.

NOVEMBER 21, 2012

The Headless Body of Nug-Shohab pauses at the Iguazú Falls between Paraguay and Argentina. The military cannot stop it anymore. There are no more armies.

As it sits, the mist of the falls gathering in droplets on its terrible skin, a nine-year-old girl approaches it.

The Nug-Shohab does not know that it destroyed the apartment block in which she lived with her mother and two sisters and stepfather. It does not know that she and her older brother were not at home when the Nug-Shohab crushed her apartment building.

Because the Nug-Shohab does not see or hear or taste or think.[a]

It does not know that her brother swore vengeance, and so they tracked it here. And then her brother died of infection because he stepped on a nail.

It does not know that the girl used to keep wounded animals to try to heal them and failed. But one time she helped a guinea pig to die peacefully, just by holding it.

The Nug-Shohab does not understand that, now that everything is gone, now that she sees it sitting senseless, without a head, that she sees how it, too, is just another wounded animal.

It does not know how tired she is, and how dehydrated.

But it feels her when she crawls into its hand.

It feels her there, a warm heart, beating, beating, beating, and then not beating. It feels her, and it does not crush her.

And so it is that even senseless creatures with iron hearts and no head at all wish, sometimes, that they were not alive.

---

a. (It has no head.)

Now he's leaning over an Irish coffee that is supporting an embarrassing amount of whipped cream. His circle of gray hair sticks up electrically. His face is tired and lined and yellowish. He eats the whipped cream delicately with a spoon as he speaks.

"I hate science fiction," he says. "Half of it is pure juvenile power fantasy. The other half takes itself so fucking seriously. It's not writing a story, it's running an experiment, it's growing crystals in a jar: very pretty shapes and colors, all sorts of elegant symmetries, but in the end pretty much airless and dead."

I agree with him, and he eats another spoonful of cream.

"Don't get me wrong," Booth continues, "I have no pretensions. There's nothing more boring than a police procedural or another old woman with a cat nosing around a dead body. But the detective story is the primal narrative. It's about making sense out of senseless events, restoring order to chaos. All fiction is a detective story, except the crime is life itself—dirty, short, mean, and random."

NOVEMBER 22, 2012
Because President Ageless Tog Aggoth is busy blood cocooning, it falls to Vice President Charnel Reign, the Skinless Priest, to perform the traditional pardon of the Thanksgiving turkey. However, instead of granting "Timmy Tom" his reprieve, the vice president withdraws a bone knife and cuts the bird open to read the still-steaming entrails. "Soon!" he cries through hissing teeth to the cameras. "Soon Nug-Shohab will be whole! Also, there will be three more weeks of winter."

"Absolutely fucking true," Billy says, nodding along. He pours me a whiskey without my asking, and I tip him well because I know it's on the house. Billy is smart. I learned last night that he's a writer, just like everyone else here this week. And like everyone else, for some reason, he's got a trilogy going. If I remember correctly, Billy's is about a family of immortal demons who've been banished from hell to Austin, Texas. But he's not pushy. He knows that he's got the best access to writers and editors and agents right here behind the bar. He's got three years' worth of business cards from some of the biggest names in the business, warm wishes scrawled drunkenly on the back, and one of these days he'll use them.

"Now," Booth says, pointing to Billy, "now, if you were a girl, you'd be going to my room with me right now, wouldn't you?"

"Absolutely true," Billy says, laughing this time.

Booth turns to me, chin jutting, eyes half closed, pleased with himself. "That line. I got two wives with that line. But of course I am impotent now."

"But what about Egan?" I say, repeating the original question I'd asked him.

"If it's her," Booth says, "if it's really her, and you can sign her, you'll make a fortune." He makes this statement with a sad little shrug, because we both know his own publishing house cannot afford a fortune.

"It's her," Billy says with the calm pleasure of knowing he's got one on us. "She was in here two nights ago."

I tell him I thought she was dead.

"Nope," he says.

934

NOVEMBER 23, 2012

In Niles, OH, Stephen King and the Gifted Child take refuge from a storm of refrigerator magnets in a strange cave. As they explore it further, they find the long-lost remains of DOOMSDAY, DC. The tiny replica of Washington, DC, is eerily well preserved, although it contains some anachronisms, such as the presence of the Washington Monument. Stephen King is surprised at how strange the monument looks to him, and how quickly he had grown used to its absence. They camp in the dry, miniature reflecting pool among these architectural ghosts of a world long dead.

"Did she mention," I ask, "if she was writing a book?"

Billy sighs, clearly realizing I am not among the initiated. Then he tells me what he does know—that everyone used to love her.

She ate magic mushrooms with Frank Herbert and together they prank-called L. Ron Hubbard. She hung out in Bradbury's basement full of knickknacks and horror-movie memorabilia and file cabinets full of thousands of stories, always stealing one before she left because, she explained, he was always writing one too many.

She spent a summer with Philip K. Dick at his doomed commune in Oakland trying to make the runaways laugh.

She spent a winter with Gerry Dunlap, telling the drag queens on Dumaine Street that in each of their hearts were two universes at war, and that in any case she was more man than any of them.

The only one she didn't love was Lester del Rey. But she did love him, in a way, she loved that del Rey hated her. He really thought she was second rate, and this amused her endlessly, especially since his wife, Judy-Lynn Benjamin, was her editor and champion.

Then everything changed. "Do you know what the Villanova Call is?" Billy asks.

I tell him I've heard of it.

Billy says that after the Villanova Call they all turned on her. One by one. No one ever confused her early stuff with genius, but it didn't matter because they were all secretly in love with her. Then after the Villanova Call, no one knew what the hell she was doing. *Silopanna* wasn't really a novel. It was a philosophy of the universe, had almost no plot, and was incredibly, incredibly long.

NOVEMBER 24, 2012

Stephen King and the Gifted Child awaken to find their legs being chewed on by tiny men. They have no way of knowing that these are the deformed, inbred descendants of the miniature congressmen who were once sent to live here, some of whom became hermaphroditic by evolutionary necessity. All they know is that they are being attacked by tiny teeth attached to tiny hermaphrodites wearing tattered doll clothing, and that is enough to freak them out. They barely escape with their legs.

"When part two came out, del Rey called it a rabid dog that no one had the guts to put down," Billy says. "But why did they really hate her? Because it sold like crazy. All these potheads got into it, college kids. And the government was watching too, because of the CIRCE stuff."

"The what?" I ask.

"Wait." Billy raises a finger and reaches for his army bag beneath the bar. "It's all in here." He comes back up with a copy of *Playboy* magazine, dated 1979. Billy flips through a few pages until he finds that photo of Egan leaning out over the balcony in what I now see is New Orleans. "This is the article Gerry Dunlap wrote about her," he says. "The famous one. I'm hoping to get it signed tonight."

For a brief moment Booth leafs through the *Playboy*. "I had this when it was new," he says with wonder.

I say, "Are you her biggest fan or something?"

Billy thinks it over. "No," he says. "I'd say I'm just a typical fan. I mean, I love the Silopanna trilogy, but I have some serious problems with it."

"Like what?" I say.

"Well, mainly that it's only two books long," and he and Booth share a laugh at my expense, because of course when I asked if she had a new book, that was exactly the question everyone had been asking since 1979. She wrote only two books, and stopped.

Still, I'm amazed by the coincidence of it all, which Billy shrugs off.

"You have no idea. This atrium? It's a freaking biosphere. My old girlfriend from Austin came in the first night of the conference.

NOVEMBER 25, 2012

Stephen King and the Gifted Child reach the remains of the semi-Domed city of Columbus, OH. What happened here must have been terrible. Stephen King stops dead in his tracks when he sees a ragged polar bear in the middle of the street. But the bear does not pay any attention to Stephen King, as it is busy eating the entrails of a deformed Pennsylvanian. When he turns back to the road, Stephen King sees that the Gifted Child has walked on.

He finds the child on the shore of the Scioto River, staring at a tourist duck boat. "We will need this," he tells Stephen King. "For the red ocean."

Haven't talked to her in three years. She had no idea I was here. It was a bad breakup. She was always saying I was going nowhere, you know, what a waste of time writing is. Then she shows up here with a book of vampire short stories and a smile. But I should have seen it coming, you know, since I'd dropped a Michelob the night before."

I ask him what he means.

"A broken bottle means old lover coming, or bad news. Usually it's the same." He dislodges the *Playboy* from Booth's long fingers and hands it to me, not without kindness, as if I'll soon see the light. "Read the article."

* * *

Excerpted from Playboy *magazine, June 1979, "Where Is Darling Egan?" by Gerry Dunlap*

Everything had already happened. That's how she explained it to me on Dumaine Street that winter. By then, part two of *Silopanna* was several hundred pages long, and she was very thin. She barely ate, just smoked grass and typed out on my balcony. Sometimes during the day I'd hear her talking to herself. And then at night we'd sit on the balcony and she'd talk to me, but it wasn't that different: that same low murmur, a transmission from another world, the end of her cigarette poking at me in the dark.

NOVEMBER 26, 2012

DOGSTORM and the 44 Animatronic Presidents of the United States reach New Brookline, MA, looking for the Gifted Child. Unable to tell humans'apart, they decide to murder all the children. Jason and Madame hold them off until the little ones can escape. But he is no match for forty-four robots and their forty-four robot dogs and their millions of nonrobotic dogs.

At last beaten, Jason and Madame are surrounded, their backs to the Pit. Robotic President James Garfield dismounts his Big Dog and crushes Madame in his animatronic hands. He puts his robotic foot on Jason's neck, takes the robotic bullet from his own chest, and then he puts it into Jason's chest.

He watches, curiously, as Jason dies. "Are you the boy who can set me on fire with his mind?" says President Garfield.

"No," says Jason. "But I can set you on fire with a flaming lawn dart."

And at that moment, a flaming lawn dart thunks into the middle of James Garfield's head, instantly re-assassinating him with fire.

And then, from all around the presidents, flaming lawn darts rain down, thrown by the last stand of New Brookline teenagers, hidden in trees and on rooftops. They will all perish by the end of the day—felled by dog or robot.

But in this last moment, as Jason closes his eyes, twenty-three robotic presidents are taken by fire, proving once and for all that the '70s were a bright and bold and dangerous time, and it was probably a good idea when they took that Flaming Lawn Darts game off the market in 1980.

A helicopter catching fire for no reason means that a party of shipwrecked men and women shall be found, and one of them shall be a visionary.

A famous scientist dying intestate means a world-killing weapon will be discovered; prices of coffee drop.

A foreigner pretending not to be foreign means all travel will stop for one year. Even if you think you are moving, you will not be.

Silopanna, the freak bible, conspiracy tract, half autobiography, bestselling trilogy of only two books, is also a list of prophecies—what have come to be known as Eganic Omens. It's the same list that is given to the novel's heroine to field test by a secret government agency, the Commission to Investigate Reverse Causal Echo Phenomena—or CIRCE ("leaving off the extra P," Egan wrote, "to obtain maximum mythological power and anacronymic potency").

Our heroine's name is Abigail, perhaps even the same Abigail from Egan's earliest stories, except now she is an

NOVEMBER 27, 2012
Though many of them have half-melted skin and singed beards, the remaining twenty-one robotic presidents and their dogs regroup, and use their computer minds to get important information from the remains of a Big Trak. They head west.

adult, jobless and alone. She seems to have no memory of her youthful interstellar adventures, and there is a strong suggestion that they may all have been imagined. At the beginning of the first book, she returns home to Silopanna Avenue in Annapolis. Her father, having died of throat cancer, has left her some money, and she has come to collect.

There is actually a street in Annapolis called Silopanna Avenue, and Egan herself grew up there. Of course Silopanna is Annapolis spelled backward, and a word spelled backward means a window of insight will soon open, and everything will be clear. Or so Abigail learns when she is approached by Duffy, a CIRCE operative who claims to have known her father and offers her a job.

Duffy explains that CIRCE has figured out a way to predict the future, and it's based on a theory that while certain events seem to have no effect whatsoever on history, others are so calamitous that they profoundly affect not only what happens after them but also what happens before them.

"It is humankind's special illness," Duffy tells Abigail in part two of *Silopanna*, "that we must see time as a river, always moving forward. But in fact it's still and glassy like a lake. We live on the surface, above unfathomable depths, and history comes like a hailstorm. Large disturbances on the surface shoot ripples outward in all directions, and we experience these waves as cause and effect. This is why history seems to anticipate those largest calamities, those wars and plagues and romances and triumphs that draw lives into them like black holes. Looking back, we always feel we

NOVEMBER 28, 2012

Having decimated most of Mexico and Central and South America, the Headless Body of Nug-Shohab reaches Antarctica. After a seven-day thaw in the Antarctic base's Experimental Huge Microwave Oven, its frozen head will be ready to be placed back upon its shoulders. Because it cannot see, the Headless Body of Nug-Shohab can't work the microwave controls very well, and so it just presses the "Giant Popcorn" button over and over again.

should have seen it coming, and in fact, we should have. World War I didn't happen because a zealot killed a member of minor royalty—Archduke Ferdinand was shot in order to allow World War I to happen. And that didn't even happen until World War I was over and done with, spreading its causal fingers forward and back, side to side."

And so CIRCE was formed by the U.S. government to sift through history, to tease out patterns and commonalities in the events that had previously announced the arrival of war or turmoil or subversion—anything that might be considered a threat to national security. They pored over millions of pages of primary and secondary sources, diaries, letters, the most respected histories and the most intimate first-person accounts. Out of an office in the Library of Congress, they have compiled a list of signs, some plain and some subtle, some banal and some sublime, that would seem to indicate "event matrix intersection at a statistically significant rate of predictability," and they now need field agents to test them.

All Abigail needs to do is take this list, watch for the signs, and report what happens to her when she sees a butterfly through a round window, for example; or a blue cloud encircling a mountain. They will also give her a government car. So Abigail takes the job and begins making her reports, the text of which make up most of *Silopanna* parts one and two. She mails them to Duffy from the road, sent as instructed to various motel rooms, which she is supposed to do because "nothing happens in motels. Time moves around them."

NOVEMBER 29, 2012

The final episode of *The Owl Shop Crowd* is broadcast. Originally recorded in 1962, Norris Goff had long since left the cast due to the loss of his throat in a boating accident. Very few people knew that he was replaced by a young McLean Stevenson, just beginning his career, especially since the final episode of the program consists mostly of Van and Chumley screaming.

But what remained a mystery was why Abigail was chosen, and how and why CIRCE began its research in the first place.

A broken bottle? An unsought-for reunion that will not end well.

An obese child on a summer street eating corn on the cob? Just turn around and go home.

Cyclops, picture or image thereof? Prepare to receive a message.

"Our entire existence is given motion by the causal waves which are emanating from and colliding between the Big Bang and the final collapse," Anne told me, the end of her cigarette dancing in the gloom. "Man's mental illness forces him to see these events as distinct, when of course they are the same: one big splash in the middle of the lake of time."

And the result of this delusion is the same sad symptom that would become CIRCE's fatal error: the mistaken belief that what we do now will actually affect the future.

* * *

All the rooms are suites at the Embassy Suites. They encircle the atrium, seven levels of balconies, up and up to the giant series of skylights. I am on the fifth floor, near the second bank of glass elevators. For some reason, the April light above travels straight down. It does not pause at the rooms, and so the balconies are dark and gloomy, and I am a little drunk. I'm skimming the *Playboy* as I walk down the hall. It's time to nap.

NOVEMBER 30, 2012

Stephen King and the Gifted Child reach a finger of land stretching north between what once was called Lake Michigan and the great Blood-Red Ocean. The Gifted Child tells Stephen King that this is the place: Chicago.

I told you," said Stephen King. "There's nothing here." And Stephen King is right: It is a wasteland of abandoned suburbs, strip malls, and empty fields.

The Gifted Child does not respond. He takes his backpack and climbs down the duck-boat ladder onto the bloody shores. He walks a few steps until he decides he's in the right place. From his backpack, he pulls out a bottle of Malort and pours it onto the ground.

And Stephen King watches as the White City rises before him. Stephen King doesn't know what to say. The Gifted Child turns back to him.

"Come on," he says. "It won't last."

There's someone standing by the door to my room. A woman, one eye glinting falsely in the dark. It's Maria Passel, the mauled novelist. She touches my arm as I approach.

"Hello," she says, like a friend. She puts her hand on my arm, just below the shoulder, warmly. At these conferences, in these long trapped hours, familiarity grows like mushrooms on a dead log. It feels like a day since I left Booth at Bowties, a week since this morning. This touch, this is how she treats old friends. But there's something more here in her gentle but desperate grasp, her long thumb moving gently on the inside. There's something else happening, something I'm hoping against but I know is coming: She's got her manuscript under her other arm.

"I've been thinking a lot about what you said." Just listening to her, I can hear her spell "a lot" as one word. "I just don't know if I'm brave enough to tell my own story yet. I mean, how does a person do that?"

Her good eye meets mine. It's sincere and searching and—I hadn't noticed before—green. The surprising deep green of a sea I know I will never see. This is the look I imagine she would use on the animals in the zoo, calming them, seeking out what was bothering them, and then finding some way to make it better. I suddenly remember the *Playboy* I'm carrying. On the one hand, I am a man destined to unravel and profit from the greatest literary mystery of our time. On the other, I'm just a guy walking back alone to his hotel room with porn. I hide the cover flat against the side of my thigh.

DECEMBER 1, 2012

Stephen King and the Gifted Child explore Chicago. It is just as Stephen King read about it story-books—the Sears tower, Wrigley Field, the Ferris wheel, the millions upon millions of authentic dive bars, the reasonable rents, and green water, and everyone reads an actual newspaper. Other pilgrims have been drawn to it. They seem like good people. He knows more will come. The Gifted Child will be happy here, and safe. And so would Stephen King. He knows it.

"Are you sure you won't stay?" says the Gifted Child.

Stephen King pats his manuscript sadly. He has wrapped it in Saran wrap and Styrofoam to protect it from the elements. "Writing isn't about sitting around being artistic. It's a job. Like putting on a roof or building a wall out of car parts or just hammering a piece of metal over and over again. You do it every day, like any other job, and you can't stop until it's done. And my job isn't done."

Stephen King boards the duck boat and sails across the Blood-Red Ocean. The Gifted Child is not surprised. That's why he got the duck boat in the first place.

"I think you are brave enough. It takes some amount of bravery just to sit down and write a book in the first place. I've never been able to do it." This is a simple thing I always say to writers, but it's true all the same. It feels especially true now, suddenly, my back against the door.

I also remind her that she used to work with wild animals every day, animals that could kill her, and that didn't scare her. (I do not mention the bear.) "And most of all, you're here."

And this is a very serious misstep. Because I mean *here*, in the atrium, at the conference, mingling, handing out business cards she designed at the mall. But she hears *here*, at my door, her hand on my arm.

"That's nice," she says, self-consciously, thinking about what I said about wild animals and wondering if I'm making some kind of comment about her face. I watch as she works out some very complex math in her head, a balancing of hopes and hard realities, of risks versus likely outcomes. It's how a disfigured person prepares for a kiss.

"Can I come in?" she asks.

"I—" I say. "I don't—" I say. "I'm not sure that's . . ."

Her hand drops.

"I was hoping I could give you my manuscript," she says, lying and not caring if it shows. "I thought maybe I could read part of it to you, if you have the time."

DECEMBER 2, 2012
SOLAR STORM SIX
The Earth's polarity reverses. The Pietra Negra—the giant magnetic mountain at the North Pole—begins to glow. Compasses around the world explode, and the mountain sinks into the earth and, drawn by an unknowable force called MAGNETISM, begins tunneling through its center.

And here I recoil instinctively. I am not disgusted by her face, I realize. I'm disgusted because she's a writer. I explain to her then that I don't have the time. If I took every manuscript that was offered to me here, I wouldn't be able to carry my own bags home. I tell her this quickly and (I hope) nicely: Why don't you mail it to me? And I scurry into my room. I even dead-bolt the door.

* * *

When I return the *Playboy* to Billy, it's nine p.m., and he's a little annoyed. He can't get really angry at me, because I may hold the key to his literary future. But it's clear he expected me earlier. I had forgotten that he wanted to get the magazine autographed, and I wonder aloud if Egan had come in that day.

"What do you think I'm talking about, man?" he says. "You just missed her."

I look at the seat half pulled out at the bar, the vinyl seat still depressed and warm, the just-crushed cigarette in the ashtray. It's instinctive: "Which way?" I say breathlessly.

Now he's on my side again, bound by a common quest. "The ballroom," he says. "Go!"

I actually run out of Bowties, scanning the atrium left and right furiously. I don't know where this desperation has come from, but after these sedentary days it feels wonderful to move, to breathe heavily. It's sad to admit, but after just a few seconds of running, I've broken a sweat.

Finally, I see her in the glass elevator climbing to the ballroom level, and I feel a kinship. She had been blowing off the awards cere-

> **DECEMBER 3, 2012**
>
> As he travels over the Blood-Red Ocean, Stephen King sees something on the horizon. It is the massive, mysterious, moving plateau known as Hohoq, the 51st United State. But now it has stopped moving, and Stephen King watches as the Thunderbirds abandon it for the darkening sky.

mony and was now sneaking in to make an appearance. It had been my plan too, and had I not overslept, I would have been sitting with her just moments earlier, a long hour alone with my brand-new, famous, reclusive, world-beating client. The one whose book I could sell quickly and get out of this job forever. Before I saw that shock of gray hair above me in the elevator, I didn't even know that's what I wanted. But now I know: I've got to get to her.

I book it back to the elevator, slam the button like crazy. There's no time. I take the stairs.

My heart is exploding by the time I make it up, and I hear a long round of applause coming from the ballroom. They've just awarded the big prize: Best Unpublished Romance or Western Novel. I run to the open door and see them all standing. There's Booth Daniels, the fraud. He'd convinced me to blow off the ceremony with him in the first place, and there he is in an ugly tab-collared tuxedo, standing and beaming with pride in himself and the whole enterprise of literature. There are my eleven one-on-ones, some of them clutching prizes, books donated by the local Borders with special gold-embroidered bookmarks handmade by the SRWWAAW prize committee. Someone's saying thank you and good night into the cheap PA system, and I still don't see Egan, and now they are starting to come—the writers are heading for the door.

This is what I notice: They are all fat. Not obese. Some of them quite attractive. Some of them, you wouldn't say fat: maybe husky, or biggish, or even slim for his age. And I say this fully admitting that I'm not the most slender tulip myself. But there's a girth there as they amble and stroll and limp and hustle their way toward me, the

DECEMBER 4, 2012
Stephen King is running out of food and water.

extra insulation that comes from spending most of one's time alone. Not just alone in a room, but alone in a fantasy, in imagined worlds, in the hope of being published. They're not used to being out. Their clothes don't fit right. The suit jackets pinch the men, and the gowns hang poorly on the women. This is not just a condition of these particular writers, I realize as they come closer, slapping one another on the back, laughing, some in happy tears. They're glad not to be alone, so glad they don't know what to do with themselves. From New York to Boston to Oklahoma to wherever: They're every writer I've ever known, and they're coming right for me.

I take a step back, feel the balcony come up behind me. They pass and jostle me and say hello, and I go up on tiptoe, pushing back, the balcony biting into my spine, the lobby below. I'm still trying to peer into the room.

Anne D. Egan is in there. I see her now, standing by a table, happily chatting away with a tall woman in a sheer gray dress. The woman's back is turned to me, but I can see she has beautiful shoulders. And then I know before she turns that it's Maria Passel. Her eye meets mine. It is not a nice feeling to be stared at by her. And then one of the writers accidentally trips the doorstop and the ballroom door swings shut.

* * *

Excerpted from Playboy *magazine, June 1979, "Where Is Darling Egan?" by Gerry Dunlap*

Anne finished part two of *Silopanna* on my porch that winter. When she was done, it stood six hundred typed pages high, not counting the twenty-three that had flown off in the wind, which she considered "editing." There are those who

---

DECEMBER 5, 2012

Stephen King reaches a mysterious island. Waiting for him on the shore is a tall young man with curly hair and glasses. He is wearing a nice suit.

"Welcome to Aspen, Colorado!" the man says.

The man does not reveal his name, but it is pretty clear from his clothing, manner, and ENOR-MOUS house that he is the shadowy figure known only as the Deranged Billionaire.

The Deranged Billionaire is very hospitable. He feeds Stephen King dinner. Stephen King admires his signet ring with a dollar sign on it.

The Deranged Billionaire is very excited to meet Stephen King. In fact, he has a complete collection of Stephen King first editions. Then he shows Stephen King his collection of Confederate coins and contemporary Bibles. He even has the stuffed, preserved body of the famous puppeteer Wayland Flowers.

"I never could find the Madame puppet," he says sadly.

Stephen King is amazed. He asks if the Deranged Billionaire would like to read the seven hundred new pages of *The Stand* that he has written.

"Not now," says the Deranged Billionaire. "You must be exhausted. Rest. I have something to show you in the morning."

---

ascribe mortal significance to the fact that the letter X never appears in the book, but it's simply not true. It appears several times. But it does not appear after page 487, when her hammer fingers blew the X key off the typewriter.

We drank that night on the porch. She propped her feet up on the manuscript and yelled at the transvestites below as they passed. We sang. Everyone wants to know if we were lovers that last week of winter. The fact is, that night was as close as it got.

Then I asked her when she was going to start part three. What was going to happen in it?

I didn't realize what a mistake this was. She stared past me. Tears found her eyes.

"I only have three ideas so far. First, I want to explain how there are good aliens who live outside of time, who want to help us to be free. Second, I want to explain how there are bad aliens also, who want us to suffer, who want us to continue to be sick because it amuses them. They're the ones secretly funding CIRCE, the ones Abigail will eventually have to beat."

DECEMBER 6, 2012

Stephen King awakens to a delicious breakfast of fried sperm-whale blubber and Utz Cheese Balls and coffee. The Deranged Billionaire says he has a confession to make.

"Two months ago, I instructed my team of scientists in Denver to open a door to another dimension," he says. "A place called NEWEST PORT."

"That . . . that is a myth," says Stephen King.

"No," says the Deranged Billionaire. "You were simply not wealthy enough to be told the truth."

The Deranged Billionaire explains that his intentions were good. All he wanted was to offer an escape to his fellow Billionaires so that they could leave this Earth until it was habitable again. At a reasonable price, of course.[a] But things went wrong, and an ocean of blood came through.

"Yes," chuckles the Deranged Billionaire as Stephen King begins to understand. "You've been floating in it."

"But . . . how did you survive?"

"I figured there was a small possibility of a BLOOD WAVE, and so I stayed safe, here in the mountains." The Deranged Billionaire explains he never would have made a billion dollars without taking risks. But he NEVER risks his OWN money. Or body.

"You're a monster," says Stephen King.

"No," says the Deranged Billionaire, pressing a button on a console on his dining-room table. "THAT is a monster."

The automatic curtains draw back to reveal a massive window, a panoramic view of the Blood-Red Ocean. And for the first time, Stephen King sees the ocean's yellow eyes. And then he sees something else: tethered to the red sand shore, a giant mass of glistening muscle and slime.

"What is it?" asks Stephen King.

"That," says the Deranged Billionaire, "is Ungolo, the Great Leech. One of the Ancient and Unspeakable Ones. They say it is twenty million years old—I bought it from a friend of mine, who had it in the basement of his chateau."

"What is it doing?" asks Stephen King, watching Ungolo as it throbs.

"Feasting!" says the Deranged Billionaire. "You see," he explains, he is not a monster. He admits his mistakes and cleans up his messes. "Ungolo will suck up the Blood-Red Ocean, and then I will launch it into space, and in seven thousand years, America will be back to normal."

The Deranged Billionaire sees that this is cold comfort to Stephen King.

"What?" the Deranged Billionaire asks him. "How long were YOU planning to live? Less than seven thousand years?"

---

a. One Billion Jerky Dollars.

I asked her, "What's third?"

"Third, I want it to be like this. I want Abigail to be calm and happy. I want her to sit on the shore of the lake of times with all her friends. I want to have them all back, all of us sitting on the shore, tossing rocks in."

By this time she was crying. I asked her to stop. I said it was beautiful.

"But how can I do it?" she cried. "You can't write a novel with only three goddamn ideas!"

DECEMBER 7, 2012

DOGSTORM and the remaining twenty-one robotic presidents reach the risen White City of Chicago. They begin their assault. The Gifted Child watches with his mind as they sweep through the city, searching for him. They face the New Chicagoans and their tommy guns without pause. The Gifted Child is the only thing they fear. He *could* destroy them, but he is saving his strength for something else. Something bigger.

* * *

It's morning at the breakfast buffet and I am eating alone. I suspect that some bad word has spread among the writers about me, for they are all keeping their polite distance, or else I'm looking particularly mean as I eat my plate of steam-table sausage. I believe either could be true.

I am considering whether to put myself through the ordeal of another cup of atrium coffee—part of me thinks I deserve it—when Maria Passel comes over with some kind of corn muffin and sits.

"Good morning," she says, very calmly, almost sweetly.

I say something in reply.

"By the way," she says, as if we were ever talking about something, "you don't have to worry about reading my manuscript."

"That's nice," I say.

"I've found someone else who's going to help me," she says.

"Naturally," I say.

"Do you know her? She's a famous science-fiction author."

"Oh yes," I say. "I've heard she's your mentor. Everyone around the atrium is talking about it."

"You don't have to be mean," she says.

"That's true," I say.

There is a long silence as she nibbles at her muffin, and I'm sure it looks like I am sullenly eating my sausage but in fact I am formulating a plan.

"Listen," I say. I explain to her that I think we got off on the wrong foot. I really did mean it when I said she should mail me her manuscript. I'm here, after all, to find promising new clients.

DECEMBER 8, 2012

Stephen King stands on the shores of the Island of Aspen, watching Ungolo, the Great Leech, as it sups on the Blood-Red Ocean. For some reason, this image depresses him.

The Deranged Billionaire joins him on the red sand. He puts his hand on Stephen King's shoulder. "I see you have gassed up your duck boat. Where do you plan to go? Do you think there is really anyone out there to read to?"

Stephen King says no. There's nothing left in this world but blood and leeches. "I'm going back to Chicago. I never should have left."

The Deranged Billionaire nods sadly. "You know I cannot let you go," he says.

"Why in the name of Red Sox not?" asks Stephen King.

"I need someone to write the tale of how I saved the world."

"I'll never do it," says Stephen King.

The Deranged Billionaire laughs. "I don't want YOU to write it! I already hired Dan Brown to do that! And that is why you cannot ever leave. You cannot ever tell what you've seen here. There are no humble, flinty Down-eastern working-class heroes standing up to the callous elites in THIS story, Stephen King."

And then the Deranged Billionaire raises his voice and calls, "Dan?"

For a moment Stephen King is confused. But he grows less confused when Dan Brown steps out from behind a tree, raises a gun, and shoots Stephen King in the eye.

The new seven hundred pages of *The Stand* fall into the Blood-Red Ocean. They float in their Saran wrap and Styrofoam coffin, and are carried away on the red waves.

She does not respond.

In fact, I tell her that I'm glad that she's hooked up with Anne D. Egan, because Egan is really amazing. "I love her work. You could learn a lot from her. And imagine if you got a blurb from her. Maybe the thing to do would be for the three of us to sit down tonight."

"Why?" she asks.

"It's the last night of the conference," I say. "We can talk shop."

"Oh," says Maria.

"I'm sure she must have told you something about her new book? *Silopanna*, part three?"

"What makes you think she's got a new book?"

"Doesn't she?"

Maria doesn't answer.

"Come on," I say. "She's written it, hasn't she? She has to have written it. Everyone has a goddamn trilogy. Why else would she be here?"

Maria stands to leave. She's still smiling in that sweet way. "I'm sure I don't know."

DECEMBER 9, 2012
A woolly bear caterpillar crosses the last road.

I can't beat her at coyness. "Just tell her I want to read it," I say flatly. My voice is cold, surprising her and me both. She stands up, eye wide, and walks away with alarming grace.

But I'm still thinking: Why else should she be here? Why else?

A few minutes later I'm standing in the back of Conference Room C with the final day's schedule in my hand. I've run into Billy there. Today he gets his *Playboy* signed, but not by Anne Egan. I should have checked the conference schedule in the first place. I should have known. Gerry Dunlap is standing at the podium.

He's a tall, extremely skinny black man with graying temples and sunken, wandering eyes. He's got the frightened, freaky air of an overgrown twelve-year-old, and he's discussing a novel he wrote about an insane asylum on an alien planet.

"I read that one," Billy whispers to me. "It's slight."

In the third row back, by the aisle, Egan's sitting there, beaming at him. Some know she's there, others don't notice. Probably a large portion of the audience doesn't even know who she is. But Dunlap's large eyes rove until they find her, and it seems to calm him as he wraps up his speech. When he's done, I watch them search for each other, find one another. They kiss—a long, deep tongue kiss, no less—and those in the know applaud like crazy. Ten or twelve people. Billy can't contain himself; he's got the *Playboy* between his knees, whistling and clapping.

As a literary agent, I know what the beginning of a book looks like, and I know how one ends. This is an ending.

* * *

DECEMBER 10, 2012
An actual Cyclops prowls the ruins of Columbus, OH.

Excerpted from Playboy *magazine, June 1979, "Where Is Darling Egan?" by Gerry Dunlap*

The next few days were slow and sad. With the book out of her, Anne was just emptied out.

I tried to take her around the city, but it's hard to go sightseeing with someone who sees signs of the future in tree shade and fly buzz. Walking her through the Quarter, with its haunted narrow streets and smells and tourist voo-doo, her head almost exploded.

Then we rode out on the St. Charles streetcar over grass-covered track to the Garden District. The streetcar still has wooden seats, I pointed out. Anne rolled her eyes meaning-fully. Like that was the last thing she needed to hear.

In that last afternoon she stared out the window at the passing mansions. I suddenly grew the nerve: put my arm around her and she didn't resist. But she whispered words to herself that I couldn't hear.

"Anne," I said, "be calm."

She looked at me, and for a second she was calm. Our lips touched just as the train lurch-stopped at an intersection and we flew forward in a tangle. When she looked at me again, her eyes were wide and wild.

"Did you see?" she asked. "The Cyclops?"

She nodded to an ordinary two-eyed man departing the train.

"He left a message for me," she said. "From the future. Under the seat." She stood up quickly and ran her hands

DECEMBER 11, 2012

The Blood-Red Ocean stares at the ugly blue sky. It feels itself being devoured by Ungolo. Slowly. Slowly. It will take more than 7,000 years, it knows. More like 7,500. But even it knows it is going to die. Even the ocean feels this fear.

under the wooden bench at the front of the train where the man had been sitting.

She nodded as she felt the old gum and splinters, forming some dirty Braille that only she could comprehend.

"Yes," she said. "Got it."

And then she looked at me, her eyes round, apologizing, seeing things I couldn't. "I have to go. I'm going." There was no arguing.

We rode along to the next stop, me still sitting, she standing, jumping on the balls of her feet. I somehow knew if I touched her she would do something hard and quick that could involve jumping from the train, breaking a window.

"Good-bye," she said at the next stop, and I rode on.

"Be calm," I said.

When I got off the train at the last stop, I knew she was gone. I knew I'd never see her again. The St. Charles streetcar stared at me with its single headlight before reversing direction, heading back to the city. I had seen the Cyclops. I had gotten the message.

* * *

Billy has *Return of the Jedi* running in Bowties that night. I'm at the bar, watching the three separate scenes, and it occurs to me that he must own three separate DVDs running on three separate machines. In my half-drunk state I decide this to be an amazing possibility, so I ask Billy if it's so. He confirms that this is true and I congratulate him on this and also on having such a good night. Not only is this the last night of the conference, but there's a whole damn senior prom on the dance floor, flush with cash and fake IDs.

Billy nods. "It's a wild scene."

Behind me, across the dance floor, I know that Maria Passel is sitting with Gerry Dunlap at a small, intimate table. She's happy, talking with the famous author at the big last fling. Situating yourself with the right publishing professional is always a goal of these last-night drinking sessions. Booth has his own cadre of admirers out on the sunken patio in the atrium and he keeps waving me over through the smoked glass window. I am alone. I know that Anne D. Egan is going to come in eventually and join Maria and Gerry. I don't know what I'm going to do when she does.

I ask Billy to show it to me again: The *Playboy* article is signed by both Dunlap and Egan.

"That'll get some cash," I say.

"No," Billy says. "I'm keeping it." He slips it back into a Mylar sleeve and moves down the bar.

And then I feel the hand on my shoulder, and I know exactly who it is.

"Hello, Maria."

"Hi," says Maria. She pulls up a stool and sits next to me. "Need a drink?"

"I'm good," I say.

"Me too," she says. "Anne's here, you know. I gave her your message."

"Thank you," I say. And I mean it. Because I know from her voice she actually did. I know from her voice that, for whatever reason, she actually pled my case. I wonder what she said.

"Thank you," I say again.

DECEMBER 13, 2012

The 21 Animatronic Presidents finally corner the Gifted Child at the end of Navy Pier.

Only a few dozen brave Chicagoans stand between the presidents and the Gifted Child, but the Gifted Child waves his protectors away.

"What have you been waiting for, young man?" asks the genial Robot Jimmy Carter, with murder in his eyes. "Why don't you just destroy us with your mind?"

"I have been waiting for a friend," says the Gifted Child. "But now I know he isn't coming."

That's when the presidents' animatronic eyes spy the pages of The Stand in the Gifted Child's hand.

Robot Theodore Roosevelt breaks the silence with a horrid, screeching bully-laugh.

Then Robot Ronald Reagan gives the command to "TEAR THAT BOY DOWN."

They advance. But the Gifted Child just closes his eyes. And the air crackles and the ground heaves. The presidents and their steeds burst into furious flames. The gigantic lost Ferris wheel from the 1892 Columbian Exposition rises from Lake Michigan behind him. With a great wrench the Ferris wheel begins to spin, faster, faster, faster, and all of Chicago disappears forever.

"I wish I could say different," she says, "but she doesn't want to talk to you. She asked me to tell you something. She doesn't want anything written down, so I had to memorize it."

"OK," I said.

She takes a deep breath. "First, you're right. She did write a part three. It's four hundred pages, and none of it is publishable, because it doesn't make any sense. Most of it is the word 'never.' She keeps it around to remind herself of how, well, OK, how crazy she got."

Maria doesn't seem to want to say the word, but she does. She was instructed.

"I see," I say.

"Next, she wants you to think what it was like for her to have a psychotic break. To have the world looking for you and calling you a genius while you were living in subsidized housing in Bridgeport, selling tea bags door to door in your pajamas."

I don't say anything.

"But she says not to worry about that, because she's better now."

I don't say anything again. What can I?

"Third, she doesn't mind if you reveal that she's alive. It was never supposed to be a secret. She's happy to give people stories to tell."

"Tell her I say thank you."

DECEMBER 14, 2012

The Final Friday Before the End: Gorgoth the Pitiless sniffs out all remaining humans who have ever eaten at TGI Fridays and devours them ravenously. Contrary to his name, he does have some pity. He does not stuff them with cheese and fry them before he eats them, but instead gives them a quick death, dipped in enough ranch dressing to numb the pain.

"But if you talk about her, she wants you to say this: Twenty-six years ago, she became herself. The voice on the other end of the phone told her to stop dicking around and just do what she was supposed to. She knew what it was, and that's what she did. The book she wrote almost destroyed her. But it was all part of a process, a path to here, where everything was plain and true and still. She's says that all her friends are gone now. They're by the lake, and the water is fine. She says in other words, if you want a book to sell, go and write your own."

"I'm not a writer," I say. "Are you sure she's not still crazy?"

"Very funny," Maria says. "That's the message, anyway."

I nod. "Thanks," I say. And then I say "You told it well," because it's true.

I twist around on the barstool. Through the bright prom dresses colliding on the murky dance floor, I see her there, sitting in the corner, her hands entwined with Gerry's. She raises her glass—it looks like soda water. I raise my blue martini and drink her health.

I turn back to Maria.

"I loved you, you know," she says, with a depth of feeling that would seem to go back years and years and not just to yesterday. Writers are dramatic.

I am almost startled, but there's no sense faking it now. "I know," I say. "Do you still want me to read your book?"

"I don't think so," she says. "I don't think you're going to be a literary agent for much longer. You're through: I can see it. I know what it's like to be burned out. You don't get mauled by a bear by accident. On some level, you have to be asking for it."

DECEMBER 15, 2012

Antarctica. The Experimental Huge Microwave oven dings. The Head of Nug-Shohab is now thawed. It blinks its twenty-eight huge, milky eyes slowly. It sees its own giant body, the scrapings of ten nations and countless lives scabbed and dried on its hands and knees. It sees the monstrous hand the little girl once touched with kindness coming toward it, reaching for it. The Head of Nug-Shohab sees her blood on its hand.

And then the Nug-Shohab knows all the things it did not know before. It becomes aware of all the damage we do simply by blindly living, and it knows that to live is to kill.

Nug-Shohab puts his head on his body, whole for the first time in ten thousand years. It remembers what it can do. It no longer hungers for vengeance, except upon itself. It wants to make the world whole and good again. It has this power. It was born in the space between worlds, in the strange amber-green light that binds universes, and was given the power to change the past and the present and the future. It has always used this power to ravage. Always used this power to sunder. But now it is time to make things whole once more.

"Huh. I really need to buy you a drink now," I say.

"No, thanks," she says. "Oh, I forgot," she says. "Anne wants to borrow your cell phone. She doesn't have one."

I don't ask questions. I give it to her and watch her walk away.

* * *

A few hours later I'm out with Booth and his admirers, under the glare of the atrium lights and the washed-out night beyond it. We get wildly drunk. The phone turns up back in my pocket somehow, and I see the last number dialed. I don't recognize the area code, but I don't need to ask where it is. Through the atrium, the moon is shining in on us. Booth is toasting the great enterprise of literature, and I'm enjoying my last moments in this strange world without gravity.

DECEMBER 16, 2012

Nug-Shohab spreads his many wings and raises his many arms, and begins to speak the incantation that will remake the world.

But before he can finish, the Pietra Negra, which has been tunneling through the inner core of the Earth, smashes out of the South Pole. It shoots out of the Earth like a giant white-hot magnetic bullet, drawing Nug-Shohab, whose very skeleton is iron, hard against its side as it speeds, endlessly, into the exile of space.

GOOD-BYE

I know you are asking: What if I am wrong?

What if RAGNAROK does not come? What if it does not happen the way I say it is going to happen?

I suppose that is a possibility.

Perhaps the Mayans WERE wrong.

Maybe we WILL enter a new era of consciousness.

Maybe we will NOT destroy ourselves with technology.

Perhaps it will be that some new old god comes. Say his name is DOZGOTH, the 701st, and say he takes pity on us. And a thousand years after all the suffering of RAGNAROK, he will retcon us back to the very day this book was published.

You will remember nothing of what happened or what you did to survive. The only evidence that any of this ever happened will be this book, and the fact that you now have a tentacle instead of an arm. But you will explain that away simply by saying you are wearing an octopus sleeve. The mind can explain so many things when it wants to close its eyes and sleep.

Perhaps only one person will remember what really happened, and he will be named Jonathan Coulton. But he cannot tell anyone, for he is but an animal.

And perhaps, in that new world, the contents of this book will all be fiction, the rantings of a DERANGED MILLIONAIRE in a book.

And you can then go home to your human children and pretend that these books were all fantasy, and you will kiss your wife, Suzanne

DECEMBER 17, 2012
"Rowdy" Roddy Piper is still punching Keith David.

Pleshette, and say to them, "GOOD MORNING. I had the strangest dream."

It could happen that way.

It is even possible that nothing at all will happen, and life will continue to undo and remake itself in all the little ways—the triumphs and failures, the births and deaths, all the little RAGNAROKS that happen day by day, the way it always does, and you will have a tentacle for some other reason.

That is what I hope will happen for you. And also for me.

And if I see you after the end has *not* come, I will be very embarrassed. But I confess I will be glad to see you, dear reader. I will be glad that you did not die in fire. And I may even shake your hand and take a moment to enjoy being alive and being human with you.

And then you will not hear from me again. I will not write any more books of fake trivia and world knowledge. There will be no reason to.

Because if it happens *YOUR* way, and the world does not end, I will leave my Park Slope Survival Brownstone. I will go and lead a normal life with my children and my wife, Suzanne Pleshette. I will enjoy whatever time awaits us. That is all we can do. And for me, knowing this fact makes all knowledge complete.

That is all.

DECEMBER 18, 2012

The Century Toad cracks the Earth as it forces itself out of the hole left by the Pietra Negra, and kicks its way out into space, its belly full of mole-men. I wish I could tell you that the cycle will begin again. I wish I could tell you that the Century Toad's secretions will attract space dust and cosmic rocks . . . that its increasing mass and gravity will, over millennia, gradually form a new, fresh Earth around it. But just because this was how OUR Earth was formed, I do not know that is going to happen again. It is impossible to say.

TABLE 53: EXPERTS CONSULTED IN THE PREPARATION OF THIS BOOK

Mark	Adams	on the subject of finishing even MORE books
Mssrs. Adsit and Lutz		on the subject of making it up on the spot
Anaheed	Alani	on the subject of telling the truth on stage
Beau and Ryan and their dog Buster		on the subject of Zombiepocalypse
Chris	Anderson	to all the Chris Andersons in my life . . . you know who you are
Lance	Bangs	on the subjects of incredible visors and Room 43
Lynda	Barry	on the subject of procrastination
Maribeth	Batcha	on the subject of "Villanova"
Joshuah	Bearman	on the subject of living in seaside mansions
Kevin	Bleyer	on the subject of presidential humor
Rich	Blomquist	on the subject of sexpertise
Casey	Bloys	on the subject of jocks vs. nerds
Charles W. "Chuck"	Bryant	on the subject of odd town festivals, and most other subjects
Donick	Cary	on the subject of Nantucket
Xander	Cassell	on the subject of foreign hospitality
Wyatt	Cenac	on the subject of mint-flavored liquors
Josh	Clark	on the subject of catfish noodling, and most other subjects
Loren	Coleman	on the subject of the persistence of cryptids
Christine	Connor	on the subject of the ancient and unspeakable ones
Elizabeth	Connor	on the subject of unnaturally cold hands
Mssrs. Corbett and Murphy		on the subject of robot monsters
Jonathan	Coulton	the Monarch of the Seas
Ted	Danson	on the subject of being the bride
John	Darnielle	on the subject of Lovecraft in Brooklyn
Charles	Digges	on the subjects of snake and eggs
Dave	Eggers	on the subject of making your own world
The humans of Essentials, Northampton		on the subject of Belgian boy detectives and unending support
Jason	Evans	on the subject of strange Arthur Ashe statues of the world
Kassie	Evashevski	on the subject of deadlines
John	Flansburgh	on the subject of echolocation
Jen	Flanz	on the subject of inspirational awesomeness

CONTINUED

DECEMBER 19, 2012

While this entire Annus Terminus is generally described as RAGNAROK, the actual battle of Norse Gods and Frost Giants and Demons technically occurs TODAY, and devours what remains of the surface of the Earth in fire, just as the Actuaries predicted.

TABLE 53: *continued*		
Katherine	Fletcher	on the subject of Scrabble
Mark	Frauenfelder	on the subjects of cigar box ukuleles and other survival devices
Stephen	Fry	on the subject of g animals
Neil	Gaiman	on the subject of building walls
Zach	Galifianakis	on the subject of kissing
Nancy	Geller	on the subject of jocks only
Martin	Gero	on the subject of plaid suits
Ricky	Gervais	on the subject of kinds of gin
Elizabeth	Gilbert	on the subject of vice presidential hug duration
Ira	Glass	on the subject of betting with confidence
The firm of Guion and Handelman		on the subject of weinermobile dynamics
Emmanuel	Haldeman-Julius	on the subjects of small books and smaller typefaces
the Harringtons		on the subject of rocking and Deadly Squires
Kasper	Hauser	on the subject of spicy pony heads
the hive mind known as HIVE MIND		on the subject of unrequested marmots puns
James	Hodgman	the motivational speaker and author of SOMETIMES YOU NEED HELP EVERY TIME
Lucy	Hodgman	on the subject of storytelling
Cynthia	Hopkins	on the subjects of entropy, electricity, and tide resistance
Mark	Jannot	on the subject of electronic reading devices
Xeni	Jardin	on the subject of spam
David	Javerbaum	on the subject of GOD
Miles	Kahn	on the subjects of skiing and the rap music of Brattleboro, VT
Eliott	Kalan	on the subject High Nerderie
Ben	Karlin	on the subject of dining at restaurants that don't exist anymore
Starlee	Kine	on the subject of California Hodgman
Geoff	Kloske	on the subjects of deftly arched eyebrows and paperbacks
Adam	Koford	on the subjects of space clowns and sperm whales
Michael	Korda	on the subject of making them wait
Tyronne	L'Hirondelle	on the subjects of doppelgangerdom, Animal Hoarders, and beer
Dougald	Lamont	on "The Theory of Many Worlds"
Matthew	Latkiewicz	on the subject of wine labels
Robert	Leininger	on the subject of Cyclopses
Ted	Leo	on the subject of cork bottling
Damon	Lindelof	on the subject of that not being all
John	Linnell	on the subject of not keeping Johnny Down

CONTINUED

DECEMBER 20, 2012

The Nug-Shohab sees the pale blue speck of the world it had planned at the last minute to save. And then he sees it split in two.

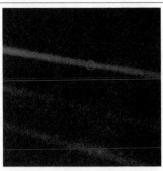

FIGURE 155: *The Earth, just before splitting, as seen by the Nug-Shohab.*

"Look again at that dot. That's here, that's home, that's us. On it everyone you love, everyone you know, everyone you ever heard of, every human being who ever was, lived out their lives. The aggregate of our joy and suffering, thousands of confident religions, ideologies, and economic doctrines, every hunter and forager, every hero and coward, every creator and destroyer of civilization, every king and peasant, every young couple in love, every mother and father, hopeful child, inventor and explorer, every teacher of morals, every corrupt politician, every "superstar," every "supreme leader," every saint and sinner in the history of our species lived there—on a mote of dust suspended in a sunbeam." —Carl Sagan

TABLE 53: *continued*		
John	Lloyd	on the subject of useful ignorance
Justin	Long	on the subject of insane clowns
Rachel	Maddow	on the subjects of comic books and labor unrest
Rachelle	Mandik	on the subject of weeping angels
Nick	Mangold	on the subject of high jockerie
Brett	Martin	on the subject of New Orleans
George R. R.	Martin	on the subject of taking your time
Nick	McCarthy	on the subjects of scary movies and raising children
Christopher	McCullough	on the subject of fried chicken and *Tron*
Sean	McDonald	who is always consulted
Sam	Means	on the subject of hobo Superman
John	Moe	on the subject of wits
The Montague Bookmill		where I first realized the world is ending
Phil	Morrison	on the subject of the end
Sue	Naegle	on the subject of warm muesli
Patton	Oswalt	on the subject of time and relative dimensions in space
Greg	Pak	on the subject of Tyrannus Flamehead
The irrepressible Paul and Storm		on nautilus docking stations and other seafaring journey
Philip Pavel and all at the Chateau Marmont		on the subject of my personal panic suite
Davin	Pavlas	on the subject of andere Geister
Daniel	Pinchbeck	on the subject of Quetzalcoatl
Ken	Plume	on the subjects of Popeye and Jeff Goldblum
		CONTINUED

TABLE 53: *continued*

Sam	Potts	on the subjects of China and Africa
Joe	Randazzo	on the subject of wine mulling
David	Rees	on the subject of karaoke
Sarah	Reid	on the subjects of home pickling and self-sufficiency of all kinds
John	Roderick	on the subject of big life decisions, such as choice of eyewear and type of ukulele
Nina	Rosenstein	on the subject of armories in Upper Manhattan
Adam	Sachs	on the subject of growing facial hair gracefully
Adam	Savage	on the subject of replicas of falcons and *Blade Runner* guns
Kristen	Schaal	on the subject of lighting rooms
Tom	Scharpling	on the subject of Four Loko
Dan	Schreiber	on the subject of museums and curiosity
Jason	Schwartzman	on the subject of hosting the set
Douglas	Self	on the subject of antique listening devices
the family Shopsin		on the subjects of cooking, parenting, drawing, building, blogging, cursing, and living correctly
Art	Siegel	on the subject of Crazy Crab
Allison	Silverman	on the subject of good counsel
Jay, Jr. and everyone at Skulls, Unlimited		on the subject of articulated ferret skeletons
Rich	Sommer	on the subject of Brownie
Caissie	St. Onge	on the subject of diligence
Jon	Stewart	on the subject of countless subjects
Brian	Tart	on the subject of maintaining patience
Jesse	Thorn	on the subject of good judgment
Hannah	Tinti	on the subject of "Villanova"
Janie F.	Tompkins	on the subject of throwing a wedding
Paul F.	Tompkins	on the subject of post-apocalyptic uses of pie filling
Richard	Turner	on the subject of British radio
Lee	Unkrich	on the subject of repairing articulated ferret skeletons
JS	VanBuskirk	on the subject of farewell
Brian K	Vaughan	on the subject of not remaking *Dune* and making new things instead
Sarah	Vowell	on the subejct of Teddy Roosevelt
Irving, David, and Amy	Wallace, Wallechinsky, and Wallace	on the subject of never ceasing to make lists
Morgan and Rob	Webb and Reid	on the subjects of video game cheats, intellectual property, and pepsico
R	Wesley	on the subject of *Happy Days* anachronisms
Jon	Wurster	on the subject of WaWa
The men of You Look Nice Today		on the subject of creepy Christmas tree salespersons

IMAGE CREDITS